STAY STRONG

Stephen Murray

with John F McDonald & Lee Martin

Gatecrasher
Books

First published by Gatecrasher Books June 2017
London – England
Copyright © 2017 Stephen Murray, Lee Martin & John F McDonald

This is an autobiography. Some names have been changed for privacy reasons.
www.stysrg.com/stephen.html

ISBNs:
hardback   978-0-9957515-0-7
paperback   978-0-9957515-1-4
ebook   978-0-9957515-2-1

5% of all profits from the sale of paperback (print on demand) copies will be donated to Wings for Life UK, Registered Charity Number in England and Wales: 1138804

Soldier by TJ Lavin
Stephen Murray Rap by John Jennings

Photos: Paul Bliss, Russ Hennings, Jasper Jones, Mark Losey, Keith Mulligan, Kevin Novak, Fat Tony, Chris Woodage
Cover Design: https://factorymedia.com
Book Design: www.shakspeareeditorial.org

For my sons, Seth and Mason
You're my life!

I sit and think of all the good times
I sit and think about the right lines
Or rhymes to say
I sit and think I'm in the right mind
And think of all the reasons for living that I might find today.
I look to the sky, god please help me now
I showed you I wanna be here
Tried to take me twice I had some bad advice but now my vision of
living is so clear
I went from zero to hero, to zero but now back to hero again,
I saw people hanging on and my brother staying strong,
Now I see the colors of my true friends, and the loose ends
Are tied up and washed, a clean slate. I'm a little bit bolder,
A changed man from the inside out for the better, should've died on
the dirt that day,
Thank God I'm a soldier.
And I told you I'm never giving up, never going down,
Got to live it up, got to make it now,
Because the whole world's on my side,
Everything inside
Gonna make this ride!
I remember sending donuts in a 745 big dirt dreams fully recog-
nised
And now I fight the fight – I fight the one for life
And now I fight the tears back for the kids and wife
And I'm here for life kid, not just tomorrow
Need a shoulder to lean on
I'm here to borrow no sorrow or sadness cause we're looking ahead
One step at a time – and one breath of a line
And one look and you'll find success with each breath of your own
Just know for me one thing my friend
You're never alone because you're never alone
And we love you.

You're on my mind and I know deep down inside – we're gonna
ride – again!

Soldier – A Tribute to Stephen Murray
T J Lavin

See the video on stysrg.com

FOREWORD

Matt Helders, founding member of Arctic Monkeys

I know Stephen and the Murray family through BMX. Me and my older brother Gary also grew up racing all over the world. Stephen grew up in a similar area to us, a working-class town in the north of England. The book begins with Stephen's final jump at the Dew Action Sports Tour in Baltimore in 2007, then goes back and covers his early life growing up in Tyneside and how that influenced him and his brother Martin.

Stephen was very successful as a BMX racer, something of a hero to the younger riders, me included. We would all hang around with each other and, as you'll find out reading this book, Stephen is a bit of a joker and loves a prank. We were once in Bournemouth at the beach and from what I remember, Stephen, Martin and my older brother convinced me, the youngest, to be buried in the sand up to my head. They then pretended to piss in a bucket and pour it all over me! Turned out to just be sea water but I didn't know that at the time.

Stephen was British Champion nine times and European Championship runner-up twice. He also came fifth at the World Champs. He achieved all this by the time he was sixteen.

One of my favourite parts of BMX was watching the King of Dirt competition between races. Basically, if there were no dirt jumps built at the track, they would choose the biggest doubles or table top and compete against each other to see who could do the best tricks. This is where Stephen first got into jumping in a big way. He raced and jumped until he was nineteen then decided to pursue dirt jumping, and the best place to do that was California.

Having saved enough money doing 'shit jobs', as he puts it, Stephen made it out to California in 1999. It was perfect, he could ride every day, and it didn't take long for him to get sponsored. It wasn't all smooth sailing though, in his first year of competing, Stephen pretty much broke a bone a month, as well as a few serious concussions.

It got to the point where Stephen was competing alongside his idols, people like TJ Lavin and Ryan Nyquist, as well as Cory Nastazio, who became his roommate, and they built their own massive trails in the back yard. This meant Stephen could concentrate on his signature trick, the double backflip. That double backflip won him the X-Games in 2001, it was the first time it had been done in a competition. Later on in that same year, he won the Gravity Games.

By the time he was 22 he was a big name in America and was living a crazy lifestyle – drugs, booze, parties, women and everything else that can often come along with fame and fortune. It all became too much to handle and he soon noticed how this lifestyle was negatively affecting his riding. All of a sudden he wasn't winning anymore. Stephen openly talks about the negatives very honestly in this book and doesn't sugar coat anything.

Stephen got married and had two sons but his career was still suffering, he was losing competitions, which meant the money wasn't coming in like it was before. This took a toll on the glamorous lifestyle that he was used to. He knew this wasn't the end of his career and over the next six months he pulled himself together, got fit and healthy again and back to the top level of BMX dirt jumping. At the Dew Tour in Baltimore in 2007, he hit his head in the second round and was concussed. Stephen's life would change forever when he attempted his famous double backflip in the third and final round.

At this point the book goes back to Stephen's crash.

Live on NBC, Stephen suffered a terrifying accident in which he severely injured his spinal cord and vertebrae. He flatlined three times in four weeks. His doctors didn't expect him to live, but he did. However, he was paralysed from the shoulders down.

The second part of the book describes Stephen's fight back against his injuries. He was told by doctors that he would never breath unaided again, that he'd never be able to sit up again or even move any part of his body again. But he did all those things through hard work, dedication and help from a lot of great people. He worked closely with the doctor who treated Christopher Reeve and now he has the use of his lungs back and movement in his shoulders. He can also sit in his motorized wheelchair, which he operates with his head.

'Stay Strong' was a phrase used by fans sending their support to Stephen and this became his motto. Stay Strong has now become a leading brand in action sports. Many people from all walks of life reached out to help Stephen – my band, Arctic Monkeys, David Beckham, Sir Richard Branson and many more. He spoke in front of crowds as big as 15,000 at venues like the Birmingham NIA, something he never imagined doing.

Stephen split up with his wife in 2008 and he moved back to the UK with his two sons in 2016. At the moment, he is seen as a role model, not only in the world of action sports, but also for hundreds of thousands of paraplegics and quadriplegics throughout the world. And he's not finished yet. Before writing this, I asked Stephen what's next and what his ambition for the future is, he said, 'I want to get out of this fucking chair and hug my kids.'

I believe he'll do it.

Contents

1
BALTIMORE 2007

Qualifying was good. I get fourth and I'm dialed.

Now I'm in the final – feeling amazing – completely at one with my bike.

Dirt's the main event in this Dew Tour and it's all going out on NBC television.

Three runs – two to count – only one point separating first from fourth place – it's real close! And I haven't dropped any of my big tricks yet.

The Dew Tour jumps at the Camden Yards Sports Complex in Baltimore aren't the best I've seen – not as good as I'm used to – and, after the qualifying rounds, I'm out there with a shovel fixing the lip of the take-off. It should be glassy smooth, but the dirt won't bind together. I guess I'm kinda spoilt with what I've built in my own yard, but when the time comes, it don't matter what's put in front of you or what's going on around you. It's the same for everybody and there's no point in bitching about it.

The place is packed – cameras – lasers – noise – adrenaline. It's huge, all lit up, ready for the night-time final. So many people – the crowd going nuts. I can feel the atmosphere – taste it.

First run and everything goes perfect. I perform a 360 turndown backflip – it's one of my signature moves. Nobody else does this trick – it's complicated, like three tricks in one – a 360 degree backflip, turning horizontally, and a turndown where you kinda get wrapped up in your bike. I nicknamed it the 'alligator wrestler'. It takes a lot of commitment.

Other guys in the final are Ryan Nyquist, Corey Bohan, Ryan Guettler and some of the best BMX dirt jumpers in the world. I don't know how their first runs go. I'm always like that, I don't look at other riders in a competition. I'm competing with myself and I always know, if I ride my best, I'll win. It's like I got tunnel vision, I don't need to focus on what anyone else is doing. There's no room for distraction, one mistake and it's game over.

I'm leading after the first run.

It's a steep roll-in – 30ft high and almost vertical. I drop in for the second run – I got some solid tricks, like a no-footer to turndown backflip and a table 360 on the first two jumps, then it goes into a long low set where you get your juice for the last. This is where we let it all hang out – right there – no holding back. Flying 25ft in the air at 30mph. We call it the showtime booter.

Four jumps ahead of me – three jumps perfect. I go for the double backflip on the fourth jump. Everything's moving so fast as I come round for the landing. I slide out on the loose dirt and fall and smack my head on the ground and get concussed. I try to shake it off. People are asking if I'm OK.

'Is your head good?'

'Sure.'

'You OK to do this run?'

I nod – things are a little foggy. I'm seeing stars, white lights – not clear. It's like being in the cage and you get hit and wobble – you're not gonna quit. OK, I've smashed myself but I'm like a dog in a fight and I'm not giving up now after coming so close. Like I said, it's two out of three runs to count, so this is my throwaway run. The double backflip's gonna be perfect on the third, then I'll establish myself back at the top after all the crap. Nothing's gonna stop me doing this.

The double backflip – my big trump card. I made that jump mine. Landed it first in Philadelphia in 2001, when I won the X-Games. Back then, no one else had ever landed that trick in a dirt competition. You approach take-off at twice the speed to a regular jump, so you can get enough height and distance to make the double rotation. When you hit it, you gotta rip back off the lip and bend your knees and elbows into a tuck position for the two flips. As soon as you get sight of the landing, you open up from the tuck and bring it in.

I'm ready.

Third run.

I'm on top of the roll-in. The announcer shouts my name to the crowd and my music's kicking in – *Soldier* by Eminem. Loud. I'm in the groove – in the mindset. I see the cheering fans, hear the noise. Then I cross my heart. Like, I don't actually remember doing that, crossing my heart, but I see it on playback later – after I come out of the black. Why'd I do it? Never done it before. Maybe God's hanging around, watching the contest – I don't know.

· · · · · · · · · · ·

Flashbacks of what happened on Wednesday streak across my memory like lightning bolts – split-second stuff. Vans Shoes were one of my sponsors and I had a big argument with Jerry Badders, their team manager, earlier in the month. Like, I was supposed to fly to England for Red Bull's Empire of Dirt contest in Devon. It was a new, groundbreaking event – the best twenty riders in the world competing on a course built like no other, with massive jumps. It was put on by Kye Forte, a good friend of mine, and everyone I knew was driving down to Devon in southwest England to see me – my family and friends – fans from all over the country. I was calling people, saying I was feeling great again and was gonna be there for sure. I was trying to make my comeback and competing in England like that'd be a great build-up to the Dew Tour for me – I hadn't rode over there for, like, five years. What better place to get dialed? I was real excited about it. I felt as good as I did back in 2002 and 2003 – never felt better.

When I got to LAX airport I went to the bag check-in.

'Your ticket's been voided, sir.'

'What d'you mean?'

'It's been voided ... your ticket.'

'I got all my stuff here ... who voided it?'

'I couldn't say.'

Because I'd been a bad boy and partying when I should've been riding, Jerry wanted me to sign a two-year contract with reduced pay, plus expenses and win bonuses, starting from the beginning of 2006. I tore that contract up and told him I'd only sign for one year because I was gonna win everything in 2006 and, after that, I wanted the same money as I was earning before – 2006 didn't go to plan and, I guess, I didn't produce what I'd promised.

Early in 2007, I'm going up to Woodward Camp to train, as part of my comeback, and I pick up a copy of *Ride Magazine* in a bike shop on the way. Cory Nastazio and Luke Parslow are with me in the car. There's a two-page Vans advert, along with a photo. Cory and Luke are in the photo and I'm not! It looked like I'd been cut and nobody told me. I tried calling Jerry, over and over, but I wasn't able to get in touch with him, despite leaving a bunch of messages. I finally got hold of him about a week after seeing the article in the magazine and when I did, I let fly!

'What the fuck's going on, Jerry? Why didn't you tell me I got dropped? I got bills to pay and two kids to feed and I'm having to chase you around.'

'You tore the contract up, Stephen. My budget's done for 2007 and I don't have a salary for you, only travel.'

I guess I was real mad and I probably said some things I shouldn't have. But I couldn't understand why I was dropped. OK, I'd been fucking about and there'd been too much partying and my head wasn't in the right place for a few years. I let things slide – got into bad habits – hung out with the wrong people. But I'd rinsed my body of everything and got back in form. It wasn't easy – I worked hard for it.

Now I was feeling amazing on my bike – all the negative stuff was gone.

Like, I'd got myself straight and now this!

What made it worse was, Jerry was my friend – he was an amazing pro rider in his day and he earned the nickname 'Bad Boy' Badders. Now he was team manager for Vans, like I said, and it was his job to get the best BMX riders in the world together to represent Vans Shoes and look after those riders at events – which he did. I'd known him since I was fifteen and we were always good friends. He was a big, loud American, but he got on with us English guys very well. Whenever we travelled to the UK to ride, he'd come to my mum's house and we'd hang out like family. I liked him a lot and he was fun to be around. That's what made it so hard to swallow when I got dropped from the team. I guess I had it coming, but I didn't see it like that at the time because my head was messed up. Anyway, after the argument on the phone, I sucked it up and apologised for the harsh words and he said he'd make sure Vans paid for me to go to England for the Empire of Dirt.

Now I'm at the airport and the stewardess is looking at me like I'm a lost dog or something. I'm tripping out. I get Jerry on the phone.

'Jerry, I'm at the airport and they tell me my ticket's voided. What's going on?'

'I cancelled your ticket, Stephen. You don't get to talk to me the way you did!'

'Fuck you Jerry! When I get to Baltimore I'm gonna knock your fucking head off!'

My wife Melissa and my young sons had dropped me off. Now I was stranded in LAX airport with two bike boxes and all my bags. I was really fucking pissed off! I had to call Melissa and have her come back for me and it stung.

After that, I couldn't have had more fire up my ass for Baltimore. Now I really had a grievance with Jerry and I had two weeks to brew on it.

OK, the LAX incident was two weeks ago. Now it's the Dew Tour contest and I want to show everyone who Stephen Murray really is – what I'm all about. I got rid of the negative stuff. I have something to prove and I've put in the hours more than ever, just riding and riding and nothing else! I know the way forward and I'm gonna do it properly. I want to show people I'm Stephen Murray and I'm back. The clouds are gonna open and the sun's gonna shine for me again!

I qualified for the Dew Tour through the rankings of the previous year – getting enough comp results to make it. I guess I'm freelance now, after being dropped – like, I'm a maverick, I'm riding for myself and no one else. That's not to say I haven't got people behind me. Steve Mateus, athlete manager for the energy drink Rockstar, pays for my plane ticket, because I'm flat broke, and Chris Gentry of Pro Riders pays my hotel and other expenses. I have a new S&M black bike that Neal Wood and Chris Moeller got specially made for me, but I travel solo and that means I don't have any pressure from sponsors.

Suits me just fine!

Chris Gentry picks me up at the airport on Wednesday 20 June and I'm trying to keep focused. But I know I'm gonna bump into Jerry Badders – it's inevitable – and I'm still angry over the LAX incident. When I arrive at the Marriot Hotel in Baltimore it's early evening and I walk into the main lobby with all my bags. The bar's full of BMXers because it's Mario Bonaventura's birthday or something and everyone's in high spirits. I see Jerry across the room. He sees me. I've just been on a six-hour flight from the west coast to the east coast and I'm fired up for the contest. I make my move toward Jerry, pushing people out of the way. I'm right in his face – like, seriously! I'm dialed, ready for anything.

I ask him outside.

We're in the parking lot facing each other – going at it – yelling at each other. Loads of people gather round us – I can feel the adrenaline running through me. Jerry's hands are in his pockets, like he don't want to fight but he's not gonna take shit either. We're about the same height, but he's a bit skinnier than me – still, he's a tough guy and I got respect for him. The BMXers are rowdy all around us.

'You fucked me up, Jerry. A lot of people got let down.'

'It's your own fault, don't put this on me, Stephen!'

I remember what my dad told me when I was younger –

'Son, if you're ever in doubt, get the first one in.'

So I stick a shot to the side of his head, before he knows what's happening. He goes down and I think I've knocked him out, but he gets up again.

'That all you got, Stephen? Do that again and you're off the team.'

'I'm already off the team, cocksucker!'

The crowd's baying like dogs, but I can't hear them. I can see their mouths moving and lips curling and teeth stripping, but there's no sound. Everything's silent. Slo-mo. Jerry's growling at me and I can see he's ready for my next move. Then I send another shot straight on to the edge of his jaw. It hurts my hand. I shake my fingers, hoping they're not broke. He sinks. Down. Down. Mario Bonaventura catches him before he hits the ground. Rodney Rambo grabs me. Jerry's ear is bleeding. The noise comes back. Loud. Shouting. Deafening. All hell's breaking loose – pushing and shoving.

The crowd converges and I'm caught up in the momentum. I get washed off my feet, like in a surf wave – a current of bodies. I see Jerry moving away to the hotel with some of the Vans riders and I know he's OK. There's a lot of people between us and that's maybe just as well – he's still my friend and two wrongs don't make a right. We've cleared the air and that's that. I don't want to get sidetracked, I want to stay focused and win the contest.

I make my way back to my gear and everything's surreal around me – voices – faces – a kind of white noise.

I go to my room to get away from the crazy fucking mayhem!

• • • • • • • • • •

That was on Wednesday.

Now it's Friday and the finals. I'm ten meters high at the top of the start ramp, ready to drop into my last run of the competition. I clear my mind and concentrate. Concentrate! This is it – everything I've worked for over the past six months – riding every day – being 100% at one with my bike and the jumps and the wind and the very fucking air around me. My bike's an extension of my body. I own it. I'm in control. Being in that kinda control's like no other feeling, and being in the moment's like nothing else on the planet.

I'm in the moment!

The first jump's amazing – x-up to turndown flip.

Second jump's good – it was supposed to be a table 360, but turned into a straight 360.

Third jump's perfect – I get mad pumped – I'm set up for the double backflip.

I get my speed up before the final jump. The showtime booter. It's what separates the men from the boys. A few people go big and send it – but there's only one or two of us who send it and let it go! Other riders settle for consistent runs – they settle for third or fourth. That mentality don't exist for me.

I take off – it's good! I'm trying to get the rotation to spin for the double backflip by pulling hard on the handlebars and throwing my head back. Out of nowhere, my left foot slips off the pedal – I've done hundreds of doubles and my foot never slipped off the pedal. It's a pure fucking nightmare! I get shot thirty feet in the air and fifteen feet past the landing. I'm not spinning. I should be spinning! Instead, I'm stuck hanging upside down in the pike position. Normally I'm like a cat and can land on my feet – but I don't know left from right or up from down.

Everything's eerily fucking silent, like time's stood still or something.

First thing to hit the ground's my neck – it shatters on impact!

. . . .

I come to lying in the dirt and a medic's breathing for me through a tube that's down my throat. My head's fully encased in a neck brace. There's a crowd around me – freaking out because I'm not breathing – saying stuff like 'serious shit' and 'life or death' and some people are even praying. Someone's telling Paul Roberts I got a 1% chance of surviving and Luke Parslow's whispering 'we love you, man'. Jerry Badders and Chris Gentry are leaning over me saying 'hang in there, Stephen'. Rick Bahr's in charge of safety and he's there too, calling for an ambulance. The medic's saving my life – breathing for me through the tube – pumping this bag. I don't take my eyes off him. It's the craziest most intense situation. Everything's fucking nuts!

Life or death?

Then I flatline.

Next thing I know I'm being lifted into the ambulance – they're still breathing for me – I'm going in and out of consciousness. There's a paramedic called Greg Steele with me, ventilating me – tubes and wires attached to me. We're speeding through the Baltimore streets – I can hear the siren screaming. Everything's a blur. I'm hovering on the ledge between life and death – teetering this way, then the other. It's touch-and-go.

All the sounds around me fade away and I slip into silence.

See the crash video on stysrg.com

2
BACK TO BEGINNINGS

OK, let's go back a bit.

I was born in Preston Grange, North Shields, a shipbuilding and fishing area of Tyneside, in the northeast of England. It was on 9 January 1980 and I reckon I must've come out of the womb riding a bike, because as far back as I can remember I knew I was going somewhere. Fast!

My dad was Jeff Murray, a firefighter and the son of a ship's stoker, who was the son of a coalminer. My mum was Cynthia, the only child of my granddad Bob, and she worked at the local doctor's surgery and played piano. My brother Martin was almost two years older than me and we were racing bikes when I was only three.

My first BMX memories are from a track at Eston in Teeside. BMX was just blowing up in the UK and there was this big ad in a local paper for an indoor race. I had a Buzz Bike with rubber wheels and stabilisers, and Martin had a Raleigh Boxer. The track was made out of cones and wooden ramps, to simulate a proper BMX track because it was winter and the weather in the north of England that time of year was pretty shit. I remember not being able to make it to the top of the jumps and rolling backwards, but my dad came and pushed me up. There was hundreds of kids all going crazy and it was like – this is fucking it, man!

From then on, me and Martin were hooked.

Not long after, we got our first proper BMX bikes –
eighteen-inch chrome Puch Invaders. My dad would take
us down to Tynemouth Haven, next to Priory Castle. There
was a downhill concrete path about three hundred yards
long and we'd rip down it. It got like I was going so fast my
feet couldn't keep up with the pedals and I went over the
handlebars and knocked myself out. My first KO! After that,
my dad realised our bikes were too heavy and we needed
new Mini Mongoose race bikes with twenty-inch wheels. I
thought they were the absolute business! I was five.

After the winter series in Eston we joined a bike club in
Wallsend called The Shiremoor Chargers and we practised
a couple of times a week at the Powder Monkey track. Doing
gate starts and sprints and building enough stamina to race
flat out. A BMX track was roughly 400 meters long, made of
crushed dirt and concrete, with jumps and turns. It was a
sprint from start to finish and you had to be fit.

Me and my brother were so connected, racing BMXs
all the time. Non-stop. Mum and dad got involved too. I
remember Jeff sweeping the track in the pissing rain, to get
the mud and excess water off it and he also did the gate
starts. Mum became treasurer of the club and kept things
ticking over. They didn't have much money, but they had
much love, and they gave what they could to get us where
we wanted to go. In return, I put everything into my bike,
even back then – I just loved it.

Loved it, man!

We did a couple of national races in 1985. Like I said,
BMX had already started to become everything for me and
I just couldn't get enough of it. Whenever I went to the
track I'd always be looking for the biggest set of doubles – I
wanted to jump the whole time I was racing. Jumping on the
track wasn't the fastest way round, but I loved that feeling of
being in the air. I remember at five years old doing shit like
bunny hops over my friends. One time I set this guy's bike
standing up next to a kerb so I could jump it. My back wheel
got clipped and I went over the bars, jamming my teeth in
between the paving slabs – I smashed my face and knocked
my front teeth out.

There was a lot more of that to come!

But it didn't put me off. Back then I'd find the biggest kerbs to do tricks on the street. I'd make jumps out of milk crates and planks of wood in Preston Grange shopping centre, just round the corner from where I lived. Even then I was going bigger than any of the other kids. It sounds kinda crazy now, but I remember all my mates started calling me Steve 'The American Boy' Murray – is that weird?

I went from racing at my club to competing in regional meetings and I qualified for a comp called The Champion of Champions at Tamworth in Staffordshire. This was where the best riders came to prove themselves, all trying to be the number one racer in England. I won that race and it gave me enough confidence to enter the national series – like, there was nine national races through the year, with the last one at the end of October and the results cumulated to a national ranking. By then I was travelling all over the UK. My mum and dad would take me out of school on the Friday; we'd leave early in the morning, heading to places like Poole and Bournemouth, and even London, all crammed into Cynthia's Nissan Prairie. And we'd be away riding the whole weekend.

I was national number two for my age when I was six and I qualified for the Weetabix World Championships at Slough Worlds in 1986. By then, dad had bought me a second-hand CW Mini and, in the run up to the championships, he started to train me seriously. He got me riding up steep hills doing sprints and I can remember the lactic acid burning my legs. I hated doing those fucking sprints, but always felt good afterwards because I knew I was getting better and stronger. We trained like that twice a week and, in between, I practised at the Powder Monkey track come hail, rain or snow.

Qualifying for the World Championships was a big deal to me and I believed it was gonna be my time to shine. I won my semi-final and was confident I could take victory in the final. But I slipped my pedal as I came out the gate and crashed and finished dead last. I was fucking devastated! Still, everyone said it was a massive achievement for a kid as young as me to be getting where I was going so fast.

Me and Martin rode our bikes every single day round the estates or at race meetings at the weekend. We made jumps wherever we could, out of whatever we could, and I started winning a lot of races in the region. In the summer of 1986 the Redcar horse racing meet had a BMX track in the middle. It was the first live televised BMX race in the UK and I won that race at six-and-under. After that, we realised we were a real BMX family and the sport was gonna be a massive part of our lives.

In 1987 I entered the World Championships in Orlando – my first trip to America. It was August and so hot I could barely catch my breath. It was like breathing in an oven, or being in a sauna. Gatorade sponsored the event and I remember drinking gallons of the stuff. I was drenched in sweat – the first time I'd ever rode in conditions like that, but not the last. I remember the track being really long and fucking exhausting. I didn't ride well and went out in the semis – my first experience of racing outside England was a disappointment.

While we were over there, Jeff and Cynthia met this guy called Bob Fury – he owned a company called Titan that made the new titanium bikes. They were lightweight and the latest thing – much easier for smaller kids to handle on the track. Mum and dad were getting more and more into BMXing and they did a deal with Bob Fury and began importing titanium bikes from America. They started up the Titan Team, which was the best team in the UK back then and a breeding ground for some real talented BMX racers. They were quality people – guys like Dylan Clayton and Jamie Staff and Neal Wood. Dylan was like no other rider, so stylish on the track – so smooth on his bike we nicknamed him 'Dr Smooth'. Jamie had legs like tree trunks – he was the most powerful rider I'd ever seen. He went on to win Olympic Gold at Beijing in the velodrome team sprint in 2008. Neal was the first punk rocker I ever met. His body was covered with tats and piercings and he looked real tough, but on the inside he had a heart of gold. The Titan Team was like a big family and we travelled all over the world together racing our bikes.

It was a crazy time and all sorts of crazy things happened – like, I was only eight but I was getting some incredible life experience even at that early age. I remember a big race that was held every year at the Pony Park in Slagharen, Holland. We went over on the ferry in 1988 and it was my first time on a boat. All the parents would meet up and party and all the riders would just run riot all over the theme park. We climbed up the roller coaster and walked the length of it on the wooden boards, holding on to the sides. It was a time of freedom, a crazy kinda freedom that's rare for kids nowadays. We got up to all sorts of mischief that was never malicious – just like kids being kids when they're let loose from the rules of adults.

I think it was the same year, 1988, that I started building jumps in the woods at Hollywell Dene. It was a steep-sided place, part of the Delaval Estate, where the River Dene followed the course of the Seaton Burn from Seghill to Seaton Sluice. I remember getting massive air over those jumps out in the woods. I'd ride with anyone who'd come with me and help me dig. One of them was this crazy Geordie dude called Mad Mick – he was also known as Mr Pants, because he'd ride round wearing nothing but his Y-fronts. He was about ten years older than me and was well known for doing mad shit. He'd fight anyone and he'd do crazy stunts on his bike, like jumping off the toilet blocks by the Grangeway shopping centre into the parking lot. I used to think he was completely fucking nuts – but I was always drawn to characters like that, people who were a bit off the norm, who didn't fit in or conform.

Around this age – maybe eight or nine or ten – other than racing, I played ice hockey and spent a lot of time at the rink in Whitley Bay. Ice hockey's a tough sport and there's always lots of barging and bashing, it's kinda like part of the game. I loved it, but sometimes the lawlessness spilled over, outside the rink. I remember a kid from primary school called Mark Lopez, the hardest kid in my year, wanting to fight me over the back field. I don't know what his beef was, but it was a big deal, all the kids from the estates were watching. We sparred around for a while and then I caught him with a sweet right cross. It was the first time I hit a guy in the face and it looked like his nose exploded. Someone went and got his big brothers and I had to make a fast getaway on my bike.

I never sat still back then when I was young – if I wasn't on my bike or playing ice hockey, I was doing something else. I was even coached in high-diving and this gave me air awareness – knowing where my body was in the air during a dive. It helped me out when I became a pro dirt jumper and was pulling massive tricks and flips. Even back then these skills were an asset to my riding. Like, when I was ten years old I entered a jumping contest at the nationals called Squirt of Dirt. It was a contest for kids aged eleven and under, like King of Dirt was for the older guys. I was real nervous, almost to the point of fear! But I faced the fear and rode up the take-off and just went for it, pulling tricks I'd never done before. The unknown's scary, but kinda contagious I guess. Like, if you face your fear, it turns into a positive force. I won the Squirt of Dirt with a 360 over a set of doubles.

It was my first dirt jump win!

Me and Martin went to Preston Grange Primary School at first. I was never what you'd call academic, but I guess I was bright enough. As far as I was concerned, fun always came before hard work at school. Martin was a good boy, but I was always around the wild kids, always in scraps and scrapes and getting up to mischief. It wasn't that I was bad, like a brat or a delinquent or anything, I just loved adventure and fun and was always looking for crazy shit to do. After Preston Grange, we went to John Spence Community High. It was a rough-arse school – like kids drinking Tipp-Ex at lunchtime to try and get high and stuff like that. It was a melting pot of fuck-off kids from all different backgrounds, but the school uniforms weren't nerdy and that suited me.

I guess school wasn't real important to me, because BMX was taking me all over the world from a young age and I was totally addicted. I loved racing, but I loved ripping jumps as well. I lost count of how many times I was British and National Champion between the ages of five and sixteen; I think it's something like nine times British Champion and ten times National Champion. I had a pretty successful amateur career in racing and I met real good friends – some

of them are still in my life now. BMXing was kinda like a cult
or a secret society for me, we all had the same passion and
shared a bond that outsiders didn't understand. Some riders
from this BMX family went on to become famous; people
like Alan Smith, the professional footballer who played for
Leeds United, Newcastle, Manchester United and England;
and Matt Helders, founding member of the Arctic Monkeys,
who raced a few years younger than me.

When I was a kid, I'd always do better than my brother
because I was bigger and stronger. I was always good in
my age group. I didn't always win, but I was always in
the top three at BMX national racing events. I made the
European Championship finals a bunch of times and got
second twice, beaten both times by a Dane called Simon
Christenson. Martin came into his own later on, when he
got bigger and stronger, it was then that it got competitive
between us. Like, Martin was real small for his age when
he was young, competing against kids who were world
champions and like grown men compared to him. When we
got older, he got bigger and, once he started doing well, he
took it real seriously. The key to Martin's racing was coming
from behind and using track skills to pass through the field.
It wasn't until I reached the age of sixteen, when me and
Martin both moved up to the pro class, that we started to
race each other for real.

There was keen rivalry between us during those later
racing years. Like, when you get on the gate for a BMX race,
it don't matter who's beside you, you just want to beat them.
We had some good races and he was always better than me.

Fitness was a key factor with racing and I think it was
1991 when I joined a grimy-ass old boxing gym. I just went
there to train, not to fight in the ring. It was where I met this
old trainer guy – he looked like Mickey out of the Rocky films.
He gave me a piece of advice I never forgot, even though I
was only about eleven at the time – it wasn't 'women weaken
legs', like Mickey told Rocky – it was 'there's no short cuts,
boy, you get out what you put in'. I did a massive amount of
push-ups and running and sit-ups and pad work in that old
gym. I'd never been so fit!

But, despite all the stuff I was into, trying to get away from the bleakness of winter in the northeast of England was sometimes a kind of longing of the soul. OK, when I couldn't ride I had diving and training at the gym and stuff, but I was always looking for something else – something new and different. I guess it's an elusive, wistful feeling that most adolescents experience. We don't really know what it is and we try to find it in different ways. Like, a few of the older kids at high school used to deal acid tabs and me and my friend Fuller decided we'd give it a try.

This particular Friday night was cold and frosty and we lay on the crunchy grass and it was like there was crystals all over the ground, like diamonds in the moonlight. It was mental. We laughed and laughed every time we looked at each other – I don't know what it was made us go into stitches, but I was laughing so hard I could hardly breathe. Afterwards we went up to my room and stared at all the crazy multicoloured rave flyers on the walls that we thought were moving. They all blended together and moved round in circles and we were locked in that trip for hours. I was only eleven when I took that first acid trip, and I didn't take another until I was a lot older and living in California.

But all this bad kinda stuff was just a diversion, the real meaning of life was always BMXing. And funny shit used to go down all the time, like what happened at the European Championships in 1992. They were held in Padova, Italy, and all the British spectators were in a grandstand along the back straight. There was a massive tree between them and the track obstructing the view and, this is crazy, but my dad decided to start cutting at that tree with a handsaw. It came crashing down and landed on the back straight while a race was going round the track. Luckily it didn't hit any of the kids, but it caused fucking uproar – like, I think the trees were protected or something. Just as I'm about to go into the starting gate I look to my right and I can see Jeff dressed in a crazy disguise – in glasses and a granddad hat – and hiding from the polizia who came rushing over to the English crowd. He hid out on the start hill for the rest of the event, like two days, while the cops surrounded the English fans and searched for him.

I ended up winning my race, but I don't know how.

The Titan Team broke up in 1992 after the quality of the bikes diminished – they were being made cheaply overseas in Taiwan and China. Cynthia and Jeff met Ron Bonner at the ABA Grand Nationals in Oklahoma, one of the biggest BMX race meetings in the world. He was a friendly, energetic guy from Florida who started a cool BMX brand called Underground Products, or UGP, and my parents brought it to the UK BMX scene. They ran the Cycle Craft Team and UGP Groove Crew Team, with riders like Ross Hill, Chico Hooke, Marco Dell'isola, Neal Wood and my brother Martin.

When I was thirteen I travelled to the European Championships in Sweden with the Cycle Craft Team, before going to the World's in Holland, two weeks later. Despite getting second at those championships – it was real close, the first photo-finish I'd ever been in – the main memory I got of Sweden is setting fire to a pile of rubbish. It seemed like a cool idea at the time, me being me like I was back then. But the wind caught the flames and spread them and the fire got out of control and half the fucking campsite burnt down. No one died or got seriously hurt, but there was fire trucks and police everywhere. The older riders got the blame, Neal Wood and Chico Hooke were banned, and it was the beginning of the end for the UGP Groove Crew Team. I guess the fire wasn't the only thing out of control that night. The wayward kinda life around North Shields and Newcastle started to cross over into my life in BMX.

Holland came after that, where I loved to race because I could go to the smoke shops and buy weed and smuggle it back in our camper van.

But, no matter where I went, I loved coming back to the northeast – it was my home and I never really thought about living anywhere else. There'd be a whole gang of us kids messing about – I can't remember all the names – we'd hang round Whitley Bay ice rink doors and get into scraps on the weekend. We'd watch the Whitley Bay Warriors play and then get up to mischief. All that crazy shit was just about getting a buzz and pushing the limits. I was all about the ultimate rush.

You can never second guess the future – I found that out the hard way in 2007 – but, in the last few years before moving south, I started doing some other stuff, apart from scrapping and smoking a bit of weed and being wild. Stuff like breaking into cars, just for something to do. We'd go across to the council estate where Mark Lopez lived – remember the kid I had the fight with? We became friends after that and we'd camp in his back yard. Once we knew his mum and dad were asleep we'd leave the tent and go 'twocing' – taking without owners consent. This was a Geordie thing, like stealing car stereos and selling them. It wasn't like we actually 'broke into' the cars, we just went around checking the doors and you wouldn't believe how many people didn't lock their cars at night. If the door opened we took the stereos to the guys on the taxi rank who always wanted them for their cabs. It was a rush. Sometimes we'd get into crazy chases with the cops and we'd ride to the quarry – we knew it like the back of our hands. We had places they couldn't come after us and we'd always lose them. We'd go buy 'tac' with the money we made, which was northeast slang for cannabis resin.

The other thing on every young guy's mind is sex – and I guess you could say I lost my virginity when I was about fourteen, at a BMX race in Coppull, near Preston. It was a Friday night and everyone was camping for the racing and there was motorhomes and vans all over the place and a massive marquee for the parents to drink and let loose on the karaoke. My mate Jim-Bob brought along his girlfriend and her sister, who was sixteen. We were drinking cider and hanging out in some caravan. One thing led to another and I ended up in a tent with that girl and a durex. Halfway through I could hear my mum shouting –

'Stephen, I know you're in there with that girl!'

But I couldn't stop. I shot my lot into the durex and ran back to our caravan without taking it off. Cynthia was waiting and I had to talk her down with lies and excuses before I could get the rubber off. The cheap fucking thing had dried up and kinda set on my dick somehow, like a second skin, and I thought I'd have to have the fucker surgically removed. I remember this being the most awkward moment of my young life up to then.

It was round about this time that my parents started
having disagreements. I don't really know what about and I
don't need to know either because it's none of my business.
I guess you could say my dad was kinda like a colourful
character. I remember once in Switzerland at the European
Championships he hired a camper van, when we got back to
the campsite after being at the track, this Belgian dude had
parked his caravan in our spot. The space wasn't marked as
ours or anything and we could've just went somewhere else.
But Jeff saw red and pulled the camper van up so close to
the Belgian guy's awning that he scratched the entire side.
The dude had to un-peg his awning to get out and there was
an altercation, to put it mildly.

The Belgian turned out to be a cop and he called the
Swiss authorities. The police arrived, but my dad refused
to speak to them. My mum gave him a slap and this kinda
shocked me – I'd never seen her get bad-ass like that before.
He didn't retaliate or anything, just turned round and said
to her –

'I da nah what yas getting' so upset aboot.'

He lost his £500 deposit because the new camper had so
much damage to it.

But my dad's always been that kind of character. He'd go
out of his way to prove a point and sometimes make a scene
and embarrass my mum. It's like, he'll always get the result
he wants and not care much about the consequences. It's his
way or the highway! Some people might say he was difficult,
even militant, but I say he was just strong – and it was his
strength that was there for me after I got hurt and is still
there for me today.

Anyway, they started having a lot of arguments and they
eventually split up. It was during the summer of 1994, when
I was fourteen. It was real hard – real hard, man. Me and
Martin had to move down to Bidford-on-Avon with my mum,
away from everything we'd known all our lives.

Goodbye to the northeast!

3
GOING DOWN SOUTH

OK, in case you don't know where it is, Bidford-on-Avon's on the border between Warwickshire and Worcestershire, about six miles downstream from Stratford-on-Avon and six miles upstream from Evesham. The place couldn't have been more different from Tyneside and we hated it. Me and Martin were working-class dudes and now we were right in the middle of all these poncified people who thought they shit Chanel. There was this guy called Tony Edgworth who used to come to the BMX races with his son Scott and Cynthia had got close to him somehow. So me, Martin and mum moved into his house in Bidford.

Our relationship with Tony wasn't all that cool. We were gobby teenagers with plenty of attitude and we never really connected with him. We couldn't understand why mum wanted to be with him, but I guess he made her happy, so we just had to go along with it. The house we moved to was small and me and Martin had to share a room. It was a two-up-two-down terraced place that was cramped and we were on top of each other a lot. This gave us an excuse to get out and ride our bikes every spare minute. We became real close and stuck together – we didn't know anyone else, except Scott, who lived with his mother in the village of Broadway, about ten miles away. He'd come and ride his bike with us whenever he could. BMX was all we took with us from North Shields and riding was our connection to the past and our escape from a world that was different and hostile.

Moving away from Tyneside was the last thing I wanted. It was like going from the city to the country and that didn't suit me much back then. Bidford was a posh area and I had to go to Prince Henry's High School in Evesham. This was completely different to the John Spence Community High in North Shields; I had to wear a blazer and a fucking tie and these really un-cool shiny shoes. I was like –

'Fucking hell, you gotta be kidding me!'

Fitting in with the kids from the snooty world down in Evesham wasn't really happening for me either. I didn't want to be like them. I couldn't relate to them. Everybody talked with a posh accent and I was the only Geordie in the school with a thick dialect that nobody understood. It was a million miles from when I rode with Mad Mick in the woods at Hollywell Dene. Like, there was a kids' TV show called 'Byker Grove' at the time, about a youth club in the tough Byker district of Newcastle, and all the stuck-up twats'd shout out 'spuggie man!' at me, which was meant as an insult. It was hard to stop myself from bashing a few of them.

Conforming wasn't on my radar and I always tried to get away with wearing Old Skool Vans instead of the shiny shoes. I kept getting called into the headmaster's office and given shit for not following the rules. It was an alien world all right, but I still had my bike. Mr Cox, the head of PE told me 'you'll never make anything of yourself riding a child's bike, Murray, you need to play rugby'. I didn't care what he said, it was like I was in my own world on that bike. I didn't care if no one understood – all I wanted to do was ride. All the other kids had their cliques of football clubs or rugby clubs or shit-don't-stink clubs and the posh twats tried to give me a rough time. Those guys had no fucking idea!

But there was a few good people hidden in among the idiots and I eventually got to know them. One of those guys was Lee Martin, he sat on the desk in front of me at form registration and I met him on my first day at Prince Henry's. He became one of my best friends and he's still here with me today. Apart from that, for the most part, I had BMX and that's all I needed.

I must've been about fifteen when I went to a contest called the Backyard Jam in Hastings. It was a freestyle event, held at a BMX track in Bexhill. BMX had dipped in popularity and was at an all-time low. This contest was organised by a guy called Stu Dawkins, who ran the biggest BMX-only distribution company in the UK, called Seventies. Stu was at the heart of BMX freestyle through thick and thin and the world's best freestylers would make a pilgrimage to Hastings every summer for the Backyard Jam. It was a mini festival and celebration of everything good about BMX and thousands of people camped out to see the event. I'd never been to anything like this in my life. The place was buzzing and I could feel the atmosphere – it was insane.

It was the first time I got to see the real US pros – riders like Taj Mihelich and Mat Hoffman and Chris Moeller, alongside the UK pros like Ian Morris and Jerry Galley – all sending it in a good-time Jam contest. I couldn't believe I was seeing them with my own eyes – I'd watched riders like this in videos but to see them in real life was something special. Thousands of people swarmed round the chasm – the biggest jump I'd ever known – probably forty-five feet long and it went from the top of the start hill right over the last straight, and the landing was on the second berm. This was only for the big boys who'd sack up and hit it, sending themselves into the unknown. Some of the crashes were gnarly, but the riding was off the chain.

I went away from that event absolutely hooked.

When my brother turned seventeen, he'd commandeer mum's car and we'd just take off and ride all the different trails. We'd go up to London to ride with Grotbags and his crew – if you don't know who Grotbags is, he's Paul Roberts and he lived close to the best trails in the country at Pinner near Harrow. He used to be a bike courier and he wore green leggings and he looked like Grotbags, the green witch from the 1980's TV series 'There's Somebody at the Door'. He was a good BMX racer and an even better BMX jumper, he was the King of Dirt and kinda like a mentor to me and Martin. A funny, witty guy and the coolest dude around back then. I knew him since I was a young kid and he helped me a lot with my riding. Grotbags moved to California in

1999 and became the 'Voice of BMX' – he commentated on all the world's biggest BMX freestyle events, including the X-Games, for ESPN.

Like I said, BMX brought me and my brother together more than ever when we moved, and helped us get through mum and dad splitting up. We built our own trails and just rode and rode our bikes all the time. Martin turned pro and he was winning races and showing his true potential. I kept on putting everything into my bike, all my energy, all my life. Mum wanted me to follow my brother and go to Worcester College. It was important to me that she was happy and I always looked up to Martin, so I went. I studied GNVQ in advanced leisure and tourism, and PE. I wanted to make Cynthia proud and do good at college, but at the same time do the absolute minimum I could get away with and I constantly skipped lectures to ride at Worcester Ramps – a community youth centre, right in the middle of Worcester City. It was built by a guy called Eggy for everyone to ride. I worked part-time at a cycle shop near there, fixing and selling bikes.

The first ever BMX race in the UK was held at Redditch in 1981. It's not far from Evesham and, when I first went down south, me, Martin and Scott Edgworth changed that track into trails and built massive jumps on it, using a digger we hired for the day and then with shovels. Some of the alternative riding spots were pretty desperate and we were trying to make something out of nothing – but we built the biggest dirt section in the UK at the time. Four massive sets of doubles in a row. We had killer sessions there in the summer of 1995.

In 1996 the BMX World Championships came to the UK and were held at Brighton on the south coast. This only happened once every ten years and it was a huge occasion for me. Martin entered the junior men's class and I entered the 16-expert class – this'd be my last chance to win the World Championships in expert class and I wanted it real bad. A few weeks before the race, my dad paid for me, Martin and Dale Holmes to stay in a caravan in Brighton so we could train there every day. Nobody rode that track more than us, we knew every line and all the places to pass. On race day I won my semi-final and was feeling real confident. The atmosphere was intense and there was, like, 5,000 plus spectators watching. In the final I got out the gate in the middle of two riders and, going into the first turn, I banged elbows with another guy and that was it – game over. I came fifth, Martin got fourth in the junior men, and Dale Holmes won the pro class. Dale winning that pro class at the World Championship on home soil was probably the biggest day in the history of UK BMX racing – it was fucking momentous!

To this day Dale reckons his win was down to my dad sending us there to live in that caravan and us spending so much time practising on the track.

One thing I gotta say about Dale here – he helped me so much with my riding and he's been a big inspiration to me – I've always looked up to him. Always! He went on to be the most successful BMX racer of all time. I had great respect for him because he was so disciplined and I could see how much hard work he put in. Some might say he wasn't the most naturally talented rider, but he'd do whatever it took to win. It was his work ethic that made him great and I have huge admiration for him to this day.

Dale Holmes, Neal Wood, Jamie Staff and all the best riders from the UK went to California at some time or other. Any serious BMX racer's dream was to live and ride in California, it was where BMX racing was founded and was the hub of the BMX race industry. Dale, Neal and Jamie were the first ever racers to move there full time and it paved the way for the rest of us to follow. Like, the weather over there made for perfect riding conditions and they all had these amazing stories that I'd listen to. That's when I started dreaming about going there myself and all the money I earned from then on went toward paying for a ticket to ride and train in California.

I'd already been to America in 1987, for the World Championships in Orlando, Florida. And in 1996 I got to go there again. This Dutch guy called Gerrit Does was known as the godfather of European BMX back in the late seventies. He ran an annual trip to the US with twenty or twenty-five of the best riders in Europe and I was fortunate enough to be on that trip when I was sixteen. All the European riders flew out to train on a track called The Fairgound in Orlando, in preparation for a race called The Christmas Classic in Columbus, Ohio, on Christmas Day. BMX riders filled all the hotels and we just ran amok. A lot of the guys stayed in the same convention centre hotel near the track and I couldn't resist the temptation to put itching powder in Robert de Wilde's bed – he was one of the top pros in the world at the time – he caught me and held me over the hotel balcony by my feet. Man, he scared the shit out of me! But trips like that always involved taking things to the absolute fucking red line.

The Christmas Classic was renowned for having the best track with a rad pro section and a long straight with difficult jumps that only the real pros could hit. I was only 16-expert at the time, but I loved riding that track because I could hit the big jumps and do tricks in practice. Usually, there was a dirt competition going on in the middle of the track where everyone came for a sick contest and I looked forward to seeing all my idols in real life. This would've been my first opportunity to ride with the Americans, but the contest was taken out of the event due to the behaviour of the pro riders in the hotel in previous years. In 1996 it was just a racing event and I was real disappointed.

I met this dude called Brian Foster there – he could do it all, race and jump and he was kinda like one of my heroes. In 1996 he was the X-Games dirt jumping gold medallist and the American Bicycle Association BMX pro racer title contender. He could win a pro main event and then smash the dirt jumping contest like it was nothing. He was a legend, nicknamed 'Blue Falcon', and one of the pioneers of dirt jumping as an organised sport. I guess I wanted to be like Brian Foster and meeting him in the flesh was something else, man.

In the race itself I got second in the 16-expert, beaten by Ryan McTaggart after leading the whole lap. But it was my first race in the US without my parents and I was pretty stoked. It was a big deal to me to come second, as it was the biggest race in the whole of America.

Around this time back home I'd be getting the bus to the Pinner trails I told you about near London and I usually stayed at Grotbags' house. I'd ride with guys like Jerry Galley and Stuart King. These dudes were the best riders on the UK Freestyle BMX scene at the time. People like that had so much talent. They were way ahead of their time, not necessarily because of the tricks they did, but because of the way they did them. They made riding look so effortless, so cool. These guys were pure skill, man, and riding with them was real special.

I guess I had trail fever back then and I'd go anywhere given the chance. A close friend called Rob Indri would drive up from Southend and take us all over the place. It'd benefit everyone, because he was able to escape from the rat race of London where he worked, and we'd escape the boredom of Worcestershire. I first met Rob racing in the nationals and he was about nine years older than me – kinda like an older brother to me and Martin and we respected him. He was just like us, an unruly hot-head. OK, maybe Rob didn't have natural BMX talent like the Pinner guys, but I never met anyone who had as much passion as him. He told me once –

'If you're gonna do something, give it everything, man. Get first or come last, don't settle for in between. Go big or go home!'

It was another piece of advice I always remembered, just like the stuff Mickey in the gym told me. We were running on pure adrenaline back then, man, riding trails wherever and whenever we could – blasting through rhythm sections and learning new tricks was the ultimate high.

We used to ride Kidderminster a lot – those trails were so sketchy. To get there, we'd hop over the railway bridge – it was littered with needles and shit and we'd try to avoid them – and pass our bikes down and climb a fence to a spot that had some sick jumps. It was here I dialed the 360 variations. Hours and hours of riding every day. We always looked after our jumps, they were immaculate, we'd fix them up before riding and never leave any junk around the place. We respected the dirt and looked after the trails.

In 1996 I signed my first contract to ride for Robinson, a subsidiary company of GT, the biggest BMX bike manufacturer of all time. It was the first time I'd seen a contract and I was wary because it was, like, things were getting a bit serious. I went to the warehouse of Shiners, who was the UK distributor for Robinson and it was like an Aladdin's fucking cave – full of the best helmets, Vision Streetwear shoes, Haro bikes, gloves, Hutch pedals and other stuff. I was just drooling over this stuff and I felt like I was a real pro. Between that and the bike shop at Worcester city centre, I was earning a bit of money at last and didn't need to get a shitty summer job in a fast-food dive. I put what I could away for California and just rode my bike all the time.

So, I guess it was from when I was about sixteen that I really started to focus more on jumping rather than racing. OK, I'd raced all my life and it wasn't something I found easy to let go of. I still had a lot of success racing in England – me and my brother once got first and second in the pro class. But I knew where I really wanted to be. I won the King of Dirt series and I started getting invited to European dirt contests. What a fucking blast, not having to go to bed at nine and be up at seven for gate practice, like with racing. At the dirt camps it was more like coming in at seven in the morning and riding early evening. Much more my kinda lifestyle.

I watched this video called 'Soil', made by Ryan Brennan, nicknamed 'Barspinner'. It just blew me away. I couldn't believe the scene, all the people I looked up to were on this video – and everyone lived at Huntington Beach. They had the life, man – they all rode Sheep Hills every day and other legendary BMX trails like Hidden Valley and Honda Hills – and it made me want more than ever to get out there to California.

My mum said I had to finish my education first. Fair enough!

There was this kid called Dave Smith from college PE and, in 1997, he came over to me and was like –

'You ride BMX? My friend has a track in his garden and he's really into it.'

He said I should go meet the guy. So I skipped college and went to meet this dude called Jason Aliano over in Upton-on-Severn. He lived in the most beautiful place called Duckswich House and he had some small jumps when I first met him. I was like –

'Would you mind if I built some real big fuck-off jumps here?'

'Build whatever you want.'

'Fucking right!'

The Alianos were the coolest family in the world, just amazing people, I can't say enough about them. Tina Aliano would feed us all every night and give us total free run of the house. It was like the old days in Newcastle and I felt real comfortable there. They had some land and they didn't mind me and Jay turning their manicured gardens into the ultimate breeding ground for what was to come.

And that started the whole DTR – Duckswich Trail Riders – scene. In the past when I built trail spots the council would always come and flatten them, ruining all the blood, sweat and tears of building and nurturing that I'd put in. Now it was different and, before you knew it, me and Jay and Scott and my brother Martin had the funnest, raddest trails ever and I knew they'd be safe on the Duckswich land. I missed so much college building and riding at Duckswich House. My mum'd get a call from college asking why I hadn't turned up that day and she'd make some excuse. She'd then get straight on the phone to Jay and ask if I was over there with him and why wasn't I at college? Even though she knew why. Jay would always lie, saying he didn't know where I was when really I was busting flatties in his garden rather than being in some crappy classroom.

After riding the trails, I'd go in and get Chris Aliano to teach me guitar and piano. I was never great, but I could hold a tune. We had loads of fun at Jay's house, riding motorbikes, flying remote control planes, playing tennis and ping-pong. It was the ultimate playgound and I felt at home there.

I really started to get good on dirt. My bike control was getting dialed and I'd be constantly skipping lectures to go spend all day at the trails. I'd be living on bags of sour candy and bottles of coke and I'd sweat so much I'd drink gallons of water. One of the main problems I experienced riding my bike was my hands sweating so much. I'd always have at least four pairs of gloves in my backpack; and I'd perspire like crazy in my helmet and squeeze the foam on the inside against my forehead and watch the sweat pour out, like it was coming from my brain.

Between 1996 and 1998 I was riding my bike on the Duckswich trails every day, weather permitting. If it rained, I'd ride at the indoor skatepark. In 1997 and 1998 me and Martin rode for Haro Bikes through a distributor called Moore & Large and I started to get proper recognised as a jumper and get paid fairly decent money to jump as well as ride. I was developing my skills all the time. Martin mixed it in pro class and was UK pro elite champion in 1999 and went on to be national 4-cross champion in mountain biking, beating the mountain bike legend, Steve Peat. He kept racing in comps up until 2001, when he retired and turned into a weekend warrior on his mountain bike. I guess he got burnt out competing and just wanted to have fun riding, without the stress of trying to be the best all the time.

Like I said, I was always attracted to the big jumps on the track and I got more and more into jumping contests. If I'm honest, I gotta say that racing was too strict and disciplined – it was a hard lifestyle that took a lot of dedication, getting up early in the morning and long training sessions. But one of the main reasons I shied away from BMX racing was the introduction of clip-in pedals, where you became attached to the bike. Clip-ins are, like, what they use for road bikes – BMX stands for 'bicycle-moto-cross' and clip-in pedals aren't very moto. They were designed so you could pull up as well as push down on the pedals, making it faster to accelerate. It became more about power and strength, rather than technique and skill. It seemed, at the time, like BMX racing was all about how much you could squat in the gym. I saw some of the racing guys as meatheads who could accelerate fast but had no technique. With dirt jumping I could still be dedicated and have a lot of fun at the same time. All I had to do was ride my bike two or three hours a day, it didn't matter when. I didn't have to do it in the morning and I could party and stay in bed late and it fitted with who I was inside. It was a loose lifestyle – kinda crazy and pushing the limits all the time. It was me, how I wanted to live my life.

So I practised and gained confidence and kinda got obsessed with it. It's different now but, at the time, there was no formal coaching in BMX dirt, like there was in other sports. So you had to adapt. We relied on each other for coaching and that support made us like a family. It's what separated action sport athletes from the rest of the universe – we had a strong bond and we loved what we were doing. We kept each other focused on reaching the next level. When one rider pushed the limits, it set the bar for others to go beyond their known abilities. The support we had for one another was stronger than in many other sports. I guess you could say in many ways we were pioneers!

People talk about 'progression' in action sports, more so than in any other discipline. Reason being, in BMX dirt jumping there's no formal rulebook, no standard arena to compete in, no set of plays to run. As much as we refine and perfect the tricks we know, we're just as much experimenting with new ones. It's like the sport's in a constant state of evolution, with new tricks being thrown, venues and jumps designed, and the bar forever being raised. I guess it's kinda like human nature at the end of the day; like ambition's driven men and women to explore and invent and drive forward. In action sports, this progression is like Tony Hawk landing the first 900, Laird Hamilton pioneering tow-in surfing, first descents in snowboarding – me doing the double backflip. It's new stuff all the time and it's what made dirt jumping special to me.

I started doing well in contests, winning a lot of them and beating people I never thought I'd be hanging with. Guys like Marcus Hampel from Germany, an amazing rider, another guy far out there, with natural talent.

The King of Dirt came back to the BMX UK racing scene in 1997, holding three contests at the national racing series. I'd go up to the race venue the day before practice and there'd be big piles of rubble with sketchy dirt and glass and concrete and stuff. OK, in pro dirt jumping, practice is where you get a feel for the jumps. You get to sus the course out, go through in your head what tricks you can do, where and when. It's where you piece your runs together, see what everyone else is doing, what the next level of riding is. I don't know what those organisers thought we were supposed to do with that course, considering some of the sessions that went down at events like this were pushing the envelope of what was possible on a bike. All the dirt jump riders got together with shovels and sorted out jumps that we could have a proper contest on – they gave us fuck-all to work with, but we made the most of what we had.

I ended up winning the King of Dirt in 1997 and people were getting to know who I was – kids were asking for my autograph and stuff. I got great satisfaction out of making the kids happy; if signing an autograph did that, then it was cool by me, because I remembered how much it meant to me when I was younger.

I became King of Dirt in England and then Europe. I got the Guinness world record for the highest air in 1998 at the European King of Dirt in Cologne, Germany. I was eighteen then and starting to travel abroad by myself or with my friend Kye Forte. We'd have a fucking blast partying before the contests and it was the time the whole race scene got played out for me – crappy tracks and shit start gates and meatheads pushing as much weight as they could with their clip-in pedals. Jumping had come along and I was having way more fun doing that and riding trails with my mates. I found something I was really good at and everything else took a back seat.

I decided it was time for my first backflip at Ipswich National Races in 1998. Normally, riders would do this on the smaller last jump, but I decided I'd go all out and land it on the massive first set. There was a crowd of about five hundred people and I wanted to go big, even then. I remember putting on the full-face helmet I used for racing – it gave me confidence. It was fucking scary. I didn't know how it was gonna go down because I'd never done one before. I also had this thing with my gloves – like crazy OCD where I'd push the gloves up off my grips, pulling them further up my hands. I'd do that three times on each hand – on the right and the left and then both together – as soon as I'd pushed both hands together I was locked and ready to go.

So, I'm on the starting hill and I crank my ass off toward the first set way faster than I need to and just go to the moon. When I'm upside down, I abort and eject the bike and come down feet first on the landing. I know I can do it, so I crank back up the start hill and try it again, landing on both wheels with just my feet slipping off. I don't reckon I've pulled this, because it wasn't pulled clean. But it was fucking close!

I slept on it.

This shit was gnarly.

4
THE ROAD TO CALIFORNIA

I won the dirt competition at the BMX Racing World Championships in France in 1998. That's where I landed my first clean backflip. That feeling was like no other, man – it was fucking insane – landing it and winning and the crowd going mental. Everyone was shouting and the music was blaring. All my friends mauled me and I'm thinking, life can't get any fucking better than this! Can it?

Back when I was a young kid, I never imagined living anywhere else but the northeast of England. Then I had to move south with my mother and I didn't like it, I wanted to go back home. Tyneside was the place I considered to be *home* for so long, the place I fitted into best. As the years went by, I came to thinking that maybe moving away was a good thing – maybe if I'd stayed there things might have went wrong for me. Looking back in 1999, I could see I was kinda going off the rails a bit in North Shields and who knows what would've happened to me if I'd stayed.

Fate's a peculiar thing, isn't it?

Now I was thinking of moving again.

In the late nineties some of the UK BMX race pros went out to California to stay with Dale Holmes and Neal Wood for winter training, to escape the shitty English weather. They'd go from about November to March and the apartment on Georgia Street in Huntington Beach was always full of BMXers. My brother Martin went out there in 1997, after he finished college. He went from January to April and stayed mostly with Jamie Staff. He rode Sheep Hills and, when he came back, he had dirt on his bike and he told me the dirt was from there and I was well impressed because, to me, Sheep Hills was the fucking coolest place in the universe.

I took a year out of education when I was eighteen and went out there for six months to ride in Huntington Beach. I slept on the floor in Dale and Neal's place, along with a bunch of other guys – riders like Kelvin Batey, Robbie Miranda and Nigel Page. We'd often ride with mountain bikers like Steve Peat and Brian Lopes, who lived in the apartment next door; and a regular visitor from Utah would be Shaun Palmer, who won gold in the X-Games snowboarding comp and was also one of the best mountain bikers in the world at that time. They were true warriors, they'd wake up, live, eat and sleep like champions – I had the utmost respect for those guys.

When I first got out there, I'd ride from Main Street down the Pacific Coast Highway bike pass, looking at the waves crashing under the blue sky and feeling the warmth of the sunshine. This was something else to me; I mean it was, like, October or something, and back in England it would've been getting all grey and dark and rainy. I was living out of a sleeping bag at Neal and Dale's, eating pasta, rice and tuna. All we did every day was ride. We'd do sprints and go to the gym; we had our own starting gate in front of the house and I'd be doing gate starts in the street with Leveque, Foster, Allier and others – the best racers in the world, bar none!

I got to ride Sheep Hills, my life-long dream. Sheep Hills were world-famous trails, located between Huntington Beach and Costa Mesa, next to the water inlet. I rode this route to get there and it was, like, six miles of paradise. The first thing I noticed at the entrance was the smell of the dirt – it had its own unique smell, you could almost taste it. I rode down a long path and my bike got covered in a film of stuff that looked like moon dust. When I got into the trails I couldn't believe it – I kept looking at the jumps and thinking how tired and knackered they looked. They were crumbling where the long Californian summer had baked the earth and they needed a whole bunch of water. The dirt there was like nothing I'd ever seen – it was so difficult to work compared to anywhere else I'd been.

So I'd ride down there every day and spend hours and hours trying to make a lip for take-off, grooming it over and over. After a few hits, it'd be falling apart again. I was like –

'Man, this place sucks!'

It was nothing but moon dust everywhere. But there was a million pros down there and I thought –

'I can't believe all these bad-asses ride such a shit place.'

I soon learnt that it wasn't how good the place was, it was the riders who went there that made the sessions. That's what made it special. I can't explain how good it was. I turned up and every pro racer was there, every pro jumper, all the different characters. It was amazing, man, and a privilege to be able to work on the jumps there.

My dream was always to ride the Sheep Hills with my brother, Rob Indri, Dale Holmes and Grotbags. Rob was supposed to come out a couple of weeks after me, but I didn't hear anything from him. Then the news came through that he'd taken his own life by throwing himself in front of a train. I was totally fucking devastated and I couldn't understand how someone with so much life and character could kill himself. Later I found out he suffered from clinical depression and I remembered what he said to me all that time ago –

'Give it everything, man. Go big or go home!'

Maybe he gave it everything he had – and decided it was time to go home.

After missing all that time at college riding the Duckswich trails, I've no idea how I got good grades and passed, but I did and got accepted into Worcester University. Once I'd spent some time in California, dirt jumping was what I wanted to go all in for and I didn't want to go back. I was just like –

'I'm not going back to University! This is me. I'm staying here!'

After a while I got promoted from the floor to the couch in the apartment. This greaser called Chris Stephenson used to come home pissed up and pour water and washing up soap and beer and other stuff on me when I was asleep – people might remember him as the S&M manager from some of the old Props videos. Anyway, I'd be like –

'What the fuck are you doing?'

I was still young then, only nineteen, and he was about thirty. The drunken sonofabitch used to push me and try to start fights with me. I guess it was because Stephenson saw the dedicated racers getting up so early and didn't like me lying on the couch while he had to get up and go to work. Or maybe the guy was just a fucking bully. He was always drunk and I wanted to smash him so bad, but I never ended up doing it out of respect for Neal and Dale.

Other than that, it was awesome. It was a real exciting time and I loved every minute of it. But it had to come to an end and, in March 1999, I came back home for a while, to make things right and get the rest of the money I needed to go out there for good. I told Cynthia I didn't want to go to university, I just wanted to go back to California.

'I'm going back, mum ... I really need to!'

'If that's what you want, Stephen, I won't stop you.'

I was real good at jumping now and that first trip to Huntington Beach made me even better. I'd ridden every day for months, like, I'd do three things every day – gym and trails, and I'd still do gate starts, because that was in my blood, at the world famous Orange Y BMX track off Chapman Avenue.

I was ready to move on.

Like I said before, I was getting paid to ride my bike for Haro and, for a long time, I'd also been selling these fake clothes – fake designer stuff that was knocked off. I got the gear from a Scouser I met at race meetings a few years earlier, he was the dad of one of the other riders. The kids in

Evesham didn't have access to this kinda stuff and I saw an opportunity to make some easy cash. This Scouser would come to the BMX events and open up his van –

'E'yer are, berds and gentlemun, straight from Italy ... Calvin Klein, Hugo Boss, Burberry ... anyth'n yous want now!'

I'd buy the stuff from him and bring it back down south and sell it to the college kids and the nerds at Prince Henry's. Snide gear was a good earner, but it still wasn't enough money to get me back to California. I had to get real work to save enough cash for that.

My first proper job was at Kane's food factory in Evesham, making garlic butter stars – classy, eh? I had to wear overalls, gloves and a fucking hairnet like an old granny. My job was to squeeze the garlic butter from a big tube thing and it came out in the shape of stars – it was shit, a robot could do it. I fucked about and stuffed some of the garlic butter into this bloke's mouth, so they moved me to the carrot line with a character called 'Barry-the-Carrot'. He was so fucking fast peeling carrots, you wouldn't believe – like a blur. Barry complained I was too slow, so they moved me to the lettuce line, cutting lettuces on a conveyor belt. Before long, I sliced my finger with this real sharp knife I was using and my glove filled up with blood and I thought 'fuck this', so I took all the shit off and rode away on my bike.

Two weeks later I had to bite the bullet and get a job in another food factory, Dawn Foods, but that was no better. I was on the muffin line, I had another big squirty thing full of blueberry paste and I'd squirt it into muffin mix and listen to old ladies yap on about their pensions and how they were gonna retire with no money and they didn't know how they were gonna manage. I fucking hated it there and I thought –

'What the fuck am I doing here, squirting horrible processed blueberry shit?'

So I said 'fuck this' too and walked out. That was it. I didn't want to be stuck in a factory, I wanted to ride.

In 1999 I won the Sprite Urban Games at Clapham Common in London, a big action sports festival with maybe five or six thousand people. All the top names of European pro BMX were there for three days. It was a sick event, man, they had a BMX park, vert and dirt and there was all sorts of other stuff going on too – graffiti and breakdancing and skateboarding and fashion. After riding in California for six months, I was always gonna win that jumping event, even though I was up against all the top European guys. I put the prize money of £1,000 toward my pot of cash for America.

I'd been making this video for nearly three years, ever since I was sixteen. It was inspired by 'Soil' and Ryan Brennan, aka Barspinner, and I called it 'Bicycles and Dirt'. I filmed it all over the world, everywhere I went. I filmed, edited and produced the whole thing myself – designed the box, the lot, everything – using all the footage from my BMX travels. I used to drive down to Devon and spend long days and nights in an editing studio, compiling thousands of hours of camcorder video footage, compressing it into a thirty-minute masterpiece with legendary tunes and BMX anthems. I managed to sell two thousand copies – personally driving round in my mum's canary yellow Citroen Saxo to every bike shop in the country to make sure 'Bicycles and Dirt' was on the counter. When I was competing in the European dirt competitions, I'd find distributors to sell my VHS. It was on sale in France, Holland, Germany, Belgium and an NTSC version in America. I was real proud of that thing!

In the end, my dad gave me some money to put with what I made from the video and what I'd saved. I finally had enough to get me on my way for my second trip to California.

This time I wasn't coming back.

In November 1999 I packed up and flew with Virgin from Heathrow to LAX. I had about $4,000 in my pocket and I headed for the BMX Mecca of Huntington Beach, California, to follow the dream that started when I heard all those older guys telling their stories years before. I was gonna go there and no way was I gonna fail. This was my time. I was already someone who pushed the envelope and was known for the go big, risky tricks. I reckoned I had self-confidence in sackfuls and I knew that'd give me the edge I needed. People were saying I was the smooth new kid – fast and stylish, 360ing doubles when I was only eleven and throwing backflips mid pack in pro motos. They said I made riding look effortless and I was the one to watch. That stuff didn't go to my head. I knew who I was, a green kid who still had to prove himself; it was OK doing what I did in the UK and Europe, but I was gonna be with the big boys now.

If America was the land of opportunity, California was the centre of it all for action sporters and the birthplace of BMX. It was home to all the big brands, in and around Orange County – GT Bikes, S&M Bikes, Fit – and the biggest media outlets as well, like *Ride BMX*, *Snap*, *Transworld BMX* and others. It was the place where all the photo shoots took place for all the magazines I'd read growing up as a kid. It was the Mecca of the BMX world and home to the world's best pros, who'd swarm there from all over to live their dream. The sun shone all the time, not like in England. I could ride every day!

But it was the end of summer again when I got to Sheep Hills and I was like –

'Man, this place still sucks!'

Nothing but moon dust, just like when I came here before, and I had to get busy again and look after the jumps with the locals. But, if something needs to be done, then it's best to get it done! So I got hold of water pumps and some hoses and got everyone out there working. What a scene, man! I rode a chrome Haro and rocked Airwalk shoes. It was sunset sessions at Sheep Hills during the week and races on the weekend. Then the racing stopped when I added some crazy moves to my trick list.

Like I said, the transition from racing to jumping wasn't an easy one for me, but it was the time now. I had the desire and bike-and-speed control, and I was prepared to put 110% into something I saw as my future.

After a week in California, I flew to Bethlehem in Pennsylvania to visit a rider called Chris Stauffer and some guys called Magilla and Sal. I met them when they came over to England to session the trails at Duckswich House. I always wanted to ride the east coast, so they invited me over. The house they lived in was roach and I stayed there for two weeks, on the couch in a sleeping bag – it was winter and freezing cold at night. But riding the most insane trails on the east coast, places like Posh and Nam, was fucking awesome. I'd never rode trails as good as these before – hundreds of jumps and turns, in and out of the trees – it didn't get any better, man. I was kinda sorry to go back to California, but I knew my future was there.

Within the first month back I got a call from my ultimate all-time hero, Gary Ellis. He was a BMX racing legend. One of the last and winningest of the old-school pros, known as 'The Lumberjack', mostly because of his size and his beard and because he came from the timber country of Tacoma, Washington State. He asked me if I'd like to ride for Nirve Bicycles, with Kyle Bennett, Dale Holmes, Christian Becerine and Mike Laird. I couldn't fucking believe it. They were starting up this new company and Dale was their pro BMX racer. He said they were interested in picking up a pro dirt jumper and asked if I was interested. Like I wouldn't be or something!

'No way, man! You're kidding.'

'I'm not kidding.'

It sounded crazy, me as a pro dirt jumper? I'd only just got here. Surely that was, like for Ryan Nyquist or TJ Lavin – it was too far out to be me. I rang my mum and dad and brother.

'Gary Ellis wants me to ride for Nirve!'

'Do it!'

'Yeah, go for it!'

So I rode down there and they had a two-year contract waiting on the table. It was $1,000 a month.

'I can't survive on that. My rent's $500 a month and I got to eat and travel and stuff.'

So they raised it to $1,400 a month. I signed on the dotted line.

My first event was a race in Reno, Nevada. GT had a dirt jump series in a shit-smelling horse arena. I made the race final and entered the televised dirt competition, even though I wasn't expecting to qualify. After I did shit in the race and didn't ride well, I just assumed I didn't make the finals in dirt. I was starving, so I went to Denny's and wolfed down two double stacks of pancakes. I couldn't have been feeling more sluggish when Brian Foster came in the diner, he was the man in BMX at the time, bar none.

'Murray, you're in the finals, dude. They're calling your name.'

I couldn't fucking believe it!

I remember how dialed the guys in the final looked – Chad Kagy and Joey Garcia and Ryan Nyquist – it was the first time I'd seen Nyquist compete in the flesh and it was overwhelming, man. But, as it was also my first time in front of TV cameras, I choked and came in eight out of ten.

Back on Georgia Street I was on a completely different schedule to Dale and Neal and they thought I just did fuck-all all day. Dale and Neal were two very different characters who'd managed to room together for years. Dale was a real pro, as disciplined and strict as any elite athlete in any sport. He was a European and world champion racer at the height of his career and on the American circuit podium week in and week out. He was a great role model and a cool person to look up to. Neal was an awesome all-round pro BMX racer who could ride trails with the best and still be a punk rocker at the same time. Sometimes the punk rocker got the better of the racer and he could drink like a fucking pirate, but he kept it under control enough to balance the image with the career. Grotbags ended up living with us from time to time too. The place was just a melting pot of personalities with BMX as our common bond.

That apartment was always full of visiting English riders who'd be in sleeping bags on the floor, getting to live the Californian dream for a short time in their lives – right at the epicentre of the BMX world. There was plenty of drinking and partying at the weekends and one night someone brought a hooker back – I'm not sure who, it might have been Andrew Lawton, aka Weasel, as far as my hazy memory of the night can recall. I'm not saying this is what *actually* happened, but this woman pulls a derringer out of her purse – I guess you all know a derringer's a small, lady's handgun, and she's like –

'You want I should blow your fucking balls off?'

I reckon it was because Weasel drank too much and couldn't perform, so he wouldn't pay her – but maybe not. Anyway, there was panic and people ducking for cover. It sure as fuck shook me up; it was the first time I'd seen a real handgun and it tripped me out. The hooker didn't shoot anyone. I guess someone must've gave her what she wanted and she left in a cab. I just hope that taxi driver didn't try to overcharge her!

We were all fuckers for taking the piss out of each other at any opportunity. Like, Dale loved to get at me and I'd have him banging on my door at 8:30am and shouting –

'Why don't you get out of bed you lazy dirt jumper!'

Trails this and trails that!

'Dale, man ... shut the fuck up, will you?'

He was an annoying fucker then, because he was on a strict racer training programme. I couldn't get out of bed because I'd be that sore and tired from riding and I'd need to refuel my body and be off again.

A typical day back then was, like, I'd get up around 11:00am and get picked up by Marvin Loetterle and go riding all day with him and Chris Slope. We'd go ride Sixty Trails and Honda Hills and a bunch of cement parks. I wouldn't go back to the house at all and I'd just be living on the cheapest food and gallons of water. Marvin taught me how to live cut-price – El Roacho, 99 cent dinners, Del Taco and all that crap. We'd go ride the Vans skatepark at night or go street riding. I wouldn't get back to the apartment till midnight and I'd be absolutely fucked.

I bought an old Ford Taurus with a bike rack on the back from Todd Lyons, a top BMX dirt jumper and racer they called 'Wildman'. It was massive inside, with leather seats and air conditioning – I'd never owned anything like it before – and now I could travel to lots of places to ride, no problem. Having air conditioning was a dream. A week later the transmission blew up and I had to buy a completely new engine. I asked Todd to help me out and he gave me $100. Wildman was a tight-ass, he was known for it, he can't deny it.

And so I settled into life in California.

It was to be a roller coaster ride for the next sixteen years!

Watch a 2000 interview with Stephen on stysrg.com

5
OVERCOMING INJURIES

In the first year of my contract I travelled all over the US and broke seven bones in eight months and knocked myself out three times – I mean, completely out, like I was concussed. In February 2000 I broke my leg. In May I broke my collarbone, my shoulder blade and my thumb in one crash. Then I knocked myself clean out and, right after that, I broke my collarbone again. In September I broke my navicular and the lunate bone in my wrist. Then a few more KOs.

When you first get injured bad, you're just so bummed. It's hurting and aching and sore when you get back on the bike and your nerve goes a bit. Then I'd get my confidence back and I'd get injured again. I'd get back on and break my collarbone. I'd get back on and break my ankle. Then it was my wrist. It was literally like that and I'm going –

'What the fuck am I doing?'

Like, anyone else might've called it quits, but I just had this crazy drive to keep on going.

During the King of Dirt contest at the seaport in New York, at the beginning of 2000, I did a double barspin and missed my bars and broke my collarbone. I was literally paralysed on the left side of my upper body and I wanted to get it fixed as quick as I could and get back on my bike and start jumping again.

This sounds crazy, right, and people can think whatever they want about it, but if you don't try things out you never know. I got referred to Mr Simpson, a chartered physiotherapist in Ipswich, back in the UK. This doctor did laser surgery and magnotherapy – there was nothing like that in America then, at least nothing that was legal. Mr Simpson started doing clinical tests on racehorses – these real rich Arab dudes would invest millions in their horses. Y'know what happens if a horse breaks its leg, it has to be shot, it has to be put down because it can't stand up any more, it's not like it can lie on a couch for six months. So Mr Simpson came up with this treatment where he'd weld the bone together with lasers so the horse could instantly start putting pressure on its leg. There'd still be soft tissue damage and the horse'd never race again, but there was the beginnings of a healed bone and the horse could be used for breeding and still make a lot of money for the owners.

So I went to the airport and waited on standby for twelve hours. It was crucial to get the treatment immediately after the injury, to stop muscle atrophy. After I landed back in England, the physio put this magnetic pad on the injuries and created a negative current through the blood – like it drew the healing properties from the blood to the injury site. He explained that it bonded the positive and negative forces together and kinda welded the bone. I don't know exactly how it worked, but it drew all the stuff that heals bones together and focused it on the fracture point. Then he brings this huge laser gun out – like, I'm sitting there shitting myself, I don't know what I've let myself in for. But it was completely painless and there was no scars or nothing, no side effects, just a mild tingling sensation. Afterwards he tells me –

'Lift your arm up and point toward the ceiling.'

I'm like –

'No way, man! It's broken.'

'Do it.'

So I lift my arm and it's pretty sore and stiff, but I can move it all the way up. He makes me do it, like, twenty times.

'The more you do it, the better.'

This went against everything I'd been taught about recovery from injury, but I guess if it worked, it worked! I got broken up in New York on Sunday, flew to England on Monday, got laser surgery on Wednesday and was riding again on Friday. Fucking surreal!

That doctor used me as one of his first human trials. I suppose you could say I was like a guinea-pig – or a test pilot!

The same thing when I broke my leg that year. Before then I couldn't put my foot down at all, I was on crutches. After the treatment, I just stood up and walked, like it was a miracle or something. Normally, if you break a bone, you get a cast put on. Within two weeks the bone forms a meshy substance made up of calcium and other things. It begins to mend. Then it takes another four weeks for it to harden up. During that process your body goes through an incredible state of atrophy and it takes another four to six weeks of therapy and rehab to get back to normal. I couldn't wait that long.

My worst injury that year was at a place called Hidden Valley, off Beach Boulevard in Huntington Beach. Hidden Valley was on the side of a hill in a wooded area and I used to session there with pro freestylers like Troy McMurray and Shaun Butler and Midget Cory. It was off the chain, man! One day I was there practising by myself – it was a time where I was confident with backflips and would take that trick and do it everywhere. There was four jumps at the bottom of the valley and I tried to flip the third mid section and carry on and jump the next. I ended up with too much speed and overshot the jump and under-rotated my backflip. I landed right in the middle of the two jumps and ate shit hard. I was out cold and woke up with three kids staring down at me saying –

'Holy crap, dude, you OK?'

I was dazed and confused and really fucked up.

'Where the fuck am I?'

They told me I'd parked my truck – it was Neal's truck – over by the kids trails. I hobbled across, got in and started it up, then I realised there was no way I could drive. I was in a real bad state.

I asked one of the kids to drive me home but I was so left-field I couldn't remember where I lived! I'd broken my collarbone, shoulder blade and wrist. The kids dropped me at the HB House – a place notorious for party animals and BMXers. I stumbled into the front room and saw Troy McMurray. He looks at me and he's like –

'Fuck me, dude, you look really fucked up.'

'You know where I live, man?'

'Sure, you live round the corner, with Dale and Neal.'

He told me where to go and I stumbled round there and rang the doorbell. Just my fucking luck, there was no one in and it was all locked up. I fell and lay on the grass staring at the sky in agony. An hour or so later I heard Neal arrive on his Harley Davidson. He'd been on a Sunday ride and only came home early because he had a flat tyre. My lucky day after all!

I got taken to Huntington Beach Hospital and they put my arm in a sling and gave me painkillers. Like, there's not much else they can do for a collarbone or shoulder blade and I didn't want them to screw my wrist back together because I'd just have had to go home and rest up for six fucking weeks. I flew back to England the following day and went straight to see the physio in Ipswich. He had this hyperbaric chamber where he'd increase the atmospheric pressure x 2 while I'm breathing 100% oxygen for an hour – it gave the blood nine or ten times as much oxygen, to heal ligaments and soft tissue damage. I was in and out of the clinic in an hour-and-a-half and, within a week, the pain had eased. I was still sore and stiff, but my bones had mended and I was able to ride my bike.

Then I got invited to this gig called the Snap Road Trip. It was sick – the blurb went something like this :-

Nine riders set out today (2nd October 2000) from the *Ride Magazine* offices on a two-week road trip up the west coast of North America – Keith Mulligan (Snap), Tim Strelecki (S&M), Van Homan (Schwinn), Pat Juliff (Little Devil/XS), Garrett Byrnes (Little Devil), Paul Kintner (K2), Stephen Murray (Nirve) and Ryan 'Biz' Jordan (Volume). They'll be visiting California, Oregon, Washington and Vancouver (Canada) on a mission to destroy everything in their path. They'll be hitting dirt and street spots as well as various skateparks as they approach the Canadian border.

You can imagine what nine riders piled into a club van for two weeks stank like! It was close-quarters stuff, sometimes sleeping in the van or on the floors of roachy hotels. But the conditions didn't matter to us, it was just about the riding. We'd stop at all the concrete skateparks and street spots and some of the best trails on the west coast. I made it as far as the sick trails at Salem, Oregon. We were having a heated session when I hit this big lip and my hand slipped off the grip. I broke my wrist – another fucking injury! I couldn't believe I got hurt again, I was just loving being there with riders who'd constantly push the limits of what could be done. Some of the guys on that trip would do things that didn't seem possible, they were oblivious to the dangers and they'd just kill it on their bikes. I was real pissed off when I couldn't keep going, because there was so many more great spots to ride with the crew of a lifetime!

Toward the end of 2000 I finally started to question if dirt jumping was really what I was meant to do. All these fucking injuries! Did I have what it took to be a pro? I questioned my mind and my body. Was I strong enough to go the full nine yards? Maybe I should go back to England and university? It was a real test of will. My sponsors were willing to release me after year one, but I had a two-year contract and my dream would've ended if I lost it. So I said 'fuck it', I'm gonna prove to myself and everyone else that these obstacles and setbacks aren't gonna stop me. I'm gonna fight back!

I travelled from Huntington Beach to Lake Perris three times a week and got that course down. I thought, after crashing so many times I needed to *learn* how to crash. In dirt jumping when you're pushing the envelope you need to know how to land on your feet like a cat. If you fling a cat in the air, it always lands feet first – I needed to be able to do that – be able to get out of dangerous situations safely. So I learnt *how* to crash. After that, I survived a lot of collisions that otherwise would've fucked me up.

I wanted to stay in California, everything was just so cool there – the weather, the quality of life, the opportunities, and beautiful women like no place else in the world. The irony of what happened to me later was, loving to ride was first with me back then. It wasn't about sponsors and money and all that – OK, it was nice to earn $1,400 a month and that was enough for me then – but it was all about loving to ride my bike and getting better and better and achieving my goals on the jumps. Money never did matter all that much to me.

I guess that's why I spent it so carelessly when I got it.

As a pro athlete, I could apply for a four-year working visa and a green card. I didn't want to deal with all the red tape and shit, all I wanted to do was concentrate on riding my bike, so I got myself an agent to deal with visas and stuff. Over that winter I practised non-stop and I felt so good on those jumps and at one with my bike. I pushed myself more and more. I got myself focused. Once I could do a trick it was done and I needed to move on and do more. Like, I saw TJ Lavin do a turndown backflip and it was a real eye-opener to me. I was like –

'Fuck! Which way did his bike go? How did he just do that?'

TJ was clean and professional and had a persona larger than life and that trick was fucking amazing. I really wanted to learn it and, when I did, it became one of my favourites. But I needed more variation. People came to contests with new tricks all the time. It was a case of who's gonna go away and put the time in and come back with the latest thing – push it further. And further.

At that time, before the double backflip, as far as I was concerned all the flip tricks in the world couldn't hold a candle to a sky-high table top. This was a trick that could be done in so many ways and styles you could make it your own – it was the best feeling trick out there. Then something cool happened. I think it was the middle of my first year with Nirve – I just seen this kid come down to Sheep Hills with his hat sideways and he was all –

'Whassssup!'

And all this crazy language –

'Dawg this! Dawg that!'

I couldn't even understand him. We were seeing each other at the trails all the time, so we started riding together and hanging out. His name was Cory Nastazio and we got on real good, we thrived off each other. We rode together non-stop. Non-stop! He influenced me and motivated me and taught me a lot of things. Like how not to be scared to go for it; to have 110% confidence, instead of 90% confidence and 10% worry about the consequences.

Fuck the consequences!

Cory was at an all-time high in his career and he bought a house out in Riverside and I moved in with him. He'd come over from West Palm Beach in Florida and was here for the same reason as me – chasing his dream. He was sponsored by Huffy Bikes and he earned megabucks and was real successful. He got second at the X-Games that year and maybe should have won it. Cory had a larger-than-life personality and we got along like magnets. We had the same things in common – BMX, partying and women – Cory always had the hottest girls and plenty of them at any one time. He had a kinda aura about him – when he walked into a room, everything'd stop and all eyes were on him. I met this girl called Mindy Pantus at his house and she was real cool and we started seeing each other regularly. I gotta say this about Mindy, she was with me before I started winning and she went everywhere with me when I had nothing.

I'd watch Cory ride down Sheep Hills and his JNCO pants would be sagging so low his whole ass would be hanging out. I'd see him go for the gnarliest tricks on the biggest jumps with his hat on sideways and a whole tub of wax spiking up his hair. I remember him going so big and looking like he was crashing, looking like he was gonna die, but somehow he'd always get out of it and go again. Cory was a loud guy and his nickname was 'Nasty', even though he was never nasty to anyone and he'd talk to everyone and had a way of making people feel good about themselves. We became like long-lost brothers – nobody said 'Cory' without someone else saying 'Stephen' and vice versa.

He had an agent called Kimarie Hunt. Kimarie was a great woman, she looked after everything for us, made sure we got to events, booked flights and cars, sorted out issues with girls and was generally there for us all the time. She took the pressure off so we could just do what we liked doing best. I didn't know it then, but Kimarie would come to my aid big time in the future.

I learnt a lot that year and I put it all into practice. I had to prove to myself that I could fulfil my dream and I had another year to do it. I knew if I could apply all the stuff I was learning and practising I could become, like, at one with my bike and everything'd fall into place for me. All over that winter of 2000/2001, me and Cory rode like crazy and just pushed each other. It really showed – my riding was getting so much better than before.

We built massive jumps in our backyard and hit them non-stop. We trained together every day, pushing harder and harder. He made me realise you gotta be serious and he motivated me to push myself to do things I wouldn't have done otherwise. I'd get up around midday and chill until about four o'clock. It could get real hot in Riverside during the day and I didn't like riding in the heat. I used to ride all day in England when I was younger, but in California I saved it all until the last two hours of daylight and went out there and rode hard until it got dark. Then, as soon as the sun went down, I'd be like –

'Man, I wish I had another ten minutes!'

Cory never got out of bed until a couple of hours before sunset. I was lucky to catch a glimpse of him in daylight. He was a true man of the night. He'd ride an hour like no other – he'd kill the session, going bigger than anyone. If you were around to witness those sessions, it'd blow your mind. Afterwards he'd come in and we'd chill, maybe order some pizza, get showered and go out somewhere and just have fun. Sometimes we'd sack early and go to bed at midnight; other times we wouldn't come in until morning.

The first person I saw trying to do a double backflip was Reuel Erickson. And I saw him eat shit hard, time and time again – just knock himself the fuck out, left, right and centre. Then I'd see Cory trying to do it – saw him on the ground freaking out and spasming, having a seizure after smashing his head at the King of Dirt contest in Huntington Beach and I'm thinking –

'Whoa ... that's crazy!'

But he came so close.

I figured, if I could do a single, why couldn't I learn to do a double? So I went to Woodward Camp – this was the home of the US women's gymnastics team in Pennsylvania – they did all their training for the Olympics there. It was a summer camp and a special place for action sports when they hit the mainstream with the popularity of the X-Games. Woodward used its gymnastics experience by including foam pits and resi landings – like, you hit a BMX ramp and do your trick and land in a pit of soft foam rather than on hard dirt. It was the first place in the world to develop this facility and that was a real springboard for the development of new tricks that really raised the bar in BMX.

Woodward had the first real foam pit I felt comfortable jumping into. In the beginning, I went flat out at it full speed and just hucked it all scorpion style – pinned to the bars – didn't know what I was doing. I tried it again and again, but I'd always get pinned. I just couldn't work it out. I was all out of form and I'd keep getting pinned in the scorpion position – there was so much G-force in the spin, and I kept getting taken out badly.

All through that first year or so in California, getting into the X-Games was my greatest goal. It was my dream – my soul's ambition. It was the Olympics of dirt riding – the pinnacle. And it seemed to me like I'd worked my whole life since I was born to get to a level where I'd be good enough to win there. I'd do whatever it took to get where my whole driving force was sending me.

The DK dirt circuit came round and it was a qualifier for the 2001 X-Games. It was at Lake Perris, the jumps I'd been practising on three times a week. This was the first contest of the season. Back then it was four runs, three runs to count. I'm riding up there against TJ Lavin and Ryan Nyquist and all the people I looked up to and admired. Two years ago I was sitting at home in England in the pissing rain, doing crappy little contests for £50 and all of a sudden I was up there on the roll-in with the best riders in the world and I'm thinking, 'I'm here!' I saw how dialed they were, how focused, how professional and composed, but it didn't faze me. I had confidence in my own ability. I knew what I needed to do.

I'd ridden the Lake Perris course so much, I could do tricks with my eyes closed by then. I'd already put the work in, so I reckoned the comp was won before I even dropped in. And that's the way it panned out. I had three really good runs and I'd already won the contest, which left me one last run to throw out, so I figured I had nothing to lose. I said to myself –

'Right, I'm going down and I'm gonna do a double backflip on the last set.'

It was a bomb hole to a big step up, I mean, come to think of it now, there's no way I could double flip it. But I was like –

'I'm just gonna try it. Fuck it, I'm gonna give it a go.'

I just hucked it, man, gave it everything. I pulled so hard I went into a scorpion. When I used to do diving, they told me the more you tuck in the faster you rotate, but it slipped my mind. I got caught up in the moment. I went into a big scorpion, you know, not tucked. I was stiff and had no technique. Got pinned to the bars and my front wheel cased it on the underside of the landing and bent my Nirve frame in two. I was concussed and seeing stars and mad lights in front of me – so fucked, man!

I'm still groggy when everyone starts diving on me and saying –

'You've qualified for the X-Games!'

And I'm like –

'Holy shit!'

I'm tripping out and suddenly I'm getting interviewed on TV for the first time. I'm like –

'Fucking right! Fucking this and fucking that!'

Lee Ramsdell was doing the interview for ESPN and he was pissing himself laughing. I reckon I was still concussed because my Geordie accent came out and no one could understand a word I was saying – apart from 'fuck'. They had to bleep the whole interview.

About a month later, they had a big contest in Venice Beach, sponsored by Panasonic, the Shockwave King of Dirt. By now, me and Cory had been landing doubles into the foam pit every time. We'd been working on technique and we figured this was it. This was the time to do it for real – in competition. We got on to the roll-in and made a pact that we'd both send the double here. He went first, landed on his wheels and, with all the force, just blew his feet off the back of his bike. He was like –

'Come on, let's do it again. This is the time. We're pulling it right now!'

He went again, landed, and his feet blew off again. He's running around all crazy. I'm thinking –

'Man, I've gotta stick this right now! If I don't stick it, I'm gonna be pissed!'

So I get the rotation down and land on both wheels – I send it. But then my feet blow off and it's not pulled clean – but I landed on my bike! That's when I know I can do the double backflip in competition. The crowd know it too, they go absolutely fucking mental.

It wasn't until I was driving away from that contest that the full realisation of what I'd achieved set in. OK, I was in the X-Games, but now I started to believe I could win it!

The DK contest at Lake Perris was a couple of months before the X-Games. After qualifying and beating the people who were my idols, I got so confident. Then, after Venice Beach, I knew I wasn't just gonna go there to make up the numbers – I was gonna win! And the way to win it was with the double backflip. I went back to the foam pit and worked on how to get that double flip around without being so disorientated. Leading up to the X-Games I must've done a thousand double backflips into the foam pit. I also learnt a no hander to turndown backflip and this'd be a world first. I was going to that contest with tricks nobody had the balls to fire out on dirt.

That's what it was gonna take for me to win.

6
THE X-GAMES 2001

Don't think I'm name-dropping or anything, but I gotta tell you about this. In July 2001 I was visiting family in England and my mum dropped me off at terminal three at Heathrow Airport on my way back. I'd just took my massive bike box out of the car and grabbed my luggage when a black stretch limo pulled up right beside me. This guy stepped out of the limo with shoulder-length grey-blonde hair and a goatee beard. I looked at him and thought I knew him from somewhere. The limo drove away and he caught my eye and walked up to me.

'Excuse me, if you don't mind me asking, what's in the box?'

'It's my bike box.'

He gave me a puzzled look, so I explained why I was dragging such a huge, odd-looking case and how I was gonna be representing Great Britain in the X-Games in a month's time. He held out his hand and I shook it.

'What's your name?'

'Stephen Murray.'

'I wish you the best of luck, Stephen. I'm Richard Branson.'

I didn't know it then, but Sir Richard Branson was to play a part in my life later on.

OK, to perfect big complex tricks like the double flip and 360 turndown backflip and the no handed to turndown flip, I went to Real Ride Skatepark in Perris. It had a foam pit that was a big square box area, stacked high with cushions and mattresses and foam from old furniture all piled up. It was pretty sketchy and dangerous, nothing like Woodward Camp on the east coast, where the foam was made of perfect square cubes. Real Ride foam pit was a fucking health hazard! The pieces of foam had been exposed to the sun and started to break down into fine yellow foam-dust. Every time I landed all the dust'd get in my eyes and ears and up my nose. I had to be careful not to breathe it in, which wasn't easy, because it'd be bad shit for my lungs. But we had to make the most of what we had and use it, because tricks were progressing faster than ever with the evolution of foam pits.

The owner, Mark Lowry, was cool and he'd let me come up there at night after the skatepark closed. It was empty then and I could focus and work on the tricks that'd put me ahead of the game. Grotbags came with me and we'd stay there until the early hours of the morning perfecting these tricks. Bags would shout out and spot me as I was coming in for a landing. I'll give him his due, he was there for countless hours, days and nights, supporting me mentally and helping me improve my technique. We'd use a video camera so I could watch the playback and see where I was going wrong. Once I had the tricks down, I'd practise them at different speeds, sometimes going higher and sometimes going longer. You never knew what the jumps were gonna be like in contest and practising the variables could only help you adjust when the time came. We'd spend so much time talking in the car about how I was gonna win the X-Games – many hours of smoking spliffs and trying to visualise what was gonna become reality.

I was living what was to come – anticipating it, eating, sleeping and breathing it.

The X-Games is a yearly extreme sports event organised by ESPN and covered by ABC. People compete for gold, silver and bronze medals, as well as prize money, and the competition side of things runs parallel with the X-Fest, with big rock bands, celeb autograph sessions and interactive stuff. After its inauguration in 1995 the X-Games started to get a lot of media exposure due to big-name sponsors and top-flight athletes and big attendances by the fans, with crowds of up to 100,000. Like, marketing at the Games was out of the box and everybody wanted to be part of it. What I'm saying is, this was it – the X-Games. Absolutely nothing like it for a rider like me, up against the best in the world and the rewards for winning were through the fucking roof.

In 2001 ESPN moved the X-Games to Philadelphia, Pennsylvania. Like I said, the comp had evolved into the premier event for action sports and it was a real big part of the youth culture of America. There was a number of changes at the new venue, like the dirt jumping being held indoors for the first time in the Games' seven-year history. The dirt was in the First Union Centre, with the street course and the flatland area outside in the parking lot. It was the same arena where the Flyers and the 76ers played their ice hockey and basketball, so it was pretty big time. The arena held over 20,000 people and it was packed to the rafters – the light shows and the roar of the crowds were electric, man. Anybody could see that the Extreme Games were here to stay for a while and I wanted to make my mark on them right now.

Most of the pro riders were happier with the way the event was going over in Philly, as opposed to previous years in San Francisco with the strong winds. I didn't know about that, as it was my first year qualifying and I was just blown away to be there. It was awesome, there was a massive composite-camera array, like the gear they used for the movie 'The Matrix'. They were using the equipment to shoot an IMAX movie called 'Ultimate X', about extreme sports, and three or four guys were lugging around a huge IMAX camera all through the week. Unbeknown to me, I signed a disclaimer, hidden in my registration contract, giving them the right to use me in the movie for free.

They took full advantage of that!

By now I was pretty confident I was gonna win in Philly. I told myself I was gonna win the X-Games and that's all there was to it! To do that, I needed the double flip, but I had to make those rotations perfect. I'd worked on the technique over and over with Cory and Grotbags – over and over and over and over until it was like clockwork in my head. I knew I had the big tricks and I knew what I needed to do to win. I had no interest in coming second. I was just there to take it. But knowing what you gotta do and actually doing it on the day are two different things. Cory said this thing to me –

'Be there *exclusively* for the contest!'

By that he meant for me to put everything else out of my mind – everything!

My Nirve team manager, Gary Ellis, is there and four of my mates from England have come over – Jay and Chris Aliano, Dave Smith and Scott Edgworth – along with my brother Martin and my mum and dad. I'm staying in the Holiday Inn with them and I don't want to let them down and not qualify for the finals – they've come all the way over and I want to give them a show they'll remember and be proud of. I'm like, I'm in the X-Games, my friends and family are here, I gotta win it! I gotta win the fucking contest! This is a once in a lifetime thing.

But I'm riding against all the odds. Only one Englishman's won the X-Games before and that's Jamie Bestwick in vert in 2000. No one else in the world truly believes I can win, except Grotbags. He says I can do it. No one but him and me know I have the ability – the will to win.

The tricks you had to do to make the finals of a dirt jumping contest like the X-Games were really getting out there. Everyone was spinning flip and whip variations, with Mike Aitken doing half-crank switches in mid-air and stuffing three variations into the same jump. I'm up against twenty of the best. Cory was riding with a fractured leg, after being told a poorly executed ejection could result in a spiral crack all the way up the bone. That's pretty nuts! He strapped it up and rode well enough, but he missed out the cut at eleventh – they only took the top ten from twenty. The course was a tough one, as you'd expect, and the prelims worked a couple of guys over real good.

But I qualify for the finals in fourth place and I'm still holding out on my secret weapons, yet to be unleashed. All the people who're top of their game get through with me and I focus like I used to in the racing days. Get my mind clear. Practice for the finals is the next day. People aren't expecting me to do much, like I said already, and they're maybe surprised I've got this far. They're just thinking of TJ Lavin and Ryan Nyquist so I'm the underdog I guess. I say –

'Right, I'm gonna do a double backflip in practice because, if I fuck it up, I'm not gonna make the same mistake in the finals.'

Next morning I wait till all the top riders get up on the roll-in, then I drop in in front of them. I know they're watching and I'm trying to mess with their minds. I dial the double backflip – I can't believe how clean I land it. Everyone goes fucking nuts! It's never been pulled clean on dirt before. Everyone's going fucking mental! That's it, I've already won the X-Games in my mind. I've psyched them all out! I know it's mine, nothing can stop me. But the last thing I want now is TV people plugging my brain, so I leave the arena immediately and go straight back to the hotel. It's the biggest high of my life! I get back to the room with Grotbags and I take a cold shower and realise it's my time now! I'm calm and relaxed and focused on what I gotta do.

The finals are at three o'clock in the afternoon and the place is crazy. I've never jumped in a venue like this. Just fucking look at it! It's like the NBA or something – the lasers and TV and media and all that. I'm just gonna block it out and pretend I'm in my backyard. The ten best riders in the world are assembled at the top of the roll-in. All of a sudden the lights go out and spotlights start shooting all over the arena. AC/DC's *Hell's Bells* starts cranking. The capacity crowd's going nuts. Each one of us are spotlighted and intro'd. Then the lights go up again and it's on!

Three runs.

I'm gonna drop the double first run – make everyone think –

'What we gonna do to beat that?'

I get over-anxious – the first run I drop in on a turndown flip to an x-up to a table 360 and go up a massive roll-in where you stop at the top to re-group for the second straight. I overshoot the pre-jump and then sailor the back jump, knowing I don't have enough speed for the double on the last. I score 82.40 and I'm just like –

'Man, I can't believe it! That's one run out the window at the X-Games finals. Fuck!'

I try to make myself forget it – forget the crowd – get into my own mind zone. And I'm thinking to myself –

'Man, this is crazy, it's just a dirt jumping competition.'

But it's more than that – it's the X-Games, and everyone wants to win.

Everyone's first runs are pretty clean and Nyquist has a strong lead going into the second round. I still have two runs to do. I gotta make them both count – no room for error. No mistakes, I gotta ride flawless.

Stay calm and focused.

Second run. I drop in and hit the same tricks over the first three sets. I know exactly what's ahead of me, what I gotta do. I'm on the roll-in, looking down at the second straight of two doubles, keeping myself composed. I can hear the crowd starting to get loud. I look to the bottom of the roll-in and Grotbags is stood there shouting –

'You better stick this!'

Then I drop in and suck up the first set, getting as much speed and pump as I can. I go for it – give it everything. The crowd's on their feet, sensing what's happening. I rip back off the last lip, pull and tuck, spinning the bike and landing with little room to spare. But I land clean! I ride halfway up the ramp and let the bike go, arms in the air and the crowd's going fucking wild!

It's the first time the double backflip's ever been done in a dirt competition.

Everyone just loses it. Since one run would be dropped, I've ended up with a score of 94.60, three full points higher than Nyquist. I'm in the game, right at the top. I'm sitting there in the infield, everyone's all around me and they're just like –

'You've won! This kid's won!'

Everyone's stoked, just to see a new face up there. But I'm thinking –

'I haven't won yet.'

You'd think if you're the first person in dirt jumping history to land a double backflip cleanly in competition, you're a lock to win – right? But with TJ Lavin and Ryan Nyquist in the same competition, nothing's a lock. Steve McCann and Allan Cooke and some others are looking strong, but it's shaping up to be a battle between me, Nyquist and Lavin for the top spots.

Third run – big and clean. A no handed flip – to x-up – to 360 turndown. One-two-three. I go up the roll-in and set up for the second straight. I drop in, x-up the first set and then do a no handed to turndown backflip. This was the first double variation flip ever pulled in contest. I ride away clean and the place is going mental again – everyone's saying 'You've won it, Murray', but TJ and Nyquist still gotta do their final runs. I'm in the lead with an average of 92.40. TJ and Ryan gotta pull something completely over the top to beat me now. The tension in the arena's crazy. It's a real contest, running down to the wire.

It's fucking awesome!

TJ's last run's some serious backflip turndowns, a 360 tailwhip that he comes up just short on, and his brand new trick, the 'nothing superman' – another world first in competition. But it isn't enough to get him any better than third place with 90.30. All eyes are on Ryan. If anyone can pull out a 93 or over, it's Nyquist. So now it's the last run of the contest. Oh my God, here we go! He comes down and does a double barspin flip first set to double barspin on the second set. He's landing everything dialed and smooth and I'm going to myself –

'What the fuck??'

He takes off and does a 720 and it looks perfect. Then his hand slips and he eats shit.

Everyone just erupts. They're going crazy, jumping all over me and I'm saying –

'Nah, nah, he's gonna get up and pull a 360 flip and beat me. I guarantee it.'

So he gets up and pushes to the top of the roll-in. The crowd brew up a deafening roar. He drops in and twists this 360 flip so dialed, so perfect, an X-Games first, and I figure if he beats me then – you know what – that was amazing. I've got no qualms about that. I know he crashed, but look at the run he just did.

Everyone's waiting for the score. Waiting. It's so close nobody can call it. It's fucking tense – never known nothing like it. The score finally comes up – 90.80 – and I almost faint. All of a sudden I've won the X-Games in my first year in the competition. I can't believe this! Robbie Morales and all the east coast riders pick me up on their shoulders and a sea of people throw me in the air. All my family and friends are there to support me when I make it happen. I'm on the ultimate fucking high.

The after party was at some club in Philly. My friend Adam Aloise had arranged it, Jonny Knoxville, Pink and Tony Hawk and some others were there as celebrity bartenders – all my close friends and family were there and we partied all night. My dad was smoking Cuban cigars with Gary Ellis and Rich Vitiello from Huffy Bikes, who was trying to sign me up to ride for his team, but I go with Vans Shoes instead. Man, what a scene! Later, I got a telegram from Sir Richard Branson congratulating me on my achievement – he hadn't forgot our meeting at Heathrow Airport in July. Next day I'm walking down the street with Grotbags and I turn to him and say –

'Y'know what ... I feel taller!'

After the X-Games, a lot of people thought I'm this kid who's just come out of nowhere. I get this vibe that people thought it was a bit of a fluke.

'Murray fluked it.'

And I'm like –

'What? Fuck everybody! I'm gonna learn another trick that's never been done and blow their fucking minds!'

I was gonna go and ride my ass off as hard as I could and learn new stuff. I'm like –

'I'm going to the Gravity Games and I'm gonna win them too! I'm gonna prove I'm not a fluke. I'm gonna do it again. And again. And again!'

I got the taste for winning big now – it's all I want to do!

Before the Crash

BMX brothers ready to take on the world

By Ian Robson

HANG YOUR heads in defeat no longer, sports fans. Raise a cheer for two young lads putting a bit of pride back into our battered image.

Brothers Stephen and Martin Murray, are only six and eight years old, but they've given a man-sized dose of medicine to sports enthusiasts knocked for six by a series of setbacks on the soccer, cricket and boxing fronts.

The youngsters are riding high in the saddle on their BMXs, bringing success and honour to their club Tyneside Chargers.

Stephen is lying at the top of the regional championships and fourth in the national tables in his age group.

Martin is placed third in his age group's regional championships and is also a serious contender for a U.K. title.

Together they have won 110 trophies this season alone which decorate the living room of their parents' home in Poldea Crescent, North Shields.

Their dad Jeffrey, who with his wife Cynthia is on the committee of the club, said: "They are both fanatics. We are proud of them both.

Both boys, pupils of Preston Grange Primary School, North Shields, compete somewhere every Sunday and practice at their own club's track at the Powder Monkey, Wallsend, several times a week.

They are waiting to hear if they have been accepted for the world championships in Slough in August, attracting 400 competitors from America alone.

Cynthia said: "Stephen has more of a winning streak in him.

Martin is more quiet and reserved but the determination is still there."

Ask young Stephen what his ambition is and there is no hesitation: "I want to be the number one in the world," he says.

Martin is a little shy, pointing out only that he would like to be more like his BMX hero, Loudoner Andy Ruffle, and simply do his best.

The Chargers are arranging a Geordie Gathering on Saturday, July 12, at the Powder Monkey track near the Coast Road, Wallsend.

Organisers hope that more than 200 competitors will turn up for the event sponsored by North Tyneside Council.

Many will also be competing in the Schweppes Grand Prix at Newcastle the following day.

Entry forms for the Gathering are available from Mrs. Murray, at 10 Polden Crescent, North Shields, telephone Tyneside 2570964.

Martin (on bike) and Stephen Murray. Picture: TON MACKIN.

1.1 First media appearance in June 1986 in the Sunday Sun.

1.2 Team Titan.

1.3 BMX Racing Gate Starts.

1.4 With some of the friends I found at Prince Henry's High School in Evesham. End of year assembly, May 1996. The girls loved it!!

1.5 Nac Nac @ Squirt of Dirt, Alvaston '91.

1.6 Winter sessions @ Hidden Valley, 2000 - these were the best apart from the worst KO over this jump.

1.7 Vans Triple Crown, Oceanside, CA. 360 flip abort ship! First set, 2004.

1.8 'Bicycles and Dirt' VHS - I was so proud of that thing!

1.9 No Foot Can Can @ my ranch in Riverside 2005.

1.10 Classic Table Top @ my ranch in Riverside 2006.

1.11 All beat up after KO in Nasty's backyard - always wear a helmet!

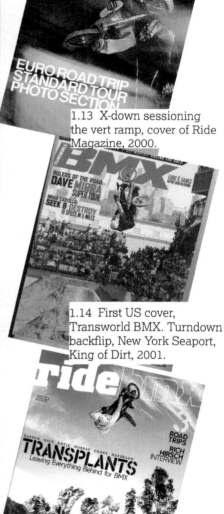

1.13 X-down sessioning the vert ramp, cover of Ride Magazine, 2000.

1.14 First US cover, Transworld BMX. Turndown backflip, New York Seaport, King of Dirt, 2001.

1.15 Ride BMX Cover shot, Riverside ranch, 2005.

1.12 Me and Nasty in the party days – full throttle.

1.16 Dirt jumpers favourite time to ride. One foot table sunset session, Riverside 2005.

1.17 Table top, Duckswich House, Worcestershire, the breeding ground.

1.18 Stag party – Riverside to Vegas, trying to keep all these knuckleheads together was impossible.

1.19 No, it isn't the campsite in Sweden behind me or the caravan in Riverside!

1.20 Building the full pipe mid section in my front yard, Riverside, 2006.

1.21 Ripping the rapids between RIverside and Vegas 200ft in the air.

1.22 Talking runs with good friend and mentor Paul Roberts.

1.23 All smiles when I'm getting ready to ride my bike.

1.24 Gate starts outside Georgia Street apartment, Huntington Beach. Snapping Nigel Page.

1.25 Hitting the fullpipe mid section, my ranch, Riverside. TJ Ellis looking on.

1.27 That was the best $200 I ever spent, racing down the waterslides on the way back from Vegas in 2003.

1.26 Perfecting the front flip on dirt, 2006.

1.28 One hand one foot dark side over the hip @ Rick's trails, Gavilan, California.

1.29 X-Games Gold, Philadelphia 2001.

1.30 On the podium with Ryan Nyquist and TJ Lavin. X-Games 2001, Philadelphia.

1.31 Whitesnake, Nasty, Ryan Guettler and me.

1.32 My little man Mason comes into the world, 30 July 2005.

1.33 Vans ad, Woodward West, 2005.

The Ultimate Road Trip Vehicle?

When Stephen Murray first moved to the states he bought Todd Lyons' old car and drove that around for a while. But after he won last year's Gravity Games and X Games dirt comps he had the money to do a little upgrading. What he ended up with may be the most tricked out road trip vehicle we've ever seen. Stephen sunk $55,000 into a 2002 Chevrolet Tahoe, but it turns out that he was able to snag so many hook ups that it's actually worth a lot more than that. Kicker hooked Stephen up with a big audio system, KMC Wheels "dubbed out" the ride with a custom set of chrome 22" wheels and Toyo tires, and Master Image Customs dropped the truck and put in an air suspension kit. We asked Stephen about the suspension kit and here's the lowdown. "It's the same principle as hydraulics, but it rides on air instead. You can hammer it up and down from wherever you want. There's a remote control that looks like a PlayStation [remote] and you can control it from up to 250 feet away." Basically, Stephen's car can bounce around just like the cars in all the Jay-Z videos. "Word!"

For long road trips the Tahoe has a seven-inch TV screen in the front, and two eight-inch screens in the headrests for the back passengers. The TV screens are from Keo... watch television, VHS tapes, DVDs... road trips. "There's also... video camera...

Stephen also has an AC adapter in the cargo section of the truck which comes in handy if you need to recharge your camera's battery. "Or if you want to eat, you could plug a microwave into the car, or if you want to keep water chilled you can bring a fridge along. I have a mini fridge I could put in, but that's taking it to the extreme a bit, isn't it?" Stephen, you don't have to worry about taking your Tahoe to the extreme—it's already there.

...n Murray and his pimped out Tahoe. Check out the pressure gauges for the suspension ...e steering wheel. Flip a switch and make that thing bounce!

...t Away

We told you last month that Stephen Murray spent some serious money on a new ride. Well, here it is in all it's glory. It's got three TVs, an insane stereo system and airbags at all four corners. Those are also 22-inch wheels.

1.34 My pride and joy, Chevy Tahoe; above, sitting on airbags.

After this bad experience, Stephen decided he was through with going on blind dates. "Man, could she eat! She ate like a...she ate a lot."

MURRAY JOINS GT

GT HAS ADDED ANOTHER talented Englishman to its team in the form of Stephen Murray. Stephen also picked up a new deal with SOBE, along with a St. Bernard puppy, bringing the total dog count in the Murray household to three. He may have to send them after the guy that sold his two trucks for him, since he skipped town owing Stephen somewhere in the neighborhood of fifty grand, which is a pretty nice neighborhood.

1.35 Feeding the horse! Just signed for GT!

1.36 Bear hug from Rocky. (photo: Russ Hennings)

1.37 Oakley ad 2004.

1.38 Persevering through adversity. Zero to Hero and broken bones.

1.39 Don't disrespect the trails if you know what's good for you.
(photo: Russ Hennings)

1.40 No hand to turndown backflip on the big dog jump at Nasty's House in Riverside, 2002.

1.41 All smiles, shovel in hand.
(photo: Russ Hennings)

1.42 Front Flip, Orlando, 2006.
(photo: Mark Losey)

1.43 I'm back! Beginning 2007.
(photo: Mark Losey)

1.44 Opposite Table.
(photo: Mark Losey)

1.45 Crankin' a turndown flip.
(photo: Mark Losey)

1.46 Me and my wife Melissa.

1.47 Favourite time to ride, sunset session riverside. (photo: Russ Hennings)

1. 48 Giving the trails some much needed hydration in the riverside sun. (photo: Russ Hennings)

1.49 On the roll-in about to take my last run in BMX. Baltimore 2007.

1.50 The Crash!
photo: Kevin Novak/Cal Sport Media

photo: Fat Tony

7
GRAVITY GAMES
2001/2002

People say it's hard coming from behind, but it's way harder staying in front. That's what I respected most about riders like Dave Mirra and Ryan Nyquist – they were true pros, always doing the job. Before Philly, I'm getting like –

> 5th place pro dirt @ CFB round 1 – Jacksonville FL
> 7th place pro dirt @ CFB round 2 – Perris CA
> 2nd place pro dirt @ DK dirt circuit round 2 – Carlisle PA
> 1st place pro dirt @ DK dirt circuit round 3 – Perris CA – where I qualified.

Now I'm trying to re-invent myself to stay on top. I start working this new trick that's never been landed before – a 360 turndown backflip. Hours and hours perfecting it at Real Ride with Grotbags. I come home from the foam pit at Lake Perris at two o'clock in the morning and I'm due to fly out from LAX at 6:45am to Rhode Island for the Gravity Games.

'Hey, Nasty, come and check this out.'

I show him a video of me doing this 360 turndown backflip. It's just dialed. I've been doing it again and again into the foam pit. I've figured out exactly where I am in the air, where the landing is. I want to silence the critics. I don't want to hear no more of this fluke shit. Cory looks at me like I'm completely fucking nuts.

Next day I'm competing in NBC's Gravity Games in Providence, Rhode Island, New York. Nobody's ever won the X-Games and Gravity Games in the same year.

Nobody!

The Gravity Games was a multi-sport competition that originally came out of Rhode Island, just like the X-Games. It featured a variety of extreme sports, like skateboarding, freestyle motocross and BMX freestyle. NBC organised it to be like an alternative X-Games, but it didn't have the same kudos, even though it was real big in itself and an important event. I guess you could say the X-Games were the Olympics of BMX and the Gravity Games were the World Championships – something like that.

When I arrive in NY I'm absolutely exhausted and spend most of the day resting and recovering in the hotel. Later, I take a long ride around the city to get my legs and body moving. The next day is practice and I go to check out the course – it's renowned for having great dirt jumps – way gnarlier than the X-Games. This is a contest I've always looked up to and wanted to ride. They have transfers everywhere and a massive 40ft first set in a line of big doubles. I spend the day getting used to the jumps and there's only a few of us hitting them. I feel great and have an early night.

The following day is qualifying and I ride well and come in fourth again, just like in Philly. The finals are later that evening, so I go back to the hotel and take a cold shower and chill by myself.

The finals are under floodlights and the atmosphere's fucking palpitating. All the riders are sessioning the jumps in warm-up and I'm the last to drop in. I know I gotta throw down the gauntlet. The last jump's pretty small, with a slight uphill on the approach, so I gotta crank my ass off and pedal fast for it. There's little air time to pull the double rotation so I spin and tuck real tight in order to get two rotations around. I'm coming in for the landing, but I over rotate and loop out on to my back, smashing my head and getting concussion. Man, it's one of the roughest slams I've taken. I feel that fucking crash, it's real hard and I'm trying to keep myself together.

While I'm trying to clear my head, I can hear the announcer calling for the first runs in the finals. The NBC host wants an interview, having seen what I've thrown down. They're asking questions, but none of it's registering. I'm trying to block it out and just focus on winning – trying to get totally zoned out. I know I'm not the only one in the final who'll hit the big sets. Now it's just about the moment – the contest. All the preparation and the planning are done.

Now I gotta throw down – I gotta deliver on the day.

It's three runs and two to count. I'm feeling confident, the crash in warm-up hasn't put me off. I know what I gotta do.

I drop in on my first run and throw the double backflip over the last set – it comes in absolutely perfect! I'm leading the points after run one. On my second run, I screw up the no hander to turndown backflip and crash over the next jump. That's my throwaway. It puts all the pressure on me for the last run.

Final run. Everything's on the line. Go big or go home!

Trying to line up the rotation of a flip and a 360 so you come into the landing straight is the hardest thing ever. That trick is so fucking inconsistent, especially on dirt, because no two jumps are the same. But I'm ready to do it! I'm gonna throw this out now! I haul ass down the roll-in and hit the forty-footer and pull a no hander to turndown backflip clean. I turn down and x-up the small set into the right hand 180 degree turn. There's a small double on the exit of the turn that I just pump the hell out of and start sprinting to the last set, where I nail the world's first 360 turndown backflip. It's fucking ground-breaking and to actually ride away from it is unreal. All the practice sessions into the foam pit have paid off. I pick up my bike and launch it and literally go nuts.

There's still one rider left to go, Todd Walkowiak. He's a real specialist, linking super tech tricks, and it's all on his last run – he needs a big score to win. He pulls his run, it's consistent and clean but I don't think it's enough to take the comp. My score still hasn't come in and the judges are delaying showing the final results. By now they should already be up. There's a real sense of anticipation and tension starting to build. Jerry Badders is my team manager for Vans and he starts shouting at the judges for taking their fucking time. Finally, they announce I've won. The 360 turndown backflip's the trick that wins it for me, it's never been done on dirt before. It's the X-Games all over again!

I'm a double gold medallist.

The feeling's un-fucking-paralleled.

The show finished on September 10, 2001 and I went out that night to celebrate and partied hard. In the very early morning I met a guy from Boston who was friends with one of my fellow riders, Ryan 'Biz' Jordan. He had this green juice called GHB and these tablets to treat ADHD called Ritalin. I was off my rocker that night, partying with the best of them and all the university campus kids. I decided I wanted to go to Boston with these guys to keep the party going over there, so I booked a ticket on American Airlines flight 11 to LAX from Logan International Airport. But I just got partied out and changed my mind in the end. The sun came up on 9/11 and I was completely wired, to say the least. I just got my original flight back from New York. Man, someone was looking out for me that day. As everyone knows now, that Boston flight was hijacked and flown into one of the Twin Towers by terrorists. It was one of those things that changes your perception of life.

I wasn't meant to die that day.

I gave Grotbags the bike I won gold on for all the help he gave me and for filming my 360 turndown backflips into the foam pit until I got them perfect – I couldn't have done it without him.

Thanks Grotbags!

Like I said before, I guess I've always been kinda irresponsible with money. Like, before the X-Games, I spent big on jet-skis – at the same time, I owed my brother $230. I mean, it's just reckless – why spend all the money I had in the world on jet-skis I don't even need instead of paying people what I owe them? After the X-Games and Gravity

Games, I got sponsored by Oakley Sunglasses and a prepaid calling card company called Dibz – and I got big pay rises from Nirve and Vans. I'm earning $1,400 a month, which is only just enough to get by. I pay $500 a month for rent and have the cheapest cell-phone I can get – like, on the fucking ten minute plan. Ten minutes spread out over the month – I had to ration them. I go from earning that $1,400 a month to winning nearly $100,000 in just two weeks. I mean, that makes no sense to my brain – I'm twenty-one years old and grew up in a place where nobody had that kind of money at twenty-one. So what's a young guy like me gonna do, except go places he shouldn't. The first thing I did was buy a Chevy Tahoe. It cost $50,000 and I walked into the saleroom with cash. I put another $20,000 into that car – airbags and killer wheels and switches and tinted screens – the lot. I got a stupid sound system that could blow the doors off and that car was worth $70,000 by the time I was finished. It was retarded. It was a beast. Fuck, man!

I did lots of things I shouldn't have with money, which I'll talk about later. But for me at that time it was like, what's money? It's just paper. I wasted a lot of it on VIP rooms and champagne tables and other stuff. Me and Nasty were living the high life for sure. We got away with things we shouldn't have. We were damn lucky our hearts were still beating, man, after some of the shit we pulled. We were definitely a pair of party animals.

My career really took off and it was crazy. The days of sleeping on other people's couches and forever digging trails had been the apprenticeship for my life as a top pro. I no longer needed to wonder how I was gonna pay the rent or who I had to hitch a ride from. I was able to pay my own way and look after myself. I was on top of the world and no other feeling came close.

I went into those two comps knowing I could win them. My dream was to get into the X-Games to start with. Once I was in, my dream was to win it. Nobody remembers who gets second in anything and I kept thinking about what Rob Indri said to me –

'Go big or go home!'

It was what motivated me and I always knew it was gonna happen. They were my goals and my dreams and I achieved them. After that I just wanted to stay on top. I didn't want to be beaten. You get a taste for being the best and you don't want to lose that feeling. It was hard, but I was focused and I did the right preparation and I knew if I got knocked down, at least I'd get knocked down trying my hardest. If I didn't try my hardest and didn't do well in contests, then I'd be disappointed in myself. It was entirely up to me – no one else.

I'll say to the kids out there, don't let anybody steal your dreams. If you have no dreams to begin with, then go get yourself some. Always live for your dreams. In your job – even if you work at McDonalds – or if you're trying to pull that manual down the street, or pot that black in a pool game, or pull the hottest chick in a club. Just be confident you can do it – and you will!

The Gravity Games was the last big event of the year and there was a lot of partying going on after it. I peaked myself out for the big comps like that, I wasn't interested in the small stuff all that much. Between Gravity Games 2001 and 2002, it's like –

8th place pro dirt @ Vans Triple Crown of BMX 1 – Salt
Lake City UT
3rd place pro dirt @ Vans Triple Crown of BMX 2 – Salt
lake City UT
10th place pro dirt @ CFB round 1 – Merritt Island FL

But I wasn't at my best for the smaller events and I didn't take them too seriously.

In April 2002 I entered the Red Bull High Air contest at the European King of Dirt Series in Leipzig, Germany. It was at a trade show and they had a height meter going up, with a bar sat over the top to measure the height of the jump from the take-off ramp. There was me, Marcus Hampel and Kye Forte – we battled it out, pushing the envelope and going higher and higher. I ended up coming first in that competition with a big winning jump of 5.55 meters and, although I didn't know it at the time, it was an

officially recognised Guinness World Record. I think that
record stood until Kye broke it in 2012.

When you get to where I was back then, about to win three
gold medals in a row, the media are all over you. There's also
a lot of downtime between comps and what's a guy gonna
do? In the run up to the 2002 Gravity Games, as defending
champion, I had to do a huge amount of interviews and
videos. I didn't mind doing the rounds of the media – it was
all part of being a champion and I just took it in my stride.
If I'm honest, I could take or leave the media attention, but it
was good for my glamour-image with the girls.

In July 2002 the Gravity Games came to Cleveland, Ohio.
At this point I was dialed and feeling unbeatable, riding at
the top of my game. The dirt course was located at the Rock
'n' Roll Hall of Fame and I consider that 2002 Gravity Games
to be the biggest win of my career. Why? Because it was 100
degrees with 100% humidity and to come through in those
extreme conditions was a *real* achievement. Riding in that
heat was like working out in a sauna and it reminded me of
Orlando when I was seven or eight years old.

Qualifying went great and I came in third. The finals
were later that night under floodlights. The dirt jumps were
big and challenging and some of the best I'd seen. But I
was sweating so much in practice before the finals my leg
muscles started to cramp up and spasm because I lost so
much sodium from my system. I remember drinking gallons
of water and Gatorade, but I just sweated it straight back
out. OK, the conditions were extreme but, like I done before,
I told myself it was the same for everyone and if the others
could push on through it, so could I.

My first run went amazing and I pulled the double flip
clean, riding away and the fans were going berserk. I had
two runs left and all I had to do was make one of them count.
The pressure was mounting and all eyes were on me. I
pedalled flat out and dropped into the huge roll-in, nailing all
my tricks down the first straight. There was a small double
going into the last 180 turn and I felt my quads cramp up
before hitting it. I cranked flat out to get speed for the last
jump – that jump was massive and I went into floating off

the lip and wrapping up into my signature move, the 360 turndown backflip, aka 'alligator wrestler'. Right when I clicked the turndown and was upside down, my quads and my forearm extensors locked up. I came down hard and ate shit, rolling to the bottom.

My muscles are contracting and I'm in so much fucking pain. Can't believe it. All I had to do was stick that jump to win! Now I'm locked up in cramp and it looks like it's over – but I'm determined I'm not gonna let my body fail now, I got too much riding on this. I tell myself there's no way I'm gonna let this slip. I'm gonna get up there and make damn sure my last run counts. I have around twenty minutes to my final run and my girlfriend, Mindy Pantus, and Grotbags go to work on my muscles, massaging them and feeding me salty potato chips and tons of water to rehydrate my body from all the sweat I've lost.

Third run and there's loads of people on top of the roll-in, the camera crews and Travis Pastrana and Pharrell Williams with his whole entourage and it's like a fucking VIP parade. All eyes are on me again. The announcer shouts my name and I'm ready to take my third Gold in a row. There's nothing I want more. I nail the first straight of jumps and hit the left hand 180 turn. I hit the jump on the exit and then accelerate for the last. There can be no fucking up now. No margin for error. I rip back off the lip, floating into a fully cranked 360 turndown backflip. I execute it perfect and see the landing and nose dive in. I clip the top and it bucks the back end of my bike out sideways, but I manage to make a last second adjustment and ride away clean.

I fucking pull it!

I can't believe it.

I'm riding away and I just stomped it.

Before I know it my whole body locks up again and I go into a massive spasm, cramping up all over. I eat shit up the roll-in and fall back down on the dirt, swarmed by all my friends and other riders. I'm in so much pain and they pick me up and make it worse. I'm soaked in sweat and I gotta keep stretching my quads to try and get some relief from the cramping.

But I did everything I'd worked for and it all came together and a feeling of euphoria floods my body and mind. I climb up the top of the roll-in and I'm congratulated by a bunch of people. I don't know who he is then, but Pharrell Williams high fives me and hugs me and he's like –

'Respect, man!'

Somebody tells me he's a singer and record producer.

I'm walking away from the event with my girlfriend Mindy when Travis Pastrana comes up to me and he's like –

'You rode amazing Murray.'

'Thanks, man.'

'Loved your three-sixty turndown and your double.'

I look at my girlfriend and I'm like –

'Holy shit, did he just say that to me?'

I always looked up to Travis and a compliment like that from him means a lot to me. I don't know it then, but three years later I'll see him pull the first double backflip on a motorbike at the Staples Centre in LA. I mean, I thought then and I still think now, that Travis Pastrana's the best all-round athlete of all time.

Defending my title in the 2002 X-Games the following month, I laid down three technically perfect runs and the judges didn't qualify me for the finals by a tenth of a point. To this day, I can't understand it. It seems like they were judging me against myself rather than the other riders. I started to realise I was up against a new challenge – getting to the top was one thing but staying there was even harder.

After Gravity Games 2002, I was claiming seconds and thirds, but I'd never walk away with that big first place again.

2nd place pro dirt @ Vans Triple Crown of BMX 1 –
Charlotte NC
19th place pro street @ Vans Triple Crown of BMX 1 –
Charlotte NC
2nd Place pro dirt @ Vans Triple Crown of BMX 2 –
Denver CO

It's like a drug and you keep trying to chase the high. I'd be non-stop, but I wasn't quite achieving it. I had everything else that comes with success – house, cars, women, everything. I was earning a lot of money and my life was nuts. I mean, you could say it was pretty much a dream life, on top of the world. I moved out of Nasty's house and bought my own place in Corona, with a pool and rock waterfalls and an oasis in the backyard. I bought a couple of Golden Retrievers, Geordie and Cassie, for $1,800 apiece, because I always loved dogs and liked having them around me. Like, you can always trust a dog, even when you can't trust nothing else.

I was getting so much stuff sent to my house from my sponsors and it was physically impossible to use or wear it all. So I figured it was best given to the local kids who were up and coming. I'd take it down to the trails and give away boxes of stuff. The same with people who came to stay. Between 2002, when I got my own place in Corona, and 2007 as many as forty or fifty young BMXers would stay in my spare rooms for free and ride with me. They could help themselves to all the stuff that was coming through from sponsors. It gave me great satisfaction to help people and having young, eager kids around meant you always had to be on your toes and open to new methods and tricks.

And so I moved into another phase in my life.

I guess I've always been kinda spontaneous. Like, one day I'd decide to patio an area of my backyard and I'd just get the sledgehammer out and start smashing up concrete. Then I'd drive to Ace's hardware and get new slabs and start laying them. I never spent much time thinking ahead about the decisions I made. I just did it! I spent $10,000 on tropical fish and another $5,000 on model aeroplanes – I had some fucking lush ones – and it was all spur-of-the-moment stuff. People always say 'look before you leap' – with me it was just leap and take a look on the way down, man!

Back then I had more friends than ever before in my life – most of them not real friends – I could never remember all the names, there was so many of them. Me and Cory would throw parties and have people over for contests in our yards, but we were always the main attraction and everyone wanted to ride with us. It was like we were kinda alternative rock stars. Life was good and I still rode every day and didn't lose that drive on my bike. I was just trying to figure out the missing ingredient to get me back winning. I reckoned that, once the judges saw me do these really difficult and dangerous tricks, that'd be it.

But they never rewarded me for it the same way again.

I got judged against myself as a rider and not against the rest of the field.

8

PARTYING LIKE AN ANIMAL

The party scene in Riverside was wild. Not like it is in England, where you go into town and you got a bunch of pissheads looking to fight all the time. Out there you had to drive everywhere – everybody drank and drove and nobody cared much about getting stopped by the cops. They didn't have breathalysers like in the UK – you just had to do a sobriety test, like walking down a straight line and putting your finger on your nose and standing on one leg. Man, I passed that test at least five times while I was plastered! It was a different vibe in California. I'd get wasted before I went out and then get even more hammered at places like Club Sevilla, a hip-hop reggaton dance venue. I could show up to any club and they knew who I was and would give me access to VIP rooms full of beautiful women and champagne and drugs. There was all kinds of people on the scene – pro athletes, film stars, party promoters, models, drug dealers, strippers, porn stars – and me and Cory Nastazio.

Then there'd be the after-parties – mansions and shit – pool parties and house parties till the next afternoon and beyond. You might not get home for days. You know the kind of thing, lots of porn-star-looking chicks all over the place and most of them wanting to bang Nasty. So I'd pretty much pick up the ones who failed to get him. There was dozens of them, and the Nastyman could only handle so many, so it was down to me to take care of business with the rest. The things we did together would top any movie that's ever been made a million times over. And, to be honest, we both should've died a long time ago.

We'd go all over – rough places like Club Gotham in San Bernardino – I've never seen more fights or shootings or people getting stabbed anywhere else in the world. It got shut down in the end because too many gangs were hanging out there. This one time we're in Larry Flint's Hustler Club with a bunch of strippers and these guys come up to us looking for trouble – it's like they hate us because all the girls are paying us a lot of attention, so they gotta grab their dicks and try to prove they're real men or something. It kicks off and we're in the thick of it, like fighting these fuckers. When the bouncers come, we get thrown out of the club – I guess the bouncers don't like us any more than the dick-grabbers, who're throwing fucking beer bottles at us from the balcony. Bunch of assholes!

After that incident, I went to get laser eye surgery.

It wasn't because I got punched in the eye or anything, although, maybe I did. But, early in 2002, I was having trouble seeing stuff. I'd look at the caller ID on my phone and I couldn't read it – like, I was long-sighted and I didn't know it. It was just normal to me because it didn't affect my riding – well, I wasn't seeing the take-off, but BMX is more sensing rather than seeing. If you're in touch with your bike and the ground and the air, then you're OK. But it was affecting my reading and I needed to get it fixed. I tried contacts but they didn't work properly with the dust from the dirt and I was talking to a friend of mine called Tracer Finn and he told me his wife had this laser surgery on her eyes and it was the fucking business.

So I went to Vegas to have it done. Back then, laser surgery wasn't a common procedure like it is now and they clamped my eyes open – all I wanted to do was blink, but I couldn't. Then they hovered over me and cut the flaps of my eyes, without any fucking anaesthetic, and re-shaped my corneas with a laser gun. Everything went black for about a minute and then bright colours appeared and I was looking at a clock that was out of focus – it was like when I dropped acid as a kid. I had to wear pads on my eyes for twenty-four hours and Mindy took me to my friend TJ's to recover.

I took the pads off when I woke up the next day and I looked at the pillowcase and I could see all the minute stitching and even the ridges of my fingerprints. I had 20/25 vision and I could see like I'd never done before. It was only then I realised how bad my sight really was. When I got back on my bike, it took me a while to adjust and I remember riding up the take-off and seeing all the grains of dirt on the lip and it kinda brought home the reality of going thirty feet up in the air.

A week later I walked into Club Metro in Riverside with Mindy, Nasty and his girlfriend Nicole. This place was very popular with would-be gangstas and that kind of crap and it could be, like, hostile. Me and Cory and the girls had been sat in my car and we done a whole bunch of blow. When we walked in I remember looking around and I could feel something was gonna kick off. We ordered some drinks and this guy came up and was like –

'Are you Cory Nastazio?'

That used to happen everywhere we went, so it was nothing new. Cory was like –

'Who wants to know?'

'Mothafucka!'

Then this kid just smashed him straight in the face. Turns out these were the same guys as before at the Hustler – Cory must've fucked his girl or something. Before we knew it all hell breaks loose and there's a whole gang of the steroid freaks. I remember falling over a table and the place kicking off big time – about twenty people fighting with chairs and bottles and glasses. Me and Nasty beat off seven of the motherfuckers and we chinned five of them before the bouncers threw them out.

We were still inside the club, but I knew as soon as we walked outside more shit was gonna go down. We left the girls inside and I told Cory to keep a watch out. As we went through the door, someone came from the right of me and smashed Cory. I kicked this kid in the head and we ended up in a massive brawl again. Luckily, Rick Lakin and Whitesnake, two BMX friends, joined in on our side. I remember being on the ground fighting this kid and I looked up and saw a bouncer with a mace spray, like, two feet away from my face. I'd just had laser surgery and my eyes weren't fully healed when I got maced point blank. The pain was intense in my eyes, nose and lungs – the burning – I was blinded and struggling to breathe, rolling round on the ground, rubbing at my eyes. Two girls came over to me and picked me up – I put my arms round their shoulders and they carried me to my car. Mindy was still in the club when I got maced and, when she came out and saw me walking off with the two babes, she came over and slapped me across the face. I couldn't fucking believe it! I tried to explain what happened, but she wasn't having any. She didn't want to get in the car but we were in a neighbourhood in the middle of an area that was sketchy as fuck, with guns and stabbings and shit, so I showed her the state of my eyes and she calmed down and came with me. I had water in the Tahoe and I washed my face, but it didn't do much good. Once everyone was in the car, we drove to a Starlight gas station and got some milk to stop the burning. It took my eyes three hours to fully recover.

The thing is, when you're on top of the game, all kinds of people want a piece of you – phoney agents, sponsors that want in at the right moment and who wouldn't touch you when you were struggling to make it, women who've seen you on TV and think you can get them in some door. None of them really give a fuck about you, all they want to do is exploit you and see what you can do for them. I was heavily involved in the LA and Orange County party scene – and it's all about what car you drive, how much champagne you buy, being seen in the VIP areas of clubs, how many rock stars you know. It's all superficial, man – shady shit, but when you're young you're stupid enough to fall for it.

But I still had a job to do and I wasn't making it easy for myself. I remember in Denver, at the Vans Triple Crown, when they introduced the drop off roll-in. It was like riding off the top of a small building. You pedalled from the back to the edge and the landing was completely blind. I'd been out boshing and raving all night and I met Whitesnake and Cory's roommate Joey Marks, a BMXer from Indiana in LA. We'd been partying till 5:00am, then caught the 6:00am flight out to Denver. I couldn't sleep because I was high as a kite on ecstasy. When I got there I sat up in the grandstand watching practice. I was sleep deprived, looking down on the course and all I could see was colours, oranges and greens. I was hallucinating and I was like –

'Fuck, you stupid idiot! Why?'

But back then I had so much confidence in my riding, I could go out all night long, run amok and pin it full throttle, and still pull it together and ride the next day. Even though I was still fucking high, I came joint first with Nyquist on points – so it went to a third run. I crashed the third and he completed all three, so Ryan won and I was placed second.

Like I said, I partied pretty much as hard as you can back then, but I wasn't finished with injuries. In April 2002 I was riding round the warm-up section of the trails in Cory's yard, with loads of rollers and berms. I usually wore a helmet but, on this occasion, I was just messing about and didn't worry about it. I hit a left hand berm and, as I went to pump round it, my front wheel slid over the top. I had no chance to get my hands out and I smashed my face straight on to concrete. I was severely concussed and thought I'd fallen backwards off the second story balcony or something. My nose was smashed sideways and I broke the orbital bone in my eye socket. My face was properly mashed up and both eyes were swollen shut for two days. I ended up getting a serious infection called scleritis, which is an inflammation of the white coating of the eye. It was excruciatingly painful and my left eye swelled up the size of a fucking snooker ball. The hospital told me to take ibuprofen, but that had no effect. So I went to an optician and he put me on steroids, which didn't help either. Then he turns to me and he's like –

'There's only one thing for it, Mr Murray.'

He starts filling up a fucking syringe and comes over close to me.

'OK, Mr Murray, look up to the corner of the ceiling and stay calm.'

I grab him by the balls as he leans in and I'm like –

'We're not gonna hurt each other, now, are we?'

'Please, Mr Murray!'

'Don't worry ... just stay calm.'

Every week for six weeks I had to have those fucking injections into my eyeball – and they did fuck-all good. In the end I flew back to London and found a specialist at Moorfields Eye Hospital. He treated me with an anti-inflammatory tablet called froben and that sorted the problem out within hours.

By the end of 2002 I had so much money coming in I didn't know what to do with it. I was still dating Mindy Pantus and she was good for me, always trying to keep me grounded. But I was twenty-two and I was flying all over the world, going to lavish, drug-fuelled parties and surrounded by hundreds of beautiful women all the time. It was too much to ask for me to stay faithful with temptation like that all around me and I didn't want to hurt Mindy, so it was best to call it quits with her – even though, looking back, it was probably a bad move.

After I broke with Mindy, me and Cory took a trip to West Palm Beach to check out where he grew up. We partied all over the place and one night I met this beautiful girl called Erica Vizzo in the downtown area. As soon as our eyes met, we had this crazy connection. We spent every second together after that, for the two weeks I was there – we were inseparable, man. When I got back to California, I flew her out to stay with me for a while. We had a great time together, like partying and having amazing sex. But I guess I was married to BMX at the time and I ended up telling her she'd break my career – I'd end up just riding her all the time and not my bike. So I shied away. When I dropped her at the airport, I was sad to see her go, but I was convinced it was the right thing to do at the time.

After Erica, I met this girl called Fleur in a sushi bar on Main Street, Huntington Beach, that was owned by one of the Linkin Park band members – maybe Mike Shinoda. There was something about Fleur, she was French-Creole, from Baton Rouge – truly beautiful, and so dialed, dressed in real high-end clothes and with this aura of incredible confidence. I had a Silverado big-lifted monster truck and that night I left it in the parking lot and we drove to an afterhours nightclub in her drop-top Mercedes SL500. Afterwards I went back to her luxury three-story house, just steps away from the Pacific Ocean in Newport Beach and we just clicked. We took some ecstasy and ended up in this deep kinda meaningful conversation until sunrise. I was due to film a commercial for Sprite and I had to catch a flight to Toronto later that morning. We hung out until it was time for me to go and, as soon as I got on the plane, it was lights out – I'd partied all night and got no sleep and I was fucked.

When I got to the hotel in Toronto, there was a message from Fleur, saying she was flying up to join me the next day. I couldn't believe it – I mean, she was so fit, so perfect, and she was chasing me! Next morning, I got on set to film the commercial – they had a roll-in and two shit sets of doubles on an athletics track. The second set of doubles had no landing, just a take-off, and there was cardboard boxes stacked up on the ground to break the fall. Some stunt men tied me to a bunch of bungee cords – they wanted me to jump the first set and then take off from the second lip. As they tightened, the bungees would pull me back on the boxes like I'd been shot out of the sky. They wanted me to repeat the stunt until they got the right shot, but after the first couple of falls, my body was getting beat up. Like, they had me getting whiplashed fifteen feet in the air and slamming into a bunch of cardboard boxes and I'm thinking to myself –

'Where the fuck are the crashmats?'

Afterwards, I jumped in a rental car and pinned it to the airport to meet Fleur off her plane. We spent the next two nights together – I'd be working in the day and she'd just go on mad shopping sprees. I never met a girl who bought so much expensive-ass clothing and accessories and stuff. She told me she'd recently got divorced from a world-famous rock star, so maybe that's how she had so much money to spend.

On the third day, I came back to the hotel from working on the set and she'd vanished.

When I got back to California, I went to see her in Newport Beach. When I asked why she disappeared in Toronto, she said she had to get back to work.

'Why didn't you say goodbye?'

'I was in a hurry.'

I couldn't quite figure it at the time, but that was Fleur. She was an unpredictable girl, and it was part of her mystique. It was what made her different, I guess. She had her own agenda and she'd just take off to be where she needed to be. We spent the night together and she gave me a xanax tablet because I was tired and beaten up from the shoot and it completely knocked me out. When I woke in the morning, she'd vanished again. I called her and she said she was in Corona hanging out. How the fuck could that be, it was 8:00am and she sounded wired and wide-awake?

'I can come back if you want, Stephen?'

'Nah. Fuck this, I'm out of here.'

Our relationship, if that's what it was, was off to a rocky start. She called me up over and over again and wanted me to go meet with her, but I said I had to get on it and ride my bike. But, man, she was the full package and hard to resist, so I went back for more. I stayed with her for eighteen months, but it was up and down, and we argued all the time and took a lot of drugs and fucked like wild animals.

I'd been awake partying in Newport Beach for four days solid, when Fleur told me about this car wholesaler she trusted called Mark Djaffe. She used to do hard-money loans with this guy, lending upwards of $100,000 to buy high-end cars like Ferraris and Bentleys and they'd get massive interest when the cars were flipped. Like, she'd lend the money to Djaffe to buy the car, then he'd sell it for a profit and pay Fleur a fixed fee for the loan. My mind was in a blender when she arranged for us to meet. I mean, I'd been doing cocaine and all sorts of other shit for four days and I just wanted to get it done and for the guy to fuck off. He's like –

'Sign here. Sign here.'

'OK! OK!'

It was just another one of the stupid decisions I was making at that time, and I signed without even reading what it was I was signing. He said he'd sell my Tahoe and Silverado within a couple of weeks and I could go buy a top-of-the-line BMW. What I didn't know was, I'd left my pink slip in the glovebox of the Tahoe, which was the title document. When Djaffe found it, he knew he was on to a winner.

A couple of weeks went by and I didn't hear anything from the guy, so I'm calling him non-stop but there's never no answer. Then I got a call from him saying he'd sold the cars for $75,000 combined and to come meet him at the beach for payment. He didn't show. He called me nine times over the next four months and I'd go to the beach but he wouldn't show. I was really pissed off by now and one day I got a parking ticket through the door for my truck. I went into maps on the internet and found out the truck was located in Newport Beach, so I went and found it. I phoned the cops and, when they arrived, this guy came out and said he bought the truck for his daughter. I asked him if he knew where Mark Djaffe was but he didn't have a clue. He said he thought the guy had drinking and gambling issues. I explained my side of the story and, as the truck was partly owned by the bank, the cops let me take it back.

I hired this private investigator to find out where the scumbag car salesman and my Tahoe were. He found out that the Tahoe changed ownership three times in one day then, a week later, it went out of state to Phoenix, Arizona. I got all the gen on the new owner, where he lived, where he worked, and the routes from the airport to his house. I got on a plane and arrived in Phoenix at 6:00am. I hired a car and pulled up outside the guy's house and waited. This massive dude came out – he was built like a fucking WWF wrestler. The garage door opened and I could hear the sound of airbags lifting up the chassis of my Tahoe. The hairs on the back of my neck stood up as I watched my pride and joy roll out into the Arizona sun. I wanted to jump out and drag the guy out of my car and work him over. But I didn't – he was way too big. I followed him to the real estate company where he worked and he parked up outside. I disabled the Tahoe with an alarm I still had and then pinned it to a GM dealership to get a key cut. The guy at the dealership saw the registration I showed him was two days out of date, so I headed back to the real estate office. I called the guy out and we talked and I explained to him what happened. He was OK and sympathetic, but he was an innocent victim at the end of a chain and I had no legal right to the car no more. So I had to suck it up.

Losing the Tahoe should have motivated me to ride harder, but me and Nasty were partying all over the place and this one time we were up all night at Fleur's place. Fleur had to go work at her real estate office job the next day and wanted to get some sleep, but she told us about this woman called Lesley who had a massive mansion on the beach. Lesley heard about us being big-time party animals and wanted to meet us. I don't think Fleur meant for us to go up there that night and I reckon she just told us about Lesley to get rid of us so she could get some sleep – but I was too out of it to realise that.

Anyway, me and Cory walked five blocks on to 45th Street in Newport Beach and rocked up at this ridiculous house with Ferrari's sitting on the drive. The door was opened by these two beautiful girls who said they were sisters. They welcomed us in and everything inside was kitsch affluence – there was about a hundred expensive-ass pillows just lounged out on the floor and the whole place just smelt of money.

The sisters took us upstairs and intro'd us to Lesley – she was mid-forties and looked like an older version of Christina Aguilera. The three women were sniffing crystal meth and it was the first time I'd come across the stuff. Me and Cory stuck to blowing lines and everyone partied through the rest of the night as high as kites. It ended up with me sessioning one of the sisters and Cory fucking the other one. Lesley was just trying on clothes in her massive walk-in closet and posing in front of the mirror, drinking Jägermeister, coffee and snorting massive lines of crystal meth. I came out of one room, dripping in sweat and Cory came out of another room and we looked at each other and we both said at the same time –

'That was the best fucking blow job ever!'

Fleur came round the next day and she was real pissed off at me because I was up all night and still riding the wave. I couldn't figure why she sent us over there – I mean, surely she must've known what'd happen? Anyway, now she was mad as a bag of polecats and we had a blazing fucking row. Cory tried to calm her down and they ended up leaving together, because I wanted to stay a while longer. After they left, I had second thoughts. I should've realised how volatile Fleur could be at times and maybe she was just feeling it or something – who knows? But I guess I wasn't the most understanding guy at that time in my life. Now I was stranded with the sisters and Lesley in this strange fucking place and they wanted to keep the party going. We took one of the Ferraris out and all four of us packed into it and headed to Irvine. We pulled up outside some skyscraper where this Asian guy came over to the car. He gave Lesley a bunch of drugs and we headed back to the pad. It was about midday by then and I wanted to escape. I called Fleur, but she didn't answer, so I walked the five blocks back to her house.

When I got there, she had a bunch of lines laid out on a CD that I assumed were coke. I sniffed these lines and it was like a furnace in my nose – like my nose was gonna fall off. That's when I realised it was crystal meth and I was really pissed off but, fuck it, now I was really on one. I was high like I never was before – I mean, fucking high! For the next three days, we painted the skies black and partied all over town – the sex with Fleur was amazing on the drugs and we just kept getting higher and higher and fucking like rabbits. The whole of the next year revolved round riding my bike, partying with Fleur, running away from Fleur, but being drawn back by the sex and her mystique. Eventually, I started to see shadows and was tripping out. I knew I had to get away from Newport Beach, but knowing it and actually doing it were two different things.

I went back and partied with Lesley five or six times after that first night and it was always just as crazy. Besides her house in Newport Beach, she had a monster pad in Corona, close to where I lived. I bought a Range Rover to replace the Tahoe and one time I drove past with my big sound system going and she was out pruning the roses in her yard. She starts to feel the music and she asks if she can borrow my car.

'You can take the Ferrari in exchange.'

'For keeps?'

'Of course not ... until I bring it back.'

'Cool.'

I ended up with that Ferrari for two weeks and I fully pinned it all over in that racecar.

Another time I hear a noise in my front yard at three in the morning. I come out and there's the Ferrari with the doors open and Lesley's clipping my roses.

'What the fuck you doing, Lesley?'

'Clipping my roses.'

'They're *my* roses.'

'Are they?'

'Yeah.'

'Oh ... sorry. I guess it's the diamonds.'

They called crystal meth diamonds in LA back then.

I liked Lesley and always got on well with her. Her husband was super successful and he owned a chain of gas stations and was worth something like a hundred million dollars when he died. He left everything to her and she was loaded. It's just that she was out of her tits on meth all the time and people took advantage of her – but she didn't seem to mind, as long as there was a party. She'd get all the beautiful girls to come to her house and she got to trust me and Cory. She'd tell us what doors were open and we'd run amok.

I was living for today and fuck tomorrow.

See the dream run video on stysrg.com

9
THE MEXICANS

There was lots of eccentrics like Lesley around LA and it was just a crazy time. I remember coming back from Vegas with Jay Aliano and Scott Edgworth – it was some time in 2003 and we'd been on a road trip. I was running low on fuel and I needed to pull over to a gas station to fill up the truck. I kinda liked the rush of thinking I might run out of gas somewhere remote and the danger I'd be in and the adventure I'd have if it happened. Everyone was telling me to pull over, but I wanted to push it to the last drop and I kept pinning it to get home. This time I pushed it too far.

Eventually, the truck started spluttering and ran out of gas somewhere in the desert, between Vegas and LA. I pulled over on to the hard shoulder. It was the middle of nowhere, man, with no other vehicles in sight and the heat was well over a hundred degrees. Away in the distance – maybe a couple of miles or so – I could see the outline of what looked like a fairground. I told Jay and Scott to grab the bikes and I locked up the truck. We started riding and the outline came closer and closer. When we got to it, I saw it was a waterpark, but it was closed and there was at least five big Rottweilers guarding it. They ran at us when we approached the fence, snarling and growling. I reckoned there must be someone about to feed them, so I started whistling as loud as I could. Finally, the park warden heard me and came over. I told him we'd run out of gas a couple of miles back and he said he could let us have some he had in a can – enough to get us to the next gas station.

I noticed that all·the water in the park had been drained off and the dry waterslides and rapids looked awesome. I'd always had a crazy dream about riding a waterpark, so I whispered to the warden –

'You reckon you'd let us ride the park on our bikes?'

'I don't know about that ...'

'I'll give you two hundred bucks.'

He thought about it for a minute, then agreed. He locked the dogs away and we came in and started riding up the rapids. The waterslides were two hundred feet in the air and we blasted down them at full speed, getting pinned to the corners and going over vert and ripping round it. My crazy dream became reality that day and it was one of the best riding experiences I ever had – it was the kinda thing you can't plan, it's something that just happens.

We stayed there for hours, until it started to get dark, then we took the gas back to the truck and drove home to LA.

In February 2003 I was back home for a couple of weeks and I went to watch England play Australia at Upton Park with Lee Martin and a few other mates. It was Wayne Rooney's debut and England lost 1-3. Before the game, we went for a few drinks at the Punch and Judy, overlooking Covent Garden in London. There's a big Oakley store right opposite and I was literally the entire shop window – a massive image around fifteen meters square of me wearing a pair of their sunglasses. My mates thought it was a big deal and treated me like a rock star, but I didn't think all that much of it.

Oakley also released a denim clothing range named after me. But I wasn't smart with the money I was earning back then – it meant nothing to me. As far as I was concerned, there was an endless supply that was never gonna dry up.

Two weeks before the Birmingham Bike Show in 2003 – around the beginning of April – I flew to Orlando to compete in a UGP Roots street contest. OK, I wasn't renowned in that discipline, but I'd rode so much with Cory in the yard on a mini spine ramp we built, and we got good real quick by sessioning the hell out of it. It was a high quality contest and I was stoked when I made the finals, but only came eighth. Even so, it was an amazing result, as it was my first comp in that discipline. A lot of Cory's friends came, as the venue was near his former home in West Palm Beach. I got on real well with those guys and we partied full throttle before meeting up with Cory, who was doing the Gumball Rally 3000.

As you probably know, the Gumball's a prestigious event, an annual 3,000 mile international celebrity motor rally that takes place on public roads. It was started in 1999 by Maximillian Cooper and the idea was to combine cars, music, fashion and entertainment. In 2003 it started in San Francisco and passed through Nevada, Arizona, New Mexico, Texas and Louisiana, before finishing in Miami. People taking part that year included Jackass's Ryan Dunn, Travis Pastrana, Tony Hawk and, of course, Cory, along with loads of filthy-rich dudes and fast car enthusiasts. We drove from Orlando and linked up with Nasty to get in on the final leg of the Gumball and the fun at the Mandarin Hotel in Miami. The place was full of celebrities from all walks of life and we partied all night.

Me and Nasty had been asked to come over to England to compete in the Birmingham Bike Show contest so, less than a week after the Gumball, we flew out from Miami. We got to Birmingham and it was fucking disgraceful, the worst dirt ever. It'd been getting pissed on by Birmingham rain and it was saturated, so they covered the jumps in wood. Me and Cory were like –

'I'm not riding this shit!'

Who wants to ride shit dirt jumps covered in plywood? There was a street course that looked OK – like I said, that year we had a mini spine ramp built in our backyard and we got real good on ramps real quick. As soon as you get something fresh beneath your wheels it's on! We'd ride dirt and ramps every day. So I was like –

'Hey, Nasty ... let's ride street.'

'Yeah, fucking right! Are you feeling it?'

'Hell, yeah!'

Nasty was boosting, like, five feet higher than Dave Mirra over the spine. It was ridiculous.

Fucking hell, every name was there, it was stacked, and we ended up qualifying second and third. We were pretty hot that year, we were tripping. That night, we went out to celebrate and one drink led to another, you know how it is. Before we knew it, we were in the middle of Birmingham on it! We met some skirt and were still shagging at six in the morning. Back then, me and him, you could drop us off anywhere in the world and we'd find the local good-time girls. We never had any intention of going to the finals the next day – we only rode street for the fun of it, just to see what we could do. The finals were in the afternoon. When we got back, everybody was getting their bikes out and we hid somewhere until they were gone. Then we sneaked into the hotel and crashed.

In May 2004 I got added to the GT bike team and I also picked up a new deal with SoBe, a brand new energy drink at the time. I bought a St. Bernard pup for $2,500 and named it Rocky, to keep company with my twin retrievers, Geordie and Cassie. That dog would dig his way out and go missing for days. Once he went missing for a week and I was tripping out. I got all these flyers printed and I put them up all over the place and went out on my bike shouting his name. Five weeks later and he's still missing and I'm starting to accept the fact that he's not coming back. Then I got sent this note –

TO FIND ROCKY, FOLLOW THESE DIRECTIONS

I jumped in the Range Rover and went where the note told me and knocked on the door. I recognised the woman who opened it, she used to be my neighbour.

'You got my dog?'

Before she can say anything, Rocky comes bounding toward me. She starts giving me excuses about finding the dog and stuff, and how it was now her daughter's dog. It was pretty clear to me that she took Rocky with her when she left my neighbourhood. Like, I knew it was my dog, and so did Rocky. I didn't want to stand there arguing with her, so I beat it, taking Rocky with me. I found out later that she split up from her husband and, when she left, she took my dog with her, just like I suspected. The husband ratted her out, it was him who sent me the anonymous note. That dog cost me a lot of money and I loved him.

Meanwhile, I'm still trying to get my winning streak back, but I can't. I pulled a 360 turndown backflip and a double flip on the last set of the 2004 Gravity Games. Nobody'd ever pulled that before – like, I had a blinding run before that with a 360 flip at the end. I thought there's no way I've lost this, but all of a sudden I look up and I'm in third position. I'm like –

'Eh?'

No one else ever pulled a 360 turndown backflip on dirt and to pull it in 2004 on a thirty-foot long jump and get an 89 was just fucking ridiculous. I'm not saying the judges ripped me off, but that score speaks for itself. I mean, c'mon, what was that all about?

Losing comps meant losing money, but I was never bothered much about that side of things – there was always cash coming from somewhere. Like, one day there'd be thousands of dollars in the bank, and the next day there'd be fuck-all. The day after there'd be more money in the bank – and so on and so on. Bills got paid late sometimes, but they always got paid. At one time, I was so disorganised my water supply was turned off because I hadn't paid up and I was still waiting for cash to come in. So I planned a little trip to Tijuana to get some money together.

I set off with Chris Mason, a friend of mine from Newcastle, and Moses, a Mexican who was rooming at my house back then. To counteract the physical effects of the partying, I was trying to keep as fit as possible and I was into pumping iron in my garage. I took steroids to bulk up, like all the bodybuilders in California, and selling them was a good way to make extra cash. I started off opening the ampoules and trying to inject the stuff into my butt, but I couldn't manage it properly, so I got Chris to do it – like, he's there sticking these syringes in my ass and it looks fucking weird, man. But I got big real quick, maybe due to my metabolism – I went from 180lbs to 220lbs fast. Someone was videoing me riding my bike and I'm like –

'Fuck it, man, nobody that big belongs on a bike.'

So I tried to get back down to normal. I had a lot of trouble losing the muscle mass – it wasn't easy and it took me a long time. I'd go running in 100 degrees heat, wearing layers of cloths and a trash bag. I ended up taking winstrol and burners like xenadrine and hydroxycut to get back to normal size. So, in the end, I decided to stay off the steroids myself and only sell them to the bodybuilders.

Moses drove us down over the border in his Chevy Silverado truck. Generally, American customs don't care much when you're going down there and Mexican customs welcome your money with open arms. So there was no problem going in. When we got to Tijuana, I went into a pet superstore and bought a load of steroids for Moses to sell to the bodybuilders back in LA. It was fucking weird buying steroids in a pet shop, but that's what it was like – the fucking place was lawless! We drove on into downtown Tijuana and had a few drinks in this strange fucking tavern that was like something out of Star Wars, then we took a walk down main street and it was heaving with prostitutes, dealers, pimps, transgenders and real rough-looking characters. I'd heard about this show where they get a donkey to fuck a hooker and Moses wanted to go see, but we couldn't find it – probably just as well.

I had my video camera and I was filming the scene when this guy who looked like a security guard went crazy and told me to stop filming and put the camera away. When we got to the end of the street, we got rushed by three cop cars and the Federalis slammed us up against a wall. As the cops were patting us down, they started shouting –

'Pariqo! Pariqo!'

They were claiming they found a big bag of coke in Moses' pocket, but it was clearly a set-up. They arrested us all, but then let me and Chris go after we paid them a $50 bribe. Moses had some previous form, so they took him off to jail. He gave me the keys to his truck before they took him away

– it was like he was afraid he wasn't gonna get back out and he wanted me to take the truck to my house.

I didn't want to leave Moses in Tijuana because the place was riddled with corruption and disease – but the truck was packed full of steroids and I didn't want to hang about either. Me and Chris went into this bar with a brothel upstairs that seemed to be catering for disabled veterans. I remember three hookers carrying a wheelchair-bound guy and he was waving his disability cheque at them. We hung out and just generally wasted time for the next six hours trying to figure out what to do – then, just before it got dark, we saw Moses walking toward us up the street. I couldn't believe it. They kept him in this dirty prison cell with a bunch of bad-asses, but he paid the cops off and they set him free. I guess he knew the drill down there. We all got in the truck and headed back to California.

Crossing the border back into America was always tense, even if you're not doing anything wrong, you feel intimidated because US customs are big, notoriously aggressive and take no shit. You never know what they're gonna do. They were spot checking cars and the vehicle in front was searched. We got pulled over into the waiting area and I'm like –

'Fuck, dude, this is gnarly.'

They had a quick look round the vehicle and patted us down, then they let us through. As we drove off, they were searching the car behind us. I guess luck was with us that day. The steroids were hidden under the steering wheel with a bunch of weed and they never even looked there. It was a fucking relief, man – I mean, I'd been down to Mexico sightseeing and boozing a few times when I was younger, because it was illegal to drink under twenty-one in America. It was always a crazy place and I could do what I liked down there. One time, coming back, I was interrogated at the border by US customs for four hours because I smelled of liquor and my visa form wasn't stapled in my passport. Those little trips were risky but, when you're that young, you don't see danger and you don't know fear.

I got on real well with Moses the Mexican and his brother, Henio. They were hard guys, covered in tattoos and afraid of nothing. They had a fucking arsenal of guns and were into trafficking coke and weed in a big way. I never had any intention of getting involved in that shit, but I didn't see it as a problem at the time. When I was away at contests, Moses and Henio and a bunch of their Mexican friends'd pack up lorries on my driveway with weed and coke that was coming in from Mexico. They'd transport it from the west coast to the east coast, where it would be three times as valuable. They took full advantage of me and my laid-back lifestyle and, when I look back now, I guess you could say they abused my hospitality.

But the good thing about it was, I had a regular free supply of strong Mexican weed. Any time my friends visited me from England, they'd take one rip of the bong and be so stoned they could barely operate. I'd been smoking the shit for a long time and it didn't bother me that much. I'd smoke it all day long and just carry on like normal – if you could call my life 'normal' at the time.

Then, when Moses was travelling back from Philadelphia in a BMW SUV that wasn't registered in his name, he got pulled over by highway patrol and they found half a million dollars in cash in the car. They arrested him and took him to the cop station, where they told him if he could prove where the money came from they'd give it back to him and let him go. He had a receipt that he got from a contact in Atlantic City, saying he won the money in a casino and, even though it was a fucking false document, there was nothing the cops could do about it – unless they called the casino. Which, lucky for Moses, they didn't. I guess it was just Moses being cautious and being prepared for the worst – which he had to be all the time. When he got back to California, he said that close shave with a long stretch in prison made him decide he was done transporting and was gonna get a regular job as a legit driver. But I noticed that, shortly after, he bought a brand new truck and his brother opened up a taco shop. If it wasn't a red flag for Moses, it should've been for me.

But the craziness didn't stop. Like I said, Moses had all these fucking guns – shotguns, handguns, M16s and everything. There was an old caravan that someone left in my yard and we shot it up. There was me and Moses, my brother

Martin, Chris Gentry, Brian Manley and Chris Mason. Brian was a freestyle motocrosser who was paralysed from the waist down. We shot all the windows out and I got inside with a shotgun and blew the roof off. Then we towed it to the top of a hill and doused it with petrol and set it alight. It burned like a fucking beacon, man, and we hightailed it out of there before the cops came. Unfortunately, we forgot Brian. He's on top of the hill in his wheelchair with a massive caravan fire and we only realised he was missing when we got back to my place, so I had to drive back up there and get him. By then there was two fire trucks pulling up and a chopper flying overhead and I had to pin it back down the hill with Brian holding on for dear fucking life.

Everybody hid inside my garage, but I didn't think it was such a big deal – like after that fire in Sweden, back in 1993, when I nearly burned the fucking campsite to the ground.

It was some time later when I went down to Santa Ana with Moses, to visit his uncle Miguel – at least, that's why I thought we were going down there. We had a few beers with the guy and some others and everything was cool. Then Moses said we should go get some cocaine, to keep the party moving along. I'm thinking he's going down the street to a dealer he knows and it'll all be cool. We pulled up at this house and the Mexican guy who answered the door told us to follow him. He got in his truck and drove away and we followed along to a rundown apartment block in the Sandpointe neighbourhood of the city that was tagged up in gang graffiti. The whole place had been shot up. There was bullet holes everywhere. We come to a rough-as-fuck gated community kinda place and our guide knocks on a garage door that's mostly cracked open and he signals us to go in.

Inside this fucking place, there's three Mexicans tattooed from head to toe and wearing three-quarter length trenchcoats and rubber gloves. They're cleaning down shotguns and an Uzi sub-machine gun and smoking crystal meth. Moses speaks to them in Spanish and the gist of the conversation's like this –

'What's happening, guys?'

'Black Dragons killed Diego.'

'You gonna smoke them?'

'Too right, mi amigo.'

'OK, we'll make tracks.'

'No, you stay!'

They wouldn't let us leave for a long time and I was struggling to keep my shit together in case they wanted us to go with them to smoke the Black Dragons. Moses stayed cool, like he wasn't worried, but I was starting to trip out. I just wanted to get the fuck out of there and I'm wondering to myself, what am I doing here in the first place?

It was so sketchy, man.

Eventually they gave us the coke and let us leave.

10
FALLING IN LOVE

I was still with Fleur in 2004. Still doing the same drugs and partying and fucking and generally having a crazy time. Fleur was a voluptuous and adventurous woman and, like I said already, the sex was incredible. I'd never been with a woman like her before. The whole thing back then was kinda surreal – it was a fabulously freaky blur of a fucked-up time, man! But the partying started to get out of control, so Fleur moved away from the beach and I moved out of my house and we got a place in Corona together. I rented my house to a band called The Kottonmouth Kings – they were a hip-hop group and I got along with them real good. They smoked a lot of weed and were generally cool people to hang out with.

Things were OK at the beginning but, after a while, life with Fleur got real difficult, with intense fights and break-ups. We'd flare up at each other and argue furiously over fuck-all. I think she liked the intensity of it, fighting like mad and fucking like mad afterwards. Looking back now, I guess it was real dysfunctional and we were living in a kinda fantasy world, distorted and unreal. As time went on, I was looking to make an escape out of a volatile situation before it went too far. I moved out twice – like, properly moved all my shit. Then she'd lure me back through a combination of emotional seduction and promises of a perfect existence together.

I had my three dogs and she thought it was a good idea to bring home the two Rottweilers she owned with the rock star. She also had a Chihuahua, so we had six dogs and it was fucking crazy. She didn't like my dogs pissing on the grass, but it was OK for hers. My retrievers were getting bullied by the Rotties and there was constant stand-offs between Rocky and them. It all sounds petty and trivial now, but I loved my dogs, they were rocks to me and stayed loyal when the world around me was going crazy and I didn't know what was happening or who to trust. I ended up moving in and out with my dogs time and time again. But I just couldn't stay away completely.

It was round about this time that me and Cory had been up all night partying and I left his house about 4:00am. When I woke the following afternoon, I found out that Nasty'd had a serious car accident. Shortly after I left, he went to get some cigarettes and blacked out while he was driving. He wrapped the car round a tree in someone's front yard. I went to the accident site and the car was completely obliterated – fire trucks and police everywhere. I thought he must be dead. When I got to the hospital he was in a coma, just laying there lifeless. It was a big wake-up call for me.

It's like, drug dealers hung with the BMX and motocross stars and that's how they got a reputation for being cool and plied their trade to people who had lots of money to pay for it. It was a match made in hell and I was mostly stoned out of my eyeballs all the time. I smoked weed because I was stressed and I blew coke to come back up again, like on a roller coaster ride that's out of control. I mean, despite the so-called 'good time' I was having, I wasn't happy about the way my life was going and I wasn't riding my bike like I should be. I was in a constant battle against pills and meth and coke and everything else that went with the lifestyle I found myself caught up in.

I decided to buy a new house and move away from all the craziness.

In July 2004 I met Melissa Giles, she was a friend of a friend and she organised home loans. I kinda knew her before that, like I knew she worked in real estate and I wanted to sell my house and buy this bigger one and I was having problems with the mortgage and shit. I asked her to fix it for me and she said she would, then we started seeing some more of each other and she was fun to be with. Melissa was a couple of years older than me and she had a son called Seth who was about eighteen months. Seth's dad was a guy called Mike Sweeney – he had a reputation as a meth addict and a big marijuana dealer. Melissa always seemed to have her son with her and she seemed like the kind of woman who'd be real easy to get along with. I was getting tired of the freakiness and she represented a kind of stability in a crazy world.

Melissa helped me buy this massive house with lots of land and stables and a sick swimming pool. It was the kind of place I'd always wanted, where I could build my dream jumps. There was too much room for me on my own, so I took in other riders as lodgers who paid me rent – Jerry Bagley and Luke Parslow, along with Moses the Mexican. I was so stoked I threw the ultimate house party – it went on for five days and nights! People came from all over and we nearly blew the fucking roof off. On day five, it was time to put the brakes on as I had heavy equipment coming in to start building my trails. So I grabbed my dirt bike out of the garage and rode it into the house, doing doughnuts and telling everyone the party was over and to fuck off.

Despite the move, I just couldn't take myself away from Fleur completely and I was fucking her and Melissa at the same time for a while, before it caught up with me. Fleur ratted on me to Melissa, who I didn't want to lose. I realised I'd fucked up big time, so I made the decision to finally end it with Fleur for real. Melissa lived in West Covina in a one-bedroom apartment. The place was fairly ghetto and I wanted her to move in with me. She didn't want to lose her apartment because she knew my reputation of being a big-time womaniser and maybe I'd dump her after I got tired of her. We began spending a lot of time together and I stopped partying as hard as I used to. One thing I noticed was, she always had a bottle of vicodin with her, but I never thought anything of this as it was on prescription.

I was happier than I'd been for a long time.

Nasty made a full recovery after months of rehab and we still partied together. But something had changed. We were both kinda calmer, like we were trying to live a more sensible existence and cut down on the drugs and being so fucking crazy and irresponsible all the time.

A couple of months later, in late 2004, I get a phone call from Melissa and she tells me she's pregnant. I'm overcome with emotion, so I jump in a cold shower then pin it to her apartment, which is about an hour away. The pregnancy wasn't planned and, when I get there, she tells me she's not sure if she wants to keep the baby. I hold her tight in my arms and tell her I love her.

'But you cheated on me with Fleur.'

'That's over. It's all over!'

'Promise.'

'I promise.'

We talked until morning, then we went over to her mother's place, which was round the corner and sat down and had a serious talk. I told Monika I loved her daughter and I'd support her and be faithful to her for the rest of my life. Her mother was cool and I really liked her and she's going to me –

'I'm happy for both of you but, Stephen, you need to start thinking with your big head and not your little head.'

It made me laugh at the time.

I remember barging into Cory Nastazio's house while he was laying in bed with his girl Nicole. I got a big smile on my face and I'm like –

'Hey, Nasty, I gotta tell you something!'

Nasty don't get up until at least noon, so he reckons it must be something important if I'm waking him at seven in the morning.

'Whassssup, man!'

'I'm gonna have a baby!'

Nasty nearly chokes on his tongue and I know he's thinking how could I let this happen?

'And I'm gonna get married.'

OK, getting married's one thing, you can always get divorced – but having a kid is real life, man! Nasty tries to tell me neither of us are ready for that kind of responsibility – we party way too hard. But I remind him of his accident and I reckon this baby's been sent to calm me down, because I'm spiralling out of control. It's a sign for me to pay attention to what's important in life.

Melissa moved into my house in December 2004 with her son, Seth. And I loved that boy like he was my own, right from day one.

Six months later, Nasty gets his girl pregnant, so it looks like we're living life side-by-side again. We found out we were both having boys and we thought that was awesome and our boys could grow up together and ride bikes together just like us.

I was feeling good when the 2005 Gravity Games were held in Philadelphia, the place where I first found fame. I was feeling confident, even though I only came third in 2004. The jumps were right under the freeway and practice was cool and went real well. After practice, I went to stay at Adam Aloise's house, who lived with Pat Juliff, another BMXer. There was a few people over that night and we had a house party and someone brought a bottle of GHB – like the stuff I took at that party after my first Gravity games win. GHB is used medically as an anaesthetic and a treatment for cataplexy and narcolepsy, but it's also used to increase athletic performance – like, bodybuilders use it in small doses to gain muscle mass and shit.

We were all doing caps and I didn't really feel a thing, so I got into this other bottle that was the concentrate for mixing the GHB and made it real strong. I necked six caps and, twenty minutes later, I was fucking flying. At first it was like the best feeling you get when you're drinking – when you're at the top of the intoxication, before you start to go over the edge and come down. Then it hit me like a fucking freight train! I had no control over my body – it went way beyond anything I'd taken before, worse than being paralytic drunk! I knew I'd done too much when I started puking my fucking brains out. All I could hear was like an engine revving inside my head and I thought I was gonna die. Man, I was scared! My body and mind were consumed by this GHB and I lay on the couch, smoking weed and drinking red bull and I got no sleep that night. I just wanted the high to be over!

Next morning the contest's on and I try to ride through the comedown – by some miracle, I qualify for the finals. It's one to count out of three runs, so I gotta hit the nail on the head and land a home run with the biggest tricks I got in my bag. I drop in and haul ass down the hill before hitting a thirty-foot set of doubles. I try a 360 flip, but get lost in the air, looking at the underside of the freeway. My mind's fucked! My head's all over the place! I come down and whack myself pretty hard. Then I get back up for the next run and do exactly the same thing, except I crash even harder. But I got one run left and, if I stomp it, I'm up for the win. I float off the lip and go into a 360 turndown backflip – I'm coming round perfect, but I don't have enough speed and I case the landing. That's game over! I've blown it!

I couldn't understand why I put myself through that shit, always making it harder than it needed to be, always making bad decisions – partying at the wrong time, like before contests, taking drugs just because they were there. Especially now I had everything I wanted – my dream house, my dream woman and my son on the way.

Melissa was amazing while she was pregnant. Over the next eight months she worked out daily and ate real healthy. But I just couldn't stop going for a blow-out every now and then. I'd be at parties and she'd come and get me and I'd say I wouldn't do it again. But I did. I was accustomed to being surrounded by loads of sycophants and bullshitters – I'd become engulfed in a world that had no soul or depth or moral grounding.

My son Mason Murray was born on 30 July 2005 and I was super pumped. Cory came to the hospital with me and I held the baby in my arms and I was so overwhelmed I was like a fish out of water. I'd been so extreme and did so much stuff that I thought at the time was cool. I'd lived through so many long nights of bad shit and, like, having a baby at that particular time was probably the craziest thing I could've done. When the doctor said me and Melissa could take Mason and leave, I wanted him to come with us because I didn't know anything about babies and I was scared shitless. Nevertheless, it was the best day of my life. It beat anything I'd done on a bike.

There was nothing like it!

The X-Games were held between 14 and 17 August that year. Once again I found myself doing the wrong shit at the wrong time. I'm partying for three days and nights over in Orange County and I suddenly realise the X-Games practice is starting in two days and the comp is the following day at the LA Coliseum. I try to get my shit together, but I'm overwhelmed by the comedown. Again, it's one run out of three to count and again I find myself having to send it and go big. So I go 360 turndown backflip over the first set that's massive and I crash three times in a row. I walk away from this event at an all-time low. Melissa always had prescription pills and I started taking vicodin for my pain. The doctor also gave me somas as a muscle relaxer and, when I took them together, I got a real comfortable sense of floating – like, complete contentment.

Me and Melissa got married in October the same year.

There's a saying that goes 'what happens in Vegas stays in Vegas', but there's another, like 'there's an exception to every rule' – this is the exception. Twenty of my best mates went on a stag to Las Vegas for my bachelor party – half of them English and the other half American. One of the US guys had a connection with Limp Bizkit and I was able to hire their tour bus for the trip. Man, it was fucking pimp – it was wild! All my English friends were there – my brother Martin, Chris Mason, Lee Martin, Jay Aliano, Scott Edgworth, Marco Del'isolla, Ben Hall, some guy called Gamble and my friend Niemi, dressed in a Newcastle shirt and three-quarter length trousers and Adidas trainers. The fucker brought no money and not even a change of clothes. The Americans included Cory Nastazio and some motocross guys, but they were mainly club promoters and LA 'gangsters' and hangers-on, the kind of people I was partying with at the time – also Luke

Parslow from Australia. We had rooms booked on the top floor of the Hard Rock Café, in those days it was the coolest place to party, and we were scheduled to stay for three or four days.

The trip from LA to Vegas in the tour bus was fucking pandemonium. The 'gangsters' had a bag as big as a flour sack full of every kind of drug you could think of – and there was a huge bottle of Jack Daniels and bottles of Budweiser and Corona and Newcastle Brown beer. By the time we got to Vegas, everyone's mangled and it was pure chaos.

After we checked into the Hard Rock, we went to the Tao, one of the most exclusive clubs in Vegas, above the Venetian Hotel. Some people got in quick and others had to wait a bit, so we got split up. They didn't want to let Niemi in, because of the way he was dressed, but Seán Dommage, one of the American guys who organised the trip, persuaded the doormen it was OK. I mean, it was a big thing to get twenty pissheads into such an exclusive club. Once everyone got inside, we kinda did our own thing. I went into the VIP area with the Americans and some of the English guys went to the bar. The Tao was real expensive and I think it was cheaper to drink at the bar than sit at a table. Motley Crue drummer Tommy Lee's fortieth birthday party was in full swing and, I mean man, there was naked women lying in baths, covered in floating petals, and crystal champagne and all kinds of drugs. It was totally crazy! Seán Dommage bought a bottle of vodka for stupid money, maybe $1,000 or something like that – he was a club promoter and I guess he had loads of dough and could do it just to show he was a big shot or something. Martin and the English guys joined up with us again after a while, but they weren't happy and thought I was ignoring them. They'd drunk all the expensive bottle of vodka and Dommage was real angry and there was a kinda standoff for a while.

I guess everyone had been up for days and no one was in the right mindset. I vaguely remember a strip club where Ben Hall buys drinks for some girls and thinks they're all crazy about him – until he finds out they're hookers. The Americans pay for a bunch of lap-dancers and it's all getting fucking frantic. Back at the Hard Rock, Martin was real angry and things were going downhill fast. You gotta understand that I was in a different place then. I guess I didn't care much about anything, not even myself. Martin could see the road my life was going down and he didn't like it. I know now that he had my best interests at heart but, at the time, I just didn't care.

All sorts of silly shit's going on in the hotel and no one gets very much sleep. I think Niemi ended up sleeping in Lee Martin's bed and Lee had to crash on the floor for two hours. We're scheduled to meet at the pool next morning and the guys are wired after so much booze and coke and so little sleep. Now this poolside's real fucking exclusive and there's all kinds of stars and celebs around it. But the English guys don't care much about that and Gamble rugby tackles a heat lamp that falls over and dents a stretch Hummer. Chris Mason's riding round on a fucking moped and causing chaos.

I'm glad when they all decide to go to a shooting range, but it's a crazy experience. The guns are fucking loud and the people shooting them are a bunch of rednecks, all talking about Afghanistan and shit like that, like they're fucking armchair Marines. It's scary to think if the English guys start anything here, it could be like the battle of Pork Chop Hill or something, with them all turning the fucking M16s on each other.

Things were getting frayed at the edges – big time. The English guys paid a lot of money to come over for my wedding and some of them, especially Martin, were pissed off with the way they thought I was treating them. The Americans didn't like the way they were behaving and it was heading for a transatlantic war – fast. Chris Mason squared up to one of the Americans and I thought he was gonna do his jujitsu on the guy. I could see the way this was going, even though I was out of my fucking head. It was fucking crazy at this point as everyone was wired and drunk and the whole thing was turning into a fucking nightmare. I was getting less concerned with having a good time and more concerned with trying to stop a fucking battle.

That night, Gamble gets naked in the casino and upsets people and Lee Martin pisses up the bar – he and Gamble are escorted to the lift by security and put under room arrest. In the end, enough was enough. I didn't want to deal with all that fucking drama, so I called Melissa and she drove to Vegas and took me home, leaving the rest of them there. If Martin was angry to begin with, he was even angrier now, being stranded in Vegas without any plan to get back to LA. He came into my room when he got back – I was in a massive comedown and I didn't want a confrontation, so I pushed him away and told him to get the fuck out. My brother had come over to be my best man, but he pulled out in protest against who I'd surrounded myself with and how my life was going.

The English guys fucked off to Huntington Beach after they got back from Vegas and hired motel rooms, even though they were supposed to stay at my place. Cory Nastazio took Martin's place as my best man and we got married at the house. The wedding was beautiful, set around the swimming pool in our yard. We lit up floating candles and decorated the whole place – I put a lot of work into it and it looked absolutely stunning! Everyone was there, all my friends and family, even Martin – though we didn't speak very much as I remember. Lots of people made speeches, including Niemi, who was dressed in Martin's suit which was, like, four times too big for him.

I didn't speak to my brother for a long time after the stag party – at least a few months, which was the longest period of not connecting in all our lives till then. I called him on New Year's Day and he answered the phone and I'm glad he did.

It's all water under the bridge now.

Despite the disastrous stag party, everyone was cool and seemed to have a good day – but I couldn't wait to get away. Afterwards, me and Melissa took off for Maui on our honeymoon. It was paradise for me, man, to be in a place like that with the woman I loved. Right then, for a short while, life couldn't be any better.

I wanted to get some weed, so the locals told me I'd have to go to the nudist beach and look for the guy with the massive dick – he was the dealer. We went down there and crossed the parking lot and climbed over some rocks to get to the place where you had to take everything off and let it all hang loose. It wasn't long until I spotted this guy with a dick like a fucking elephant's trunk and I reckoned he was my man. It was awkward with him standing in front of us while he took the weed from his satchel and sold me some, with this enormous tool swinging in the breeze. Melissa was embarrassed and she's whispering like –

'Just get the stuff and get rid of him.'

'What? Don't you like it?'

'No, it's grotesque.'

Women, eh!

So we're on the naked beach and we smoke some weed while watching the sunset. Then, for no particular reason, I start singing – it's this song from West Side Story that my grandma used to play all the time, only I'm using Melissa instead of Maria –

> ♪Melissa ...
> *I married this girl called Melissa*
> *And suddenly her name*
> *Will never be the same*
> *To meeeeeee*♪

Then I'm on my feet –

> ♪Melissa ...
> *I'm in love with a girl called Melissa*
> *And suddenly I found*
> *How wonderful a sound*
> *Can beeeeeee*♪

Then I'm dancing, like I'm in some schmaltzy fucking musical or something –

> ♪Melissa ...
> *Sing it loud and there's music playing*
> *Sing it soft and it's almost like praying*♪

Melissa's holding her hands in front of her face in embarrassment and I'm prancing round naked with all these people on the beach thinking I'm fucking crazy.

And I am.

Crazy in love!

See Me and Mason on stysrg.com

11
HITTING BOTTOM

All honeymoons come to an end and now, after Mason's born, I find myself caring for two kids – him and Seth – even though I'm still getting fucked up on prescription pills and it's becoming a massive problem for me. The whole Riverside scene was, like, prescription drugs and stuff at that time – and I was so pilled out! Melissa got caught up in it too and she found this 'special' doctor who gave her whatever she wanted – a bit like the guy who supplied Michael Jackson, I guess.

I remember my mum and granddad coming over to Riverside to visit us and I'd be on the kitchen floor with codeine and other shit in me – all kinds of stuff, like painkillers and norcos and somas and hydrocodone and duexis and shit I can't even remember. One time I took so many pills there was nothing left, so I started drinking cough syrup. That's how bad it was, man!

Cory's son was born in January 2006 and it was like two kids raising kids. We were still partying fairly hard, despite previous good intentions, and pilling and trying to focus on BMX, with wives and kids and bills – it was like we were trying to have our cake and eat it too. But it was all taking more and more of a toll on my performance as a rider. Like, going to a contest, everyone's waiting for Stephen Murray to bust out these big tricks and if he don't, he's messed up. I was known for the do-or-die tricks – all or nothing. Sadly, they like to see guys smashing themselves just as much as seeing the big gnarly tricks and they knew with me it might go either way. For years, I could party for days and nights on end and then ride, but it got to a point when I wasn't handling it no more. It was really affecting my ability and sooner or later I was gonna get hurt real bad. The people in the crowd knew it and were waiting for it to happen.

That was the professional side. On the personal side, I was pretending like everything was OK. Each year I held a big BMX jam in my front yard where I'd invite all the riders to come and party. In late Spring 2006 I wanted to make it even gnarlier and build a full pipe in the mid rhythm of the dirt section. I didn't know how I was gonna do it, so I contacted Ron Kimler and Nate Wessel, the best ramp builders in the game, and I got some financial support from GT, who were still sponsoring me at the time. I got a knock on my door one day and, when I answered it, there was this guy called Hollywood Mike Miranda, a BMX legend from the early eighties who was in the motion picture 'Rad'. He had Ron and Nate with him and we went to work. It took them two days, working day and night, to construct the full pipe and, once it was formed, a whole gang of us would stretch it out, making it into a corkscrew.

I painted it white and put plywood up over the top to build a fourteen-foot lip and a landing on the other side. It was seventeen feet high and you could ride right over as well as upside down round the loop. It took nearly six months to get everything dialed so we were ready to hit it. Nasty said I was crazy and he wanted no part of it – that only threw down the challenge for me to do something no one else had done before. The morning we were gonna hit the full pipe I noticed three big crash mats on my neighbour's drive – don't ask me what they were doing there, it was just random, they just kinda appeared. So I got on my motorbike and blasted over there and offered them two hundred bucks to borrow the mats.

All the guys came round that day and everyone was game to nail the full pipe. We laid the crash mats down so we'd just smash into them when exiting the loop. Kevin Robinson was the first to get the party started and he came round the full loop clean and crashed into the pad. It was my turn next and

I went down the roll-in, hit the first double and pulled back on the second, before cruising up to what looked like a wall of death that turned slightly to the left. Before I know it, I'm exiting the full pipe and smashing into the crash bag. I did this a couple more times to get used to it, giving myself dead legs from the handlebars jamming into me.

The time came for me to hit the whole thing – no fucking up or I'd get seriously hurt. I hit the loop again and got stuck in a compressed position coming round, from all the G-force. After four or five attempts, I managed to make it all the way through the section. What a fucking trip, man! I was the only one to make it all the way round that day, but everyone else managed to overcome the fear and send it round the loop.

I was still trying to have fun on my bike, even at that stage.

But I wasn't winning comps! The 2006 Red Bull Elevation was held at the Whistler Mountain resort in Canada, with one of the world's best ever dirt courses ending in the centre of Whistler Village, near Vancouver, in British Columbia. It was invite only and all the world's best riders were there – including me. The jumps were massive and you had to be on top of your game, going downhill real fucking fast! But I wasn't really with it. I remember practice sessions where everyone'd be riding and I just didn't feel right on my bike. I wasn't able to ride the way I wanted to and it felt fucked up watching Nyquist and Bohen and Mike Aitken murdering it.

Before the main event, Red Bull threw this big party and all the riders went out and got pretty hammered. But that wasn't enough for me, before long I have this bag of cocaine from one of the bar staff and it was all bad news from there! I partied all night on coke and came in at 5:00am. I was still wired, but I knew I had to get some sleep. I took eight tylenol PM's and closed my eyes, but the cocaine had flooded my system and I couldn't switch off. My eyelids were fluttering, but they wouldn't close. When reality finally dawned, I knew I'd fucked up and was in a sketchy situation.

It's 9:00am and everyone's waking up in the apartment. Jerry Badders is there and Cory and everyone's slept well –

except me and Whitesnake. We're both ruined. When Cory sees me he shakes his head and I know I gotta do something about the state I'm in. There's dozens of cases of Red Bull all over the place, so I crack open a couple and try to snap out of it. I'm feeling really edgy and I know I'm playing with fire – it's gonna be suicide riding a seriously dangerous downhill course the way I am.

Then it's 10:00am and only an hour to the contest. I jump in a golf cart to get a lift to the starting point. There's total disconnect between me and my bike and I couldn't be in a crappier mindset if I tried. I'm riding sketchy and the first couple of runs are scary as fuck. I get through and somehow manage to qualify for the finals later that afternoon. So I go straight back to the hotel and try to get a couple of hours sleep. That kinda steadies me and I manage to pull some tricks out of the bag in the finals. But it's still disappointing by my standards and I know I've blown a golden opportunity to get back to where I was. I'm starting to realise what Cory meant all those years ago when he said –

'We go there *exclusively* for the contest!'

I didn't, and I get eighth.

Over the next year, the prescription pills became a bigger and bigger problem. I stopped riding my bike competitively for the first time in my life. Every time I looked at it, I had no motivation to ride. I was completely burnt out. The money stopped coming in from sponsors, which wasn't surprising, considering I was rarely riding for them.

One day in 2006 Melissa went to work and I put Seth and Mason in the truck and went to drop them off at the babysitters, as I wanted to try to get back on my bike and ride. I was on some prescription shit, I don't even remember what, and my foot slipped off the brake pedal. It was at a T-junction and it was wet. I went straight across the intersection, through a bush and hit a wall. Luckily, the kids weren't hurt, but it brought me back and I got out of there fast, before the cops showed up. The kids looked at me and it was like they knew I was hitting rock bottom.

As I said, I'd stopped riding my bike by then and lost a lot of my sponsors. It was like I'd lost my drive and I wasn't winning comps no more. I wasn't high profile enough and, I guess, you can't blame them. It was my own fault. I gotta say here that Vans and Oakley stayed with me through thick and thin, and I'll always be grateful to them. But I lost my motivation. I lost my fire and I didn't have what it took to go big no more – if Rob Indri'd been there, he'd have told me to go home! I'd been riding my bikes since I was three years old and I'd achieved pretty much everything I'd ever dreamed of achieving – more than I'd dreamed. I'd partied with rock stars and all that shit, but after my son Mason was born, it was a full-time job looking after a young kid and a baby and keeping my wife happy and trying to snap out of it – trying to find the reason why I was falling out of love with riding. All the negative stuff sent me down the wrong roads. I was making mistakes with my life – I had everything I'd ever hoped for, but now I was fucking it up.

Looking back, you could say, what if I did it differently? What if? But I can't change anything. I lived life to the craziest, like it was the only way for me back then. I'm not ashamed of the things I did and I'm not scared to tell anyone, as you can see from this book. I got nothing to hide and even if I did, I wouldn't – if you know what I mean. If anything, I hope my mistakes are something young guys can learn from.

I stopped training like I should have been. Most of my sponsors left, except the few who stuck with me. I had a high expenditure lifestyle and money started running short. You could say I was chasing the high I got back in 2001 when I won the X-Games for the first time, and then the Gravity Games two weeks later. But I never got that same feeling again. It was the same with drugs – eventually they don't work.

Things kept sliding and I remember taking 'oxycotton', which is a form of opium, for a whole week – five tablets a day. I didn't know the fuck what I was doing. When I finally realised what I was dealing with, I stopped. But I was smoking loads of weed as well as doing the prescription stuff. I was a person I didn't want to be, but I couldn't see any way out of it. It's like, taking drugs starts off being cool with your mates, then it gets lifestyle, then it goes to a different place. It gets to be something else.

By then, Melissa was sliding too, she was on norcos and other shit, and some people were trying to say it was her fault. It wasn't. She was my beautiful wife who I loved so much and she came into my world because she loved me. Now that world was destroying us both. To make things worse, we had two wonderful sons who we were trying to protect from it all. It's like a downward spiral. I guess we were both scared because we were losing everything – losing ourselves, who we really were. At least, that's the way I felt. The further down I spiralled, the more I depended on the crutch of the drugs. Nobody made me bad, I got there all by myself. I made myself that way. I guess I felt like a failure and, when my sons grew up, they'd see me like that. I wanted to get it back, that winning feeling.

But didn't know how.

The drugs took the sadness away – for a while.

But it always came back.

Melissa was working long hours and bringing in some money but that, along with what I was earning from Oakley, wasn't enough to pay the mortgage. I had to find another way to make some dough, I had a family to feed and bills to pay. Then I met this kid called JJ, a dude from the Riverside party scene who got me the oxycotton, and I sold a bike to him to make some cash. He put me in touch with another guy called Scotty who was a horticulturist and electrician, he blew up all the houses for the Mexicans – I mean he lit up the houses so they could grow weed and tapped cables straight into the electricity mains so nobody noticed the high usage. I wanted part of it – I didn't want to ride for a living no more. Fuck riding, this was easier! Scotty intro'd me to Mexican weed growers, guys with names like Marcos and Santiago – I knew them already from being with Moses and Henio. I took money out of the equity on the house to finance the operation and it wasn't long before I was growing weed in my house too. Scotty took a cut out of everything and I thought he was cool at the time, so I let him move in with us.

The Mexican weed operation was big-time. Marcos had a fake track in his back yard – his house was four times as big as mine and lots of guys hung out there. There was four or five Mexicans, all big fuckers and covered in tats from head to toe. As far as I know, they were all legals in America, but they lived under the radar and were into drug dealing big time. I mean, at one stage Marcos had, $50,000 worth of pure refined coke in a transparent sack, like it was a shopping bag and he was just strolling back from the mall with his asparagus. Santiago got my back when I was involved in a massive fight in Club Gotham and they were like my new friends now and this was my new life.

Melissa was working so she wasn't home a lot, the kids got sent to day-care to be away from it, and I'd go sit in the weed room and just smoke. I had a huge grow of weed going on, maybe as much as $30,000 in one room alone. There was all kinds of lighting rigged up by Scotty and tapped into the grid. I was a grower now and I was done with bikes and all that stuff!

During 2006, when my career was at rock bottom and I was dropped by most of the sponsors, my brother Martin came over to visit and we went out riding trails at Rick Lakin's house. We're coming back with the bikes in the back of my beat up Ford Ranger truck that I bought from Brian Foster, with bent axles and broken windows from driving to the trails. Anyway, we gotta pass through a place that's just been built and the roads aren't finished properly, like they're just gravel in places. About half a mile from my house, I have this habit of doing a handbrake turn on this sharp bend – like, I'm doing it all the time. So I handbrake it hard and the truck spins round too far to the right. I let go of the handbrake and spin the steering wheel too much to the left and we shoot straight through this fence into a front yard, almost through the window, and nearly end up in some guy's living room. I'm like –

'Fuck!'

So I ram it into reverse and wheel-spin out of the yard and I'm about to put it in first and rip it away. But Martin's going –

'Stop! Stop!'

The guy's come out of the house already and Martin's like –

'He knows who you are, Stephen. He knows where you live. You can't just fuck off! He'll send the cops straight to your front door and you know what you got going on in there!'

I reckon he's right, so I tell him to hold his hand out. Martin holds his hand out and I grab a bunch of weed from my side of the truck and stick it in his fist. He's looking at me with his mouth open, going –

'Fucking hell!'

So I get out of the truck and walk up to the guy.

'Man, I'm so sorry. I came round the corner and lost control on the gravel surface.'

And the guy's like –

'Ya mothafucka! Ya do that all the time. It ain't the first time ya've done it!'

A few doors down, this other guy's come out shouting –

'Joe, that's the dude! That's the dude who does it every damn day! We got him, Joe!'

Joe goes to me –

'See that guy? He's an ex-sheriff and I'm an ex-cop. Ya're fucked, buddy!'

Martin's still in the truck with a fist-full of weed and Joe's like –

'Give me yar ID.'

'I haven't got any ID.'

'What d'ya mean, ya gotta have ID.'

'I got my passport, back at the house.'

Martin gets out of the truck and comes over to us. He's stuffed the weed into his pocket and he goes to Joe –

'I'll take one of the bikes and go up the road and get the passport. Stephen will stay here with the truck.'

Joe seems OK with that and the sheriff's fucked off to call the police.

'Ya do that. The cops are coming, they've already bin called.'

So Martin gets on the bike and rides off. At the house, he tells Melissa to bolt up the weed-rooms and not to open the door to anyone. If the cops come in and smell the stuff, we're all fucked. He gets the passport and blasts it back down the road. When he gets to Joe's house, I'm sitting on the front porch with him drinking a coke, all friendly like. Joe's going –

'So, listen Stephen, when can my kids come round and ride their bikes with ya?

'Anytime, man. You send them round my yard and I'll coach them.'

When Joe found out who I was, he's impressed because I'm like a hero to his kids. Martin's going –

'What about the police?'

And Joe's like –

'Nah don't worry. I'll talk to them.'

We got back into the truck and drove home. The cops never came round, but it was a close fucking call! I went round a few days later and fixed Joe's fence.

When it comes to drugs and money, people will do anything. Anything for a hit of meth or a snort of coke or a tug on a bong, and it all become unstable and volatile. Marcos owed Scotty some money, so a bunch of guys gathered at my house, including a white supremacist with swastika tats, and they went over to Marcos' and took a load of stuff from his place. After all the commotion that caused, Marcos got raided. He was only two streets away from me and, after he got popped, I took down my growing operation and got rid of all the weed. It was getting far too risky – I didn't want to go to prison for a long time. That still left Scotty but, without the lure of the weed, he gradually disappeared from the scene.

After that, me and Melissa started making alternative plans. We decided to sell up and move to a smaller place in Lake Perris, across from the skatepark, in the hope that I'd get the hunger for BMX again. This guy called Larry, who had a couple of marijuana shops, agreed to buy our house and he started moving all sorts of shit in and doing his own thing. Larry had been coming and going for three months and he just started to take the piss, running up bills and leeching off me.

One day I came home and Melissa's crying on the phone because he's been bitching her out. I grabbed the phone and told him to come get his shit and fuck off. So, I'm in the shower and I can hear Melissa screaming –

'Larry's here and he wants to fight!'

'Pass me my Vans.'

I tied them up tight as fuck so they didn't fall off when I volleyed him in the head. Cheeky fucker opened the door and walked straight into my house, past my kids.

'C'mon Murray, you want to handle this outside?'

OK, this guy's twice my size and supposed to be hard as nails. I'm like –

'Yeah, let's go.'

When we get outside, he moves into a fighting stance and he goes –

'You want to do this in front of your kids?'

For the second time, I remembered what my dad told me when I was younger –

'If you're ever in doubt, get the first one in!'

That was it. I head butted him straight in the face, with all the power I could muster up. Instant knock out. Smashed. I hoofed him all the way down the drive like I was kicking a field goal, then I beat fuck out of his Sand Rhino quad with a shovel.

'Fuck off you glamis, sideways-hat-wearing cocksucker!'

He came back later with the cops, sirens blaring and all. Pussy! And I'm thinking –

'Shit, this is it! I'm getting deported.'

They questioned me and I explained it was self-defence. It turns out this lunatic had a record for twenty-one assaults, three with knives.

Fucking hell – thanks dad for that piece of good advice.

They say you gotta hit rock bottom before you start to come back up again. After a while I began to take stock of my life and where it was going. How did I get to be such a fucking mess? How was I gonna get my career back on track? I was a ship without a rudder. One of my fans sent me a Bible, because I was trying to look for direction, but it was hard for me to connect with it back then – like, it didn't make much sense to me. I started to stress out. How was I gonna take care of my family? Life's a precious thing and I had a precious life – a precious wife and precious kids. I was throwing it away, along with my career in a sport I truly loved. I lost my fire for that, fully pinned fifth gear, full throttle.

I'm burnt out and it's hard to re-focus.

I want to understand how I can get back on track.

How?

12
THE ROAD BACK

It wasn't until the end of 2006 that I fully realised how fucked up my life had become, drifting in all the wrong directions, any which way. It took me a long time to come to terms with what I was doing, but I finally hit the nail on the head. The realisation came about six months before the 2007 Dew Tour. I was still smoking stupid amounts of weed. I was getting up in the night to smoke, smoking while I was driving – stupid dumb shit! It was like I went from being a fully fledged party animal to being a husband and father and having responsibilities so quick, I couldn't adjust to the transition. It took me completely by surprise and I thought weed and meds would help me through it. I should've been on a whole other level, but I wasn't.

Guys like Ryan Guettler and Corey Bohan and Luke Parslow were dominating the dirt contests. There was an influx of young, fearless Australian riders and watching them was like a wake-up call for me. I could see myself in them when I first came to California. It was like looking at me then and now. And it was a shock to my drugged-up system. This started to mess with my head – what was left of my head after all the pill-popping and weed-smoking. I was known as a rider who'd give 110% going for first place. I was never one of those people who just settled for something. I heard Rob Indri inside my brain –

'Go big or go home!'

I was looking for a way to reignite the fire. I had to prove to myself that I could win at the top level again. I had to take a step back and try to process what I was doing. I had to find some way to snatch my life back out of the jaws of assholeness. But I'd made things real hard and weighed myself down with the painkillers and the weed and shit and it'd take a big effort to change my ways and get back on the level. I knew what I was doing wrong – I was in with the wrong crowd and out of BMX. But knowing what you're doing wrong isn't enough, you gotta know how to get back to doing right.

There was this best-selling book called *The Secret* that was written by Rhonda Byrne and published in 2006. Melissa got me the DVD and I started to watch it. It was based on what they called the 'law of attraction'. All about positive thinking bringing you health, wealth and increased happiness. OK, I was sceptical, I'd heard all that shit before. There was loads of motivational stuff like that out there – especially in California, which is the home of the guru and the gullible. But I watched it and what it did tell me was that I was responsible for the way my life was. I was responsible for the negative elements that were bringing me down. It told me that, if I spend my time wallowing in regret and feeling sorry for myself, then things were only gonna get worse. But if I got off my ass and did something about my situation, I'd find the 'silver lining' in my life. I had to start living and thinking in a more positive way – a more optimistic way. If I did that, I'd find what I was looking for – the way back.

I watched that DVD over and over again, until it sunk in and I understood. I also opened up the copy of the Bible the fan sent me and tried to understand it a bit more than I'd done in the past. It was difficult. I never was much of a god-botherer and some of the stuff in the bible seemed ridiculous to me – like the animals going into Noah's Ark and Jesus parting the Red Sea and stuff like that. Until I realised it was symbolic; these stories were all part of the sacred science that's encoded in the book. To get the real meanings, you had to know how to read the code. Noah means 'rest', so we need a rest from ourselves and the chaos in our minds. The Ark's a safe haven when shit hits the fan, so we need to be ready inside ourselves for when bad stuff happens. I wasn't ready when the flood of bad shit hit me and I had no Ark and nearly went under. But now I understood and the other stories in the Bible began to make sense to me on a personal level. I started to apply it all to my life, in the hope of getting to a better place.

I start to talk to myself. It's like the old me talking to the new me and I'm like –

'You're not happy with your life?'

'No.'

'Then do something about it!'

'Like what?'

'For a start, stop feeling sorry for yourself and get off your dumb ass!'

And that's what did it for me. In the midst of all the shit that was going on. Like, I was gonna lose my house, I couldn't pay the bills, I didn't have any money and I was massively stressed out. I had to get away from it all.

Luke Parslow was living with me at the time and I'd wake up every morning and see him killing it by himself in my front yard. I once took a pay cut to get that kid sponsored and on the Oakley team – that's when he started to place in finals. Now, watching him and the other kids riding in my yard began to inspire me. I realised the only way to get out of the mess I was in was to do what I did best and, at the beginning of 2007, I did just that. I stopped fucking about, flipped a switch, put my feet back on the ground and found my bike again.

I began to train. A little at first, then every day.

The first couple of weeks getting back on track didn't come easy. I had to be patient and try to understand that, little by little, making small adjustments to my daily routine'd end up changing the person I'd become. As far as coming off the drugs was concerned, apart from having the major shits, I was generally OK. I guess I wasn't what you'd call a hardcore addict, so I didn't get that cold-turkey comedown. The worst was after the oxycotton – I got sweats and muscle cramps and felt nauseous but, overall, it wasn't as bad as I thought it was gonna be. I'd get up very early every morning and take care of my boys before dropping them off at the babysitters. This gave me a window of seven hours to concentrate on my riding and keep pushing forward in the right direction. Melissa was still working in real estate and the money she made helped out, but I'd be finding bottles of norcos all the time and I knew she was still doing the meds.

All the guys came over to ride with me – Luke and Nasty and TJ Ellis and Andre Ellison and Larry Edgar and Shane Dog. I started to work out in earnest and my fitness was coming back. I got on to a strict diet, giving my body the nutrition to expel the shit from my system and the fuel it needed to perform the way I wanted it to. Months went by and living clean and sensibly became second nature. I got connected with my bike again. Riding became fun again and I was getting back in control. Eventually I was able to have killer riding sessions, especially in the mornings before the hot Riverside sun came up. I started pushing the boundaries again – asking what was possible, trying the impossible. I was nailing it every day. From the moment I opened my eyes, I started to think like a champion again. Everything I did, every decision I made, I asked myself –

'Would a champion do that?'

I felt brand new – a brand new rider. I never felt so dialed.

Risk is all around us – everywhere and every day. Everyone sees and feels it in one way or another. For some people, it's in trivial everyday stuff and they'd never dream of doing anything as dangerous as action sports. Risk could be said to be a kind of 'gatekeeper', stopping most people from taking part in stuff that could hurt them real bad. It's something that don't show itself so obviously in many other sports, and this gives a high level of respect and kudos to action sports athletes.

I learnt at a young age that I couldn't afford to worry about taking risks. It wouldn't have won me any championships or brought me to California or skyrocketed me to the top. For BMX dirt riders, talent's only part of what you need, you also gotta have that mental toughness needed to attempt each run, each jump, to push the limits, to go further than anyone else. Some people might think that dirt jumping's reckless – but it's not as reckless as getting into a car drunk or high on drugs. Dirt jumping's a kind of calculated recklessness – it's countless hours of practice and planning. It's knowing yourself and what you're made of. You know the risks and you sign off on them. And there's no way you can anticipate or prevent the fluke – the one-in-a-million.

And the risk factor brings its own high – that rush of adrenaline in an increasingly over-sanitised, risk-averse world. Senses heightened to the level of wildness that very few people experience. It's what makes us want to go further, higher, faster. But even after practising for thousands of hours and measuring and calculating and planning, accidents and crashes are inevitable in a sport like BMX dirt jumping. No matter what you do, injuries happen. You just gotta be prepared to do what you do and not think about it too much. And you gotta take the bad with the good, the downs with the ups. If you're all the time worried about injury, then you're gonna fail. If you're talking of a career-ending or life-altering injury, or even thinking about it, then it's already game over. Time to hang up the helmet.

The scariest trick I've ever done in my life was the double backflip. You can ask any person in BMX dirt riding, 'what's the scariest trick?', and I guarantee they'll say the double backflip. It's so quick, there's a lot of G-force involved, and it's real difficult to pinpoint the landing. I always tended to do the first flip quick, then open out on the second to give myself plenty of time to spot the landing. In Nasty's backyard one time I slightly under-rotated it and hit the underside on the landing. My ribs hit the bars and then I went on to my head. I had concussion and broke two ribs – I still got up and tried another one, over-rotated it and then tried again and landed it. Once you crash it and you were so close and the adrenaline's pumping, you just want to go for it again. The adrenaline masks the pain till later. But there's no way it should be tried unless you're 100% sure in your mind that you can pull it – there's no ifs or buts with that trick. It's one thing doing it on a box in a closed environment, but it's another thing doing it on dirt, where you got the elements and other things to take into account – wind and climate conditions, the dirt, the lip, the ruts.

Scary as fuck, man!

All my attention and focus was on the first round of the Dew Action Sports Tour in Baltimore. The Dew Tour was a joint venture between NBC Sports and Live Nation and, in 2007, it was a series of five events at Baltimore, Cleveland, Florida, Oregon and Salt Lake City. OK, the tour's not as glitzy as the X-Games, but there's a prize of $15,000 for each leg, plus an additional $75,000 and an off-road, four-wheel drive vehicle for the overall winner. I could win $150,000 and a new car and get most of my sponsors back.

That's the place I want to be at and I reckon I can do it.

I'm ready to make a statement at the first venue and, and on June 19, 2007, I flew out from LAX. By coincidence the guy sitting next to me on the plane to Baltimore was Brian Deegan. He was a big influence in freestyle motocross and had a similar reputation to me for taking big risks. He was one of the first people to flip and 360 a dirt bike. Deegan was a real party animal but, during a 2005 taping of MTV's 'Viva La Bam', he under-rotated a backflip and the handlebars hit him hard in the stomach, almost killing him – the accident was cut out of the show. He lost a load of blood and a kidney and he found God. When I met him on the plane he had a long scar across his entire abdomen that he called his 'zipper' and a clothing line called Metal Mulisha that was real successful.

Anyway, Brian had turned a corner, like me, and he was completely different to what he was before. We got to talking about stuff.

'I hear you're making a comeback, Murray?'

'You heard right.'

I was telling him how good it felt and all about the partying and how it was behind me now and I was going to the contest to win it.

'Yeah, sometimes you gotta hit rock bottom before you realise who you really are.'

When he said that, it rang a bell with me. It felt like someone understood me. For a long time I'd felt really alone, like I couldn't talk to anyone about what was inside me. Now it was like someone else knew where I'd been and was maybe there themselves. I don't know why, but it made me feel real confident.

I was back!

I get my speed up before the final jump. The showtime booter. I take off and it's good! Out of nowhere, my left foot slips off the pedal –

I'm not spinning. I should be spinning!

I don't know left from right or up from down.

Everything's eerily silent – time stands still.

My neck hits the ground – it shatters on impact!

. . . .

Now I'm lying there and they're all around me – paramedics and people I know. Luke and Rick and Jerry and Chris and Grotbags – coming in and out of focus. I can't breathe – someone's doing that for me through a tube. The medics are there immediately. They have a trauma centre on site because what we do is dangerous and guys crash and get hurt all the time. Staff are positioned along the course and they have visuals on all parts of the track. I'm unconscious to begin with, then the noise comes back and someone's with me in a matter of seconds. More seconds and everyone's with me – all around me. They're telling me to relax. I'm trying to move, but I can't. They keep telling me to relax. Rick Bahr's talking to me, I'm trying to understand what he's saying.

'Calm down, Stephen.'

I can't speak – can't answer him.

'Let them breathe for you. It's life or death, man.'

I do what I'm told.

The trick that made my career ended it – the double backflip.

It finally got me – in Baltimore.

It nailed me. Took me down. Claimed me, like I once claimed it.

Now I'm flatlining in the back of this ambulance.

The shock/trauma unit at the University of Maryland Medical Centre is the best in the world and it's only five minutes away from the crash site.

If it hadn't been so close, I wouldn't have survived.

I guess I wasn't meant to die that day either.

13
INTO DARKNESS

I'm on a stretcher, prepped for surgery. I'm lucid, at least I think I am, stringing words together. I can still speak – barely – until later, when the trachea and ventilator fuck up my vocal cords. I keep asking Grotbags the same questions, over and over again –

'What happened? Where am I?'

But his answers aren't registering inside my head.

Into darkness.

I have seven hours emergency surgery that Friday evening. I have fractures in four vertebrae. Three are clean breaks, but one is shattered to pieces and they have to pick fragments of the bone from my spinal cord.

They need to stabilise my condition minute by minute.

• • • • • • • • • •

Melissa don't take it well. She's staying in a hotel with my mum and dad, who arrive on Saturday on the first available flight from England. It hits her hard and she's struggling to cope. The hospital calls the hotel on Monday 25 June because they need her consent, as next of kin, to start a second operation. Nobody can find her. Cynthia tells the hospital she'll give *her* permission and they agree because it's real important that the operation goes ahead. They perform the second op, to release the vertebrae from the front of my neck. It'd pushed my spinal cord into the back of my vertebrae, so they had to drill from C2 to C6, to set in titanium support rods to stop C3, C4 and C5 from moving – like, a titanium tube that had eight titanium rods and sixteen titanium pins. The surgeon was this Iranian doctor called Bizan Araabi who specialised in spinal cord injuries after learning his trade during the Iran/Iraq war. They reckoned my injuries were so severe the surgery couldn't have been done by anyone else and I was lucky I had him.

Thanks Bizan!

I'm in ITU, in a corner room of a unit with the nurses station's in the middle, surrounded by other rooms in a square shape. I'm in an induced coma and it's real quiet, apart from the continuous pumping of the ventilator that's keeping me alive. I have tubes coming from every orifice in my body and it's surreal. Apart from all the medical equipment, I don't have a mark on my face and it could seem to people like I'm just sleeping. I don't know it, but my brother Martin's arrived – and Scott Edgworth and Marco Dell'isola come over from England with him. Travis Chipres, Fuzzy Hall and Ryan Guettler fly in from LA. Dale Holmes, Neal and Kelly Wood from California, Jamie Bestwick, Travis Pastrana, Steve Matheus from Rockstar, Jerry, Nasty and many others who'd been at the contest and saw what happened. They all wait for news of my condition – all nervous, trying to keep cool, hoping for the best and anticipating the worst.

I come out of the black after the operation and I panic. There's bleeping machines, and tubes in my nose and jammed down my throat, and IVs in my arms and a feeding tube into my stomach. I get this feeling inside me that something's controlling my body. I can't see, everything's blurred. I can't swallow, feels like I'm choking. The worst part is, I can't move. It's like gravity's pinned me down. I go into a massive panic. I try to get up but I'm pinned, like someone's strapped me up in a duct-tape straitjacket.

What the fuck's going on?

I'm vaguely aware that there's people in the room with me – then I see my mum and I know something's real fucked up

– Melissa's in the corner. I can't speak now and the surgeon's telling my dad about the operations and how they went.

'He's on life-support, mister Murray. He'll never walk again!'

'That's what yee fucking-well think!'

Mum's got this letter board, she tells me to blink when she points to each letter so I can communicate with her. Everything's hazy. I'm on the life-support machine and I'm literally hanging on by a fucking thread. The first thing I spell out is 'bible', so she reads me this Psalm 21 from the Old Testament –

> *The Lord is my shepherd; I shall not want.*
> *He maketh me to lie down in green pastures;*
> *he leadeth me beside the still waters.*
> *He restoreth my soul;*
> *he leadeth me ...*

They're the first memories I have from waking up in Baltimore shock/trauma unit.

Everything goes black again.

When I come back into the light they've transferred me from recovery to a private suite in shock/trauma. There's a place inside the suite called the crying room, where people can go so they don't have to cry in front of me. My mum's still there, so's my wife, and my dad – they're listening to the doctors. I can't move my arms, I can't feel my legs. They've had a clinical meeting to discuss who's gonna tell me I'll never walk again or have the use of my arms again and I'll be on a ventilator for the rest of my life. They've asked Cynthia if she wants to do it or if she'd prefer a member of the medical staff to tell me. It's a heart stopper for mum, but there's no contest – that's what mother's are for, isn't it!

She tells me I snapped my neck when I overshot the landing of the last set of doubles. She tells me about the vertebrae and the spinal cord. She tells me I'm paralysed from the neck down – like, I'm a quadriplegic. I've never heard of a quadriplegic, what the fuck's that? I don't understand what she's saying. It's not sinking in. I just want to get up and get out of here, like I did when I had crashes before. I spell stuff out –

'Am I disabled?'

'You're only as disabled as you want to be.'

Even small changes in routine can throw people off –
can knock the wind out of people – but this is a complete
mind-fuck. Doctors and surgeons saying I'll never walk or
breathe by myself again. I'll be on a ventilator indefinitely.
They're giving me no hope, but my mind's so messed up I
don't believe them. Mum's talking to me, explaining things,
but I don't believe her. It's not true – what they're saying – it
fucking can't be! I reckon I'm hallucinating or something.
Somebody's slipped me some shit that's causing this freak-
out. It's not real! I can remember stuff from before and after
– but not the accident itself. Not the impact.

Back to black.

I come to again and I'm locked into some kinda metal
frame to support my head and stop my neck moving and
causing more damage to the spinal cord. They tell me
I flatlined twice, once lying on the dirt and again in the
ambulance. People are in and out of the crying room. When
I finally realise the extent of what's happened, my mind goes
into survival mode. All I'm thinking about is escape from
the paralysis. I'm trying mind over matter to make my limbs
move. Move! Move! But there's nothing. Nothing. Nothing!
How the fuck can I live like this? How am I gonna cope?
I've pushed through tough stuff before, but how can I push
through this? Nothing's ever come close to this! I'm trying to
apply all the discipline I used in physical competition to the
state of my mind now. If I could overcome setbacks before, I
can do it again.

Can't I?

After the tracheostomy, my voice box is damaged and the
only noise I can make is a croak, like a frog. I croak to try and
get attention and help, because there's a balloon inflated in
my throat to prevent any fluid going down into my lungs and
I can't drink anything for six fucking weeks. Fluids are going
into my body intravenously and it's not good that I can't
drink. It's fucking horrible, man! All I can think about is the
days when we'd finish riding and we'd go to 7-Eleven and get
massive ice-cold Gatorades. Having a drink's something you

take for granted, but it's not an option for me now. Like, my brain's telling me I need a drink so I'm constantly signalling to the nurses to bring ice chips. Sometimes they hear me croaking, but lots of times they don't and I can't use a buzzer because I'm paralysed.

Over the next three days, I'm pumped full of drugs, but I still suffer from the worst pain I've ever felt. I'm surrounded by doctors and surgeons and my own special 24/7 nurse. They get a suction pump down my throat and into my lungs to draw out the built-up mucus. They can't understand what the yellow particles are that're coming up the suction pipe and I'm too fucked to tell them how much time I spent in the pit at the Lake Perris skatepark, breathing in the dust from the sun-baked foam.

They turn me on my side and beat my back every fifteen minutes – they called it chest PT, for fuck's sake! I was totally exhausted, but something at the back of my mind was telling me I had to keep fighting if I was gonna come through this. Then they appointed a designated senior nurse called Colleen Flanaghan to look after me. Colleen was a tough cookie and took no shit from anyone, but she was also a guardian angel. My mum was in the room with me when my arm slipped off the bed and hung down the side. She was still in shock and denial and she waited for me to lift it back up, but I didn't. So she moved round the bed to lift my arm up for me. It felt so heavy to her, so unreal, like a prosthetic limb with no life in it. I guess that's when the reality of what had happened to me began to set in.

She went back to the hotel and lay in the bath and tried to stay still and not move for as long as possible. After a few minutes, the tap dripped, so she automatically reached out to turn it. Then her hair fell into her eyes and she automatically brushed it back. It was impossible for her to be still for more than a few minutes. She wondered how I was gonna cope – an over-the-top, fully active young guy. It was gonna be impossible. Would I really want a future entombed in a body I couldn't move? Her mind went into overdrive and she rushed back to the hospital to see Colleen.

'Colleen ... I don't know if Stephen can live this new life ... I mean, how do quadriplegics kill themselves?'

'They don't.'

'What do you mean?'

'How can they, Cynthia? The only way it can happen is if someone helps them.'

Colleen told my mum that life would be real different now, not just for me, but for the whole family. She said my medical situation was highly critical and everyone should just think fifteen minutes ahead. Get through the next fifteen minutes and move on to the following fifteen. If that goes OK, move up to thirty minutes and so on, until they have the strength to think ahead and start planning a future.

After three days with no sleep, I go into a state of psychosis – I'm hallucinating and having confused and disturbed thoughts. Like, I'm on the seventeenth story of a skyscraper – my room's slanted on an angle. There's a sliding glass door on the back wall and my hospital bed's on bungee cords and I slide out over the street. I can see the sidewalk down below and I'm dangling there. I start tripping out. It's all real to me and I'm going nuts.

Then I'm thinking I'm in this drug lab and this crazy witch who looks like an ex-girlfriend's put a spell on me. She's evil – a methamphetamine witch. I'm trying to run but, like in a dream, my legs are lead. I believe the doctors are injecting me with meth. I freak out every time I see them and I'm like –

'Fucking leave me alone!'

The guy in the room next door to me is an Amish dude who dove into a pool and broke his neck, and there's candles burning and they're all singing hymns. He dies and they take his kidney out and start passing it around from one to another – like, his dad has his own son's kidney in his hands. After a while I fall asleep and I wake up on an evil pirate ship. My son Mason's floating in the water and they kick me off the ship. If I can't reach him we're both gonna die. I wake up just as I get to him. I start going mental. Then I'm thinking I'm at Woodward Camp in the snow. I'm on a mission with

Travis Pastrana to find parts of Christopher Reeve's body. I know I'm awake and I'm digging through the snow. Every time I find a bone, his family give me five grand to pay for my recovery. I guess Travis Pastrana's in my psychosis because he came to visit me early on, but I don't understand where the rest of the stuff's coming from.

Then there's Melissa, she's totally gone off course and taking some kinda meds, but nobody knows what. Cynthia asked her to get her mother to come and support her and on Wednesday 27 June, her father turned up. He was a quiet, unassuming guy who had an immediate calming effect on my wife and it was obvious she was happy to have a member of her own family there with her. He only stayed a couple of days and then Monika arrived. My mum reckoned I should go back to England to live as soon as I was well enough, but Monika wanted me to stay in California. She reckoned I was a married man with two kids and Melissa would die if she had to move to the UK, with no friends and no support. I made it as clear as I could, under the circumstances, that I wanted to stay with Melissa and the boys.

But, mostly, things were a confused mist to me in those early days.

Like, time blurs into itself. Minutes become days and hours become seconds.

There's a diary – here's how it goes –

Thursday 28th June – MRI scan – tracheostomy to allow me to swallow and talk cancelled – IV filter inserted into carotid artery to stop blood clots travelling to my brain.

June 28th was my mum's birthday and Jamie Bestwick invited her and my dad and brother, along with Marco and Scott, out to The Cheesecake Factory in Baltimore for a meal and a glass of wine. It gave them a break from the hospital nightmare they were living through.

Friday 29th June – breathing concerns – bleeding from artery in neck – needs to be stabilised – fifteen minutes at a time.

Saturday 30th – tracheostomy – breathing on my own – ventilator as backup – I can communicate verbally – a few words at a time – I try to sing – Oasis – Wonderwall.

Sunday 1st July – CO_2 emissions increase to a dangerous level – ventilator turned back on – roller coaster spiralling down again – bad dreams are back.

Cynthia was emotionally drained and I remember her crying at my bedside when this beautiful lady walked through the curtains. She was Travis Pastrana's mother, Debbie, and she could see what a mess my mum was in. They went out into the corridor and Cynthia just let it all out. She poured out her soul to this stranger who she never met before, but Debbie listened to her and took my mum out in her car to visit a rehab facility. She gave my mother the courage to pick herself up and carry on. It's like, there's some extraordinary people in life who seem to appear out of nowhere when they're needed.

It's just something else!

The number of visitors coming to see me was crazy and everyone'd sit on chairs in a long line outside my room until it was their turn to visit. I guess they were all a bit nervous about coming in the room, not knowing what they were gonna find – if I was the same Stephen Murray or if I had head trauma and was someone else? Some of those guys were reduced to tears when they saw me, but most were relieved to find out that my brain function was OK.

I remember my family looking anxious – like they're saying 'hang in there' and counting down, 8 : 7 : 6 : 5 ..., it goes to zero and I black out. I think that's when they first try to take me off the ventilator. They were testing to see if I could breathe by myself. I couldn't. My phrenic nerve was damaged and wasn't sending a signal from my brain to my diaphragm – the phrenic nerve starts in the neck and passes down between the lung and the heart. Actually, there's two phrenic nerves – I guess neither of mine were working properly. I think my right diaphragm was completely paralysed and my left one was 50% paralysed – so I only had half capacity in my left lung, nothing else.

It's like, when you breathe, your diaphragm tightens. This increases the space in your chest cavity, so your lungs can expand when air gets sucked in. Oxygen from the air gets passed to the blood vessels and, without this process, you die. This wasn't working with me and I had to have a machine do it for me. It was a constant life-or-death situation – touch-and-go for days. But the support from the BMX community, along with family and friends, was overwhelming. Tens of thousands of messages of support and a lot of them said 'stay strong!'

Monday 2nd July – on vent again – bad dreams again.
Tuesday 3rd July – pneumonia – hallucinations – temp 103 – horrible day.
Wednesday 4th July – more IV – antibiotics – fever.
Thursday 5th July – anxious – no sleep all night – swallowing, spitting – temp 101
Friday 6th July – CO^2 down to 48 – peaceful.

Let me say something about pneumonia here. It's the quadriplegic's biggest killer. Real scary, working on half a lung function. It hurts my lungs just thinking about it. Inflammation of the lung tissue caused by bacterial infection – mucus – breathlessness – rapid heartbeat – fever – sweating and shivering – horrific chest pain – coughing up blood – headaches – fatigue – vomiting – wheezing – muscle pain – feeling confused and disorientated. If it's not controlled, death comes quick.

Saturday 7th July – temp under 100 for first time – pneumonia subsiding.
Sunday 8th July – 4 hours sleep – exhausted – temp 97.7

They decide I've recovered enough to get out of the room for some fresh air. OK, Baltimore shock/trauma's as dodgy as fuck! There was Bloods and Crips – a few rooms down the corridor a Blood had been shot in the spine but was still alive and a bunch of Crips were trying to get to him to finish him off. Another guy three doors away had hung himself – he was paraplegic. There was cops with guns and people were dying left, right and fucking centre! My dad detoured past all that and wheeled me round the hospital block in the sunshine and it felt so good, man – just to be outside! The air and sun were beyond words and it was like the world's brand new again for a while. But it was the only time I got to go outside for months to come.

After two weeks of being pumped full of steroids in shock/trauma, to give my organs a chance, all the skin comes off my hands, feet and body – like, where I had calluses from bike riding. I shed all my dead skin, like a fucking snake, man!

At the end of the second week, this dude comes to see me. He's wearing a brown chequered old-school suit and he's got glasses and wiry hair, like some mad scientist. He's intro'd as Dr John McDonald, a neuro-scientist who's famous for his work with Christopher Reeve, the Superman actor who fell off a horse in 1995 and was paralysed. Dr McDonald was a world renowned stem-cell researcher and he pioneered clinical treatment into spinal cord repair.

Like, when I crashed, it just so happened that a lady called Bernadette Mauro, who was education director of the Christopher Reeve Foundation, was watching the event on TV with her sons, Seán and Zac. Seán pestered his mom to reach out to me and she did – Bernadette was the one who put Dr McDonald in touch with me. I was real lucky the Mauro family was watching TV that day, without them, I wouldn't be where I am now. Angels were watching over me and paths were made for me, without me knowing.

There was this other guy with Dr McDonald, called Patrick Rummerfield, who was in a near-fatal car accident in 1974, when he was twenty-one. He'd fractured all his ribs, broken his neck in four places, shattered his collar bone, suffered massive head injuries and had to have one of his eyes shoved back into its socket. He was completely paralysed and given seventy-two hours to live. The doctors wanted to send him to a convalescent home to die, but he wouldn't go there and chose intensive rehabilitation, against the doctors' orders. He said he was lying in bed one night dreaming about playing basketball, when his big toe moved. Three years later, he was learning to walk and using his hands again.

When he came to see me with Dr McDonald, Pat Rummerfield walked into the room. He was able to jog and ride a bike without falling over. He went through six knee surgeries and total reconstruction of his right ankle and wrist and they reckoned his recovery was due to his commitment – with intense physical therapy like weightlifting and jumprope and exercise bike. This dude had 85% of his spinal cord destroyed. OK, he still had loss of sensation in his lower back and some bowel and bladder problems, as well as reduced strength in his hands – but, hey, what the fuck! I'd settle for that.

Dr John McDonald showed me my MRI and said it was strikingly similar to Pat's. He told me you only need 5% of the spinal cord to regain full motor function. This gave me a lot of hope, man. The light started to glimmer again.

OK, here's how it works. The cervical vertebrae, or neck bones, are the top eight bones in the spinal column. They're part of the backbone and they protect the spinal cord. If these bones are broken, but the spinal cord isn't damaged, then no problem – just set the bones and let them heal. If the spinal cord's bruised or partially damaged, this can lead to quadriplegia. If the cord's severely damaged and the injury's at or above the fifth cervical vertebra, C5, then it can cause asphyxiation and death. The part of the cord that controls breathing is C3 through C5. If the cord's cut or torn in half, there's a sudden loss of nerve supply to the entire body, including the heart and blood vessels. There's a sudden drop in blood pressure and sudden death – called spinal shock. So, if you break your neck, you could be OK, apart from a cervical fracture, or you could be partially paralysed, or you could be quadriplegic, or you could die from asphyxia over a few minutes, or you could die instantaneously from spinal

shock. It depends on which and how many of the cervical
vertebrae are damaged and how badly.

I shattered C3 to C6 – and survived!

Monday 9th July– hospital psychosis – staring at
the ceiling day
and night.
Tuesday 10th July – hallucinating and calling out
in the night – Colleen is there.

Dr McDonald told my parents the best two rehab
hospitals in the US were Craig Hospital in Denver and the
Shepherd Centre in Atlanta. Craig Hospital's a rehabilitation
centre for spinal cord injury in Englewood, Colorado, and
it's the number one hospital in America for weaning people
off a ventilator. My dad had to go back home for a week,
so my mum and Grotbags flew out to Denver in the second
week of July and met the clinical team there and saw the
facilities. Atlanta also had fantastic facilities, but it was
too far away and the weather was too humid down south.
Denver was dead centre between the east and west coasts
and it'd be easier for Melissa and the boys to get to. The
weather there was also more conducive to my condition.
They came back full of confidence and, if I could get over
there to Craig Hospital, I might be able to start breathing by
myself permanently.

Wednesday 11th July – final sensation test –
intermittent – arms, upper chest, legs, toes.
Thursday 12th July – given the OK for Denver –
Melissa and two nurses to come with me.

It was arranged that I'd go there on the following
Thursday. Two specialist flight nurses came into the room
with a mobile life-support machine. They needed to transfer
me from the bed life-support so I could go on the plane. I was
in the elevator when the mobile machine started making
weird noises – sounded like air was escaping through a valve
on an oxygen cylinder that was connected to the ventilator.
The nurses were tripping out on the noise, it was making the
vent equipment vibrate. Then one of them said to stick some

duct-tape round the leak and it'd be OK. So they did, like it's
no big deal, even though any mistake could cost me my life.

There was an ambulance waiting and we headed for
Baltimore airport. I was supposed to fly in a superfast Learjet
to Denver. Melissa was in the ambulance with me and the
flight nurses and I'm lying down looking up at the roof and
it's real bumpy. Then the roof starts to spin, like when you're
wasted drunk and everything goes round and round and you
feel sick and close your eyes, but the room keeps spinning.
I'm trying to get it under control and stop the spinning roof,
but it's like a roulette wheel, getting faster and faster. Faster
and faster!

Then I flatline for the third time.

I remember a piercing white light coming into my vision,
then colours – different blurred images. Next thing I know I
wake up and they're pushing on my chest trying to resuscitate
me and Melissa's reading scriptures from the Bible. I don't
know where she got the Bible from, or what scriptures she's
reading, or whether it's happening at all or I'm hallucinating
again. Everything's fucking surreal. They're going –

'Are you there?'

'Sure, I'm fine.'

They bring me back and I'm just gasping and croaking out
stuff like –

'I'm fine, man. Just take me to rehab.'

The paramedics tell me my blood pressure fell through the
floor, I flatlined and they nearly lost me. The tube the flight
nurses taped up came undone again and I'd been dead for
two minutes and forty-two seconds.

They didn't take me to Denver, they took me to Baltimore's
Washington Hospital where they closed the room off and
stabilised me. My blood pressure was dangerously low and
I had to stay there till it normalised. They were pumping my
lungs and shitloads of dirt from all the digging I'd done in
my life were coming out – bash, bash, bash – it's just fucking
dirt coming out and they're saying 'what the fuck?'

After being stabilised, I'm back to shock/trauma with the Bloods and the Crips and the gunshot wounds and stabbings and all the rest of the fucked-up shit. I couldn't believe it, the place of my worst nightmares. They took me back up to the top floor and there was my room, right in the corner, waiting for me. I was there for another week, trying to push through the crisis and fight on. It was like I was living on borrowed time.

> **Friday 13th July** – swallow test, positive, then negative – move
> right big toe!
> **Saturday 14th July** – movement in both legs (striking sole effect) – malfunction of ventilator.
> **Sunday 15th July** – sleeping a lot – dizzy in chair.
> **Monday 16th July** – sleeping all day – on ventilator 6 hours.

You gotta understand, I can't regulate my temperature like able-bodied people do automatically. I don't sweat like I used to – I don't sweat at all from the point of the injury downwards. If I even get a slight chill, my temperature goes haywire and I'm in danger. But, one week later, I leave shock/trauma again and this time I get to the airport. My dad's lost all trust in the ward nurses at Baltimore and I want Colleen to go with me instead of Melissa – that nurse has been real good to me and I trust her. Jeff does some kinda deal with her and she gets permission from the hospital to go. I board the Learjet and they ask me if I want to be sedated. I'm OK with that. They try to sedate me, but my body fights it and I stay awake for the whole four-hour flight to Denver.

Those four weeks in shock/trauma were the worst of my life – a patient would die, on average, every thirty minutes. I went from a hundred and ninety pounds to a hundred and thirty pounds in that time. I reckon I really shouldn't have lived, but I did.

I made it.

14
AGAINST THE ODDS

I had a temporary bed at Craig Hospital to begin with and Colleen stayed with me for the first three days, to keep an eye on how I was being treated. She flew back to Baltimore when she was satisfied the transition went smoothly. There were curtains dividing me from three other guys in the room. There was a fifty-five year old from Chicago in the bed next to me. He had similar injuries to mine that happened when something fell on his head when he was putting up power lines. He was awarded crazy money, like eighty million dollars in compensation and he had a private male nurse to look after him. But, for all that, he couldn't handle it. He was suffering badly and crying all the time. Funny how I can't remember the other two guys, just him.

When I signed registration contracts and waivers for competitions, they were pretty watertight, so it was impossible for me to sue the organisers. You enter at your own risk and I always knew that. I just signed to take part, I never thought about the consequences. To be fair to Dew Tour and NBC, they did cover my family's hotel bills while I was in Baltimore.

In the months leading up to the Dew Tour in 2007, money was tight and I cancelled elements of my insurance cover, trying to cut back as much as I could. As a result, immediately after the crash, the mortgage payments stopped. I had to go bankrupt and we lost our million-dollar dream house. But that wasn't important to me – most of the time, the only thing

I was focused on was making sure I was gonna be around for my sons. Like, it's not until you're stripped of everything that you find out what's really important in life. What was left of my insurance policy only covered part of my medical bills, as my 'occupation' was so dangerous. So, financially as well as physically, I was in a bad way.

The connections I made throughout life and my BMX career helped me out at the beginning of my new journey. Friends and family mean a lot in times of hardship and trial. My friends and family were there for me. I used to be the one encouraging people to go for the limit – the impossible – now it was them telling me the same thing.

Fuck, man, there's no way I could've got through this by myself. I was hanging on to my life by a thread and if it wasn't for my family, my close friends, the BMX community, skateboarders, motocross riders and everyone else supporting me, I don't know what I'd have done. Sir Richard Branson arranged hundreds of discounted transatlantic flights for my family to fly back and forth – thanks Richard! Mat Hoffman came to visit me in Denver and he told me I inspired him – I mean, that's Mat Hoffman, a legend, telling me the shit he's been through is nothing compared to what I've been through. He said he died twice, but I beat him because I died three times. This guy's the godfather of BMX to me, and being in his company was an inspiration that helped build my spirit. I can't thank everyone enough for all the support I got. I couldn't have got this far without you – much love to you all. I mean it!

Then there was the other side of the coin. Before my house got repossessed, some people broke in and stole lots of my clothes and other stuff. It didn't bother me all that much at the time – if some scumbags want to do that to me when I'm down and fighting for my life, karma will catch up with those fuckers.

Melissa was practically sleeping in a chair by my bed for the first month or so in Denver and she's like –

'Move your finger.'

Every day –

'Move your finger. Move your finger.'

And I'm like –

'Shut up! Stop saying that!'

They arranged a family room at the Four Seasons Hotel, three miles from the hospital, where she could stay, as they reckoned I'd be there six months minimum. The kids were staying with family friends called Dianne and Eric Eckland in California and they came to visit me on weekends so it didn't affect their schooling. I seriously missed my sons so much and when they came to visit, it was like a breath of fresh air that lifted my spirits up to the sky.

After a few weeks I moved out of the four-man room into a private suite, and that's when I really knew I was gonna be there for a long time. The walls got covered in photos of me, my dogs, my kids, my wife, mum, dad, brother – so I could always be reminded of what I was fighting for. I still wasn't able to breathe on my own – I needed the ventilator to provide me with oxygen and take away carbon dioxide. But the problem with the ventilator was, although it was keeping me alive, the muscles in my diaphragm weren't doing any work and they'd keep getting weaker and weaker, until they'd be no good to me anymore. That's why it was important for them to get me off the vent as soon as possible – why they took the big risk of moving me to Denver in the first place.

I gotta say here that Grotbags was a rock for me after the accident – he was in Baltimore and Denver a lot and stuck by me for as long as he could. He drifted after Denver and I didn't see him much again, I guess it was kinda like he never came to terms with my accident, like he couldn't handle it – couldn't handle seeing me the way I was then. And who could blame him?

I was real frustrated and getting more anxious all the time. I still couldn't talk and I wasn't in control, waiting for the machine to deliver my next breath, and I was being fed by a tube connected to my stomach. The first time they took me off the ventilator was supposed to be for two minutes. I lasted twenty seconds. My lungs didn't function and it just fucked me up – my respiratory muscles hadn't worked in six weeks. It was a big mental blow – I was in a no-holds-barred fight and it was the beginning of many intense battles.

One battle was gonna be to get off that vent. The weaning process to do it wasn't easy – it was hard work. It started with twenty seconds off the machine and they lengthened the time by tiny amounts every day. Gradually, I built it up to eighteen hours off, but the carbon dioxide levels in my blood got too high and it fucked me up again – I got knocked back down to three hours off. But they kept trying and I kept making progress. Slowly. It was the battle of a lifetime, I took six months to get off that ventilator and every second was a massive fucking effort. But I gotta say that my family and friends were so positive and encouraged me every step of the way. I was real lucky to have them.

In the past I could go out and make shit happen, but this was a whole other animal. It was one small move forward at a time. The only way to get through this was, like nurse Colleen said, to take each hour as it came. It was a different process to anything I'd done before and I just had to push on, stay strong and fight through it. My dad said it was like a seed that gets water and light and eventually it turns into a flower – you don't see it changing in front of your eyes, but it's happening all the same. You just gotta be patient. But this took a long time to sink in with me. I guess because I still really hadn't come to terms with the reality of being paralysed.

After the third week in Denver, they brought me a wheelchair. It was a pretty standard spare chair that anyone could use. It wasn't customised to my shape, but I reckoned at least it could get me around. They brought this sling over and rolled me in the bed, back and forth, until the sling was underneath me. Then they got this lift that hoisted me from the bed and put me in the wheelchair. OK, there's wheelchairs and wheelchairs, but this one was around when Methuselah was a kid. People had to push me in it and, after twenty minutes, the blood left my head and the whole picture started fading. My blood pressure dropped through the floor and I was about to pass out when I felt a jerk from behind. The nurse realised what was happening and tipped the chair back so I was laid flat with my back on the ground. The picture started to come back and everything returned to normal – if you could call me lying in a tipped-up wheelchair, parallel to the ground, normal. Once I was OK, the nurses raised the back of the chair a bit, not fully upright, and wheeled me round the room. I kinda let them know by blinking and making croaky noises that I'd like to see the rehab gym. I didn't think they'd agree, but they did.

When I was being wheeled down the corridor, I could see other quadriplegics for the first time. Some were in good shape, but others looked completely fucked, like they were ready to die. Others had halos attached to their heads – this looked crazy, it was basically screws and bolts and rods stabilising their necks. I was fucking glad I didn't have that – things were bad enough without having my head in a crazy cage. When I got to the gym, it was full of patients. I was keen to see what they were doing and how they were working out. Most needed a lot of help from the staff, but some were able do the exercises by themselves. I was determined to get back to that level myself and I remembered the days in the grimy-ass old boxing gym doing all those push-ups and running and sit-ups and pad work. I remembered the old trainer guy and what he said to me –

'There's no short cuts, boy, you get out what you put in.'

Man, I wished I could've been back there again!

I was still on life-support and I couldn't cough. There was always a build-up of phlegm in my lungs and the suction nurse'd push the hose through the trachea to suck up all the mucus. One thing I fucking dreaded was when it was time to change my trachea. This was the tube that went into my windpipe and was connected to the ventilator. It had to be changed every two weeks. It felt like they were ripping my guts out through my throat when they removed it. They had another trachea waiting to go in because they couldn't leave the hole exposed, as it'd close up. They'd jam this thing into my throat and I reckoned I knew what torture felt like. At the end of October, they inserted a smaller trachea and, once I was able to cough up secretions on my own, they took the trachea out altogether.

First battle won!

There was two types of therapy, physical and occupational. Like with most people, the day began with a crap and a shower – that's where the similarity ended. They lifted me out of bed and into a commode chair that had a hole in the middle, just below my butt, and they shot a kinda bullet up my ass and all the crap would come out. Then the nurse'd wheel me into the shower-room, still attached to the life-support machine. After showering, they'd get me dry and back into bed. Breakfast took about thirty minutes – I'd been fed through a tube for two months, then soft food like a baby, and I was dreaming about calamari. So, after they did a swallow test and I could eat properly again, I went for what I always loved best, steak and fries and calamari. Man, that tasted fucking good!

Then they'd lift me into my chair and push me to the gym and get me on to a bench. In the beginning I thought rehab meant I'd be lifting weights at Craig Hospital like Rocky Balboa. Shit, it wasn't like that at all – there was a lot of stretching exercises on the bench to get my body moving and keep my limbs active to stop my bones demineralising and my legs pooling. They stuck pads to my quads, hamstrings, glutes and calves and put my feet into straps. The straps were attached to a function electrical stimulation bike and, when they sent electric shocks to my leg muscles, I'd pedal the bike. This was to help avoid atrophy and prevent the loss of too much muscle mass and I was the first person in the world to do the FES bike on a life-support machine. Man, I loved it and looked forward to that shit, it was as close as I could get to riding a real bike.

It was an intense two hours every day and it really took it out of me.

Occupational therapy lasted two hours. It concentrated on simple things, like learning to get in and out of the chair, with help of course. Learning how to operate a power chair with my head and going to lectures about disability and how to cope with it. Then I'd have a lunch break. Between them, my dad and Melissa came to all the lectures and classes with me, to learn about spinal cord injuries and care. Jeff was always there when Melissa wasn't around. He only left my side three times in the whole six months I was in Denver.

He was determined I was gonna stay alive. He'd feed me in the cafeteria and it kinda felt like I wasn't in hospital while I was there with him.

Thanks for everything, dad!

There was a period in Denver when I was in a really bad way, mentally. I mean, when reality sinks in that you're gonna be like this for the rest of your life, you say to yourself 'what the fuck kinda life is this?'. Especially after the kinda life I led up till then. Also, you don't want to be a burden on people, where they gotta do every single little thing for you. So you start thinking, maybe I'd be better off dead. Not only that, but maybe everyone else'd be better off if I was dead. Then I'd think about my sons, and the feeling would go away – hide itself away at the back of my mind.

And I'd pretend it wasn't there.

For the first three months I had a catheter permanently up my dick. I fucking hated that – it was a fucking nightmare. Then they told me about a simple operation where they made an incision in my bladder and inserted a suprapubic catheter, with a balloon on the end filled with sterile water to stop it ripping out if it got pulled. I had loads of urinary tract infections and they had me on antibiotics a lot of the time. It seemed like it was one thing after another and I was beginning to wonder if staying alive was worth all this fucking hassle. I mean, if the accident had happened to me in an earlier time, without all the medical know-how, I'd be dead. Maybe that was the natural thing? Maybe trying to stay alive in my condition was unnatural?

The doubts came back again.

My ex-girlfriend, Mindy Pantus, called me and we talked for an hour – that really cheered me up. It's the little things like that. She won't know how much she helped, but the lift she gave me was incredible. Mindy was always, and still is, a sweetheart – looking back, maybe breaking up with her was a mistake.

Then I got my 'sip and puff' chair. It's got, like, this pipe thing and I puff on it to go and suck on it to stop – two puffs to go right and three puffs to go left. And I can barely fucking breathe! I never really got the hang of driving that thing properly – it had high and low gears and I always drove it in high gear and I'm all over the place and continuously smashing into walls and trolleys and nurses and patients and anything that was in my way. After a while, they tried me in a chair with head controls. If I took my head away from the pad it'd go forward and if I moved my head further forward it would stop. It had pads on the side to go right and left and it was an improvement on the sip and puff chair, but it was shit going over bumps because it was hard to keep my head in the same position and it gave me bad neck pain. It had a button to change the chair functions and I had massive problems finding and hitting that button with my head, like, I had to make it lean backwards every fifteen minutes to take pressure off my coccyx. I used that chair for about a year and it was a fucker!

One day, I'm in the middle of rehab when this call comes in for me. I'm being helped on a standing frame and I ask the staff to tell the caller to ring back. I only get two hours rehab a day and, even though it's tough, the time's precious to me – I don't want to lose none of it. But they keep asking me to take the call – maybe three times. They say it's important, but I think it's just one of my mates and I can call them back when I'm finished. Anyway, it takes twenty minutes for them to get me off the frame and back into my chair, and another twenty minutes to get to the phone and get attached to Bluetooth so I can talk. All that time, the caller's on hold and I'm like –

'Hello, who's this?'

'Hi Stephen, it's David Beckham.'

I don't believe it's him and I'm like –

'Fuck off! Who *is* this?'

'David Beckham.'

'Fuck off and stop playing around!'

Kimarie was there at the time and she's waving her arms around and screaming –

'Stephen, it really is David Beckham!'

So I'm like –

'Fuck, Becks ... I'm sorry, man. How are you?'

Like he's my long-lost friend or something.

He was at the X-Games in Los Angeles when they showed a short documentary about my accident on the big screen. It kinda touched Beckham and he found out where I was so he could give me a call – and I made him wait forty fucking minutes! We had a good half-hour chinwag about how I was getting on and he wished me well and a speedy recovery and said he'd like to intro his family to me. He also asked to be updated on my progress. He never sought any publicity for what he did that day – he did it in his own time and out of the goodness of his heart. That call made my day and it made me wonder how much other stuff he'd done without shouting about it. Beckham's a superstar and for him to make that effort and hang on the phone for so long meant a lot to me. What a genuine guy!

Thanks David!

I first experienced spasticity waking up one morning when my legs started to contract real hard. This moved through my whole body until I became completely spastic. I didn't know what the fuck was happening and I thought maybe it was my legs coming back and my muscles starting to work again. But it wasn't. They were powerful contractions that came out of nowhere and they were uncontrollable. Like, my whole body shook and it took my breath away. This lasted about thirty seconds and I had to wait that long for my next breath. Once it started, it happened randomly throughout the day. My hands contracted and all my fingers had to be pulled back so far I'm sure some of them were broken. It was so bad they tied my arms to the chair and my legs as well, so they wouldn't kick out. They put me on a cocktail of pills to try to control it. The pills reduced the intensity, but they didn't stop it altogether.

It usually started about 4:30am, when my body was beginning to wake up and I had to put up with it for three years, until the spasticity got too much to live with and they decided to implant a baclofen pump. Baclofen's the medication used to control spasticity and it's usually taken orally several times a day, which I was doing. Then they sent me to Loma Linda Hospital in San Bernardino and put the pump into my abdomen. It has a catheter that delivers the medication straight into the spinal cord. The pump's a round, metallic disc, a bit like an ice hockey puck – it has a battery, a reservoir for the baclofen and a microprocessor. One end of the catheter is connected to the pump and the other end into the spine – it goes up my spinal column to C6 and the medicine's dispensed there. The pump's programmed with a kinda wand thing and a small computer. This still don't stop the contractions completely, but it's an improvement on taking the meds by mouth.

I wasn't getting much sleep at all, because they had to turn me on my side every two hours for pressure relief. I'd be real tired and there was this sky-bridge with a main road going underneath that connected the quadriplegics with the paraplegics and I'd go to the middle of that bridge and look out the window at the world passing by. I'd look out at it for a long time, until I fell asleep from exhaustion in the wheelchair.

OK, it was finally sinking in that my life'd be very different from now on. I was a C3 quadriplegic – incomplete. Incomplete means only partial loss of function or sensation below the affected vertebrae, because my spinal cord wasn't completely severed. There's stuff I won't be able to do, like coughing or blowing my nose or scratching an itch. I can't go to the bathroom by myself, brush my hair or my teeth, or hug my kids. The fucking list goes on! Like I said, I got to be turned in bed every few hours to prevent pressure sores – a dangerous breakdown of the skin due to pressure on that area. It can get real ugly and result in infection and tissue death. They told me lots of quadriplegics die as a direct result of complications related to pressure sores. It was fucking scary! As well as that my bowel and bladder had to be manually emptied every day at a specific time, to encourage what they called a habit programme. I felt constant pins-and-needles and it's like my skin's burning over most of my body. For me, the thing that happened to me was a 360 degree about face. I had to learn everything all over again. I needed to learn to live with all this shit and just get on with it.

Melissa stayed with me most of the time, but she went back to Riverside every two weeks to check on the kids. One time, on the way back to Denver, she got thrown off the plane at LAX for being under the influence of something and aggressive to the stewardess. I guess she was just pissed off with her life and snapped. Melissa was under extreme pressure because her whole life had changed completely, just like mine. I guess it was natural that she'd get depressed and just snap from time to time. She was only human, after all, just like me.

It wasn't all crap at Denver. There were good days and I made some friends in Craig Hospital – we had a little crew and started to have some fun. Chris Mason, the guy who went to Tijuana with me, came to see me and stayed for a week in my room, sleeping in the corner. They taught him how to help me with my exercises and it was great having him there. The nurses encouraged us to do art and I got Chris to make a life-size gingerbread man with a massive erection and we stuck it up on the door of the proctology department. The doctors went fucking crazy! Every time the nurses took the gingerbread man down, it'd appear somewhere else. We even put it in people's beds – we'd sneak into the rooms and pull all sorts of pranks, moving stuff around and shit.

Some of those quads were fucking nuts, man – one got bitten by a shark, another was shot, but most were there because of traffic accidents. They had this thing called 'social rehab' where you were supposed to learn how to get along with people all over again. We sure did that – then we went round causing mischief and tormenting the nurses and doctors. We'd tear around, crashing chairs into stuff – I wasn't used to the basic chair I had then and I'd turn it over all the time. We did shit like that and other stuff and generally played up and had a laugh, to keep our sense of humour and stop everyone from going stir crazy.

I guess it's important to keep things in perspective when your whole life is changing. There was a guy called Doug Smith who was a concert pianist – he crashed his car into a ditch one night coming home from the studio. He couldn't use his hands no more to play the $90,000 baby grand piano he'd just bought, but he was always cracking jokes and was the life and soul of the place. He was a hilarious guy who had a great outlook on life, despite his injuries. He left before me and I hope he's doing fine. Another of our crazy group was Tara Llanes, one of the world's best mountain bikers. She was planning to come see me in Denver shortly after I was moved there from Baltimore shock/trauma. As it happened, she had a bad crash at a big mountain bike event a few days before and was paralysed from the waist down. We ended up spending three months together in rehab.

We'd tell blatant lies and keep it going – like, there was dozens of movies we could watch when we were doing exercises and me and Chris Mason would insist on watching Beetlejuice all the time. We'd tell the American nurses it was a true story and that kinda stuff happens in England all the time; like, there's loads of places haunted by weird fuckers and witch doctors who shrink heads and shit. I don't know whether they believed us or not, but I think they weren't sure.

We were the bane of the nurses' lives.

Then I heard about the Make-A-Wish Foundation – a non-profit organization that arranges 'wishes' for kids with life-threatening illnesses. To qualify for a wish, the kid has to be between three and seventeen years old. A little boy had a poster of me on his wall in St Jude's Leukaemia Hospital, which was also in Denver, and his wish was to meet me – so I arranged to go to the hospital and surprise him. It was me who got the surprise because the poor kid had passed away two days earlier – if only I'd known in time. I was devastated. I stayed in that hospital all day with the kids, just in case there was someone else who wanted to meet me. I learnt about what they were going through and the battle I was fighting didn't seem so tough anymore. When I was with those brave kids I put myself and my problems aside for a day and I tried to make my visit count for something. I couldn't take their pain away, but I wanted to show them that they could fight against it. Afterwards, I got sponsors like Vans to donate a bunch of stuff for the boys and girls in that hospital.

So you see, no matter how bad things are, there's always someone worse off than yourself. I guess this was how, mentally, I was trying to deal with everything. Step by step. Doctors and surgeons told me I'd never walk or breathe by myself again. I'd be on a ventilator indefinitely. They gave me no hope but, three weeks before I'm due to go home, they take me off the vent and I'm able to breathe by myself. This is the best feeling in the world! I'm away from the machine that's kept me alive for six months and, though I'm grateful, I'm glad to see the fucking back of it.

That was the second battle won!

The truth is, I really loved my wife but, after a while, it looked like she was really struggling. She was causing problems in the hospital with the staff because she was taking too many meds and they were affecting her judgement. One day Jeff found her in a nearby bar buying drugs from some guy, but she was my wife and my parents had no legal rights to get anything done without her. Yet the doctors always talked to my dad, because they reckoned Melissa was too traumatised to be relied on. The hospital even took the keys of her car away from her because she was in such a bad state. Some nights she wouldn't show up and that kinda fucked with my head a bit, but I knew I had to stay focused and positive – it was the only way.

After about four months, they put me in this family housing unit on the other side of the hospital, where Melissa had been living, so she could get used to looking after me before going back home to California. It was a small apartment, like a little house, with a wooden exterior and a kitchen and lounge, so I could get used to living 'normal' again. By now, Melissa was self-medicating most of the time. It was clear to everybody except me that she was losing it, and even the doctors were worried in case she became a danger to my survival. But, for now, they were prepared to give her the benefit of the doubt and see how she coped. When my parents came to visit they were shocked. Washing was piled up everywhere, pizza boxes all over the place, the whole apartment in a complete shambles. Melissa had gone into complete meltdown and things were getting out of hand.

I gotta say here that Melissa was a victim of what happened as much as I was. I have a lot of sympathy for the situation she found herself in, even if I couldn't see it back then because of all the trauma I was experiencing. It takes a strong person to cope with life changes like that and Melissa just didn't have that kind of strength. She had very little backup either and too much was expected of her.

After the Crash

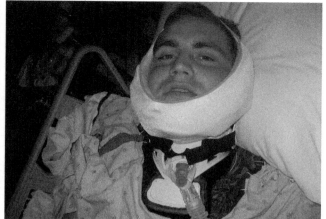

2.1 When I thought it couldn't get any worse I had to have six teeth pulled, including all my wisdom teeth, while trying to get off the ventilator.

2.2 Finally off the ventilator.

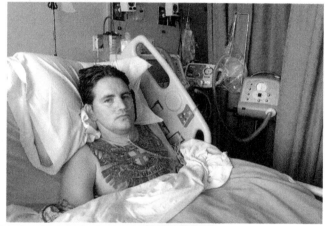

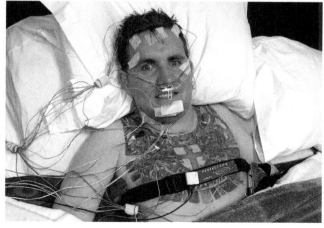

2.3 All wired up – sleep/breathing study.

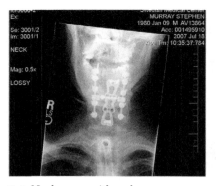

2.4 Neck x-ray with rods.

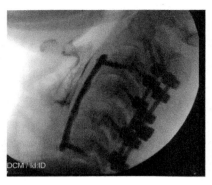

2.5 Rods with screws.

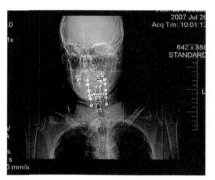

2.6 Rods with skull.

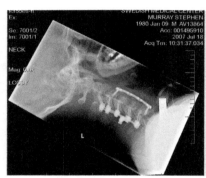

2.7 Rods and screws from the side.

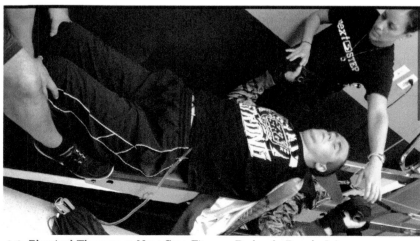

2.8 Physical Therapy at Next Step Fitness, Redondo Beach, LA.

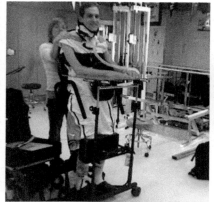

2.9 Physical Therapy @ Denver, Standing tall!

2.10 Locomotive Training @ Next Step Fitness.

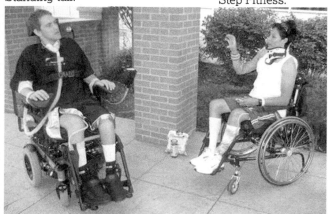

2.11 Me and Tara Llanes hanging out @ Craig Hospital, Denver.

2.12 Me and the boys with Gold Olympic medalist Maris Strombergs.

2.13 Mat Hoffman – my hero – me and Chris Mason hanging out.

2.14 Hanging with Nick Diaz, my favourite UFC Fighter.

2.15 Me and Erica.

2.16 NORA Cup, I'm presenting the Number One Dirt Jumper of the year award with John Jennings.

2.17 Uncle Martin, me, Seth and Mason in my yard, Riverside, 2015.

2.18 Getting interviewed at the 2008 Dew Tour in Baltimore.

2.19 Signature Hijinx Sunglasses by Oakley.

2.20 Put on by my boy Shane Dog.

2.21 Bangers and Mash annual jam at my yard in Riverside, put on by Aaron Cooke – good times!

2.22 Remembering Dave Mirra.

2.23 Me and Nasty reminiscing the good times.

2.24 Adam Aloise, me and Nasty.

2.25 Chillin' with Brian Foster.

2.26 Red Bull Empire of Dirt, Alexandra Palace. Ben Wallace Wall rides over my head.

2.27 Hanging with The Nitro Circus Crew in my yard.

2.28 DTR Crew, back at Duckswich House, Worcestershire, 2013.

2.29 Graffiti mural on the streets of Barcelona. Love this!

2.30 Reppin' Stay Strong!

2.31 Skiing at Big Bear with my brother Martin.

2.32 Stay Strong van thanks to Aaron Cooke, The ARF and my sponsors.

2.33 Road Trip with Erica and her family and my boys. AJ in the background.

2.34 Me, Erica and our kids – Seth, Mason, Chance and Brooklyn.

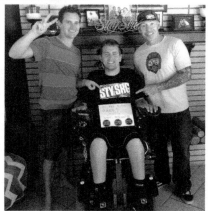

2.35 Martin, Dale Holmes and me at my house in Riverside, California.

2.36 On a Vegas road trip – me, my brother and Lee Martin in The Stay Strong van, February in 2016, going to TJ Lavin's House.

2.37 Nurse Betty, Seth, Mason, me, my dad and Adam Aloise at LAX just before flying home to England in June 2016.

2.38 BMX Pros Brandon Dosch and Hucker flew from the US in August 2016 to ride @ Lakefest and support Stay Strong. Great guys and sick riders!

2.39 The London ambulance crew and my family @ Jay Aliano's for our 'Welcome Home Murray boys' party in June 2016.

2.40 Stay Strong Crew @ Corby Skatepark, April 2016.

2.41 Mum's birthday dinner in England, 2016.

2.42 Melissa came to London with me and the boys in February 2017. The boys rode their scooters all the way from Leicester Square, Trafalgar Square, down The Mall, past Buckingham Palace, then to see Big Ben and right through Covent Garden back to Soho. Great day being tourists!

2.43 @ Red Bull's HQ in London with Lee, Ben Hall and Tarek Rasouli. March 2017.

2.44 Helping hand to drink my Starbucks.

2.45 Partying at [Spunge] gig in Birmingham, January 2017

2.46 My Dad, my brother, Lee and my boys watching The Geordies! It was January 2017 in England so I am properly wrapped up!

2.47 @sethmurraybmx

2.48 @masonmurraybmx

15
COMING HOME

In December 2007 I left Craig Hospital and flew with
Melissa to John Wayne Airport in Orange County. Cory
Nastazio met us at the airport. We moved into a rented
house on Grace Street in Riverside that had been adapted
so I could get around easily in my chair. My mum found
the property for us – she went to LA the week before I
left Craig and got the place ready. It was a nice house,
but a lot smaller than the other one. Everything was open
plan on the ground floor and I had a wheel-in wet room
with a hoist fitted so I could shower. The boys were young
and were OK with this, but one tough thing was my dogs
didn't interact as much with me when I came home. Mindy
Pantus was looking after them and they knew there was
something wrong with me – I wasn't the same guy they
last saw leaving for Baltimore. I loved my dogs and I was
real close to them and it was like they didn't recognise me
– at least that's how it felt. I guess it was probably that I'd
been away for so long.

We had a welcome home house party and that was kinda
emotional, because people were struggling to engage with me
as a quadriplegic. I'm telling them, just act normal and say it as
it is. Don't shy away and pretend things are the same. Don't try
to blank it out or ignore it, just hit it straight on and talk about
it. I'm trying to make people feel comfortable in my company,
but I guess it's not easy for them, considering I went from a
hyperactive crazy man to someone who can barely move.

When the party was over and everyone went home, it was just us on our own – me and Melissa and the boys.

We had no call button, no emergency cord to pull, no nurse – nothing.

We were home alone!

One of the crew I fooled around with at Craig Hospital, a guy from Iowa, had a nineteen-year-old brother called Clint. He wasn't a professional carer, but he wanted to help, and we needed all the help we could get. Clint came to live with us and he was a serial internet dater, constantly having girls coming to the house. When my mum visited, she got a bit annoyed and banned him from bringing women back. Might have been the worst thing she could've done because she woke one night jet lagged and wandered into the front room. Clint had fallen asleep mid-wank and she found him lying there with porn on the TV and his dick in his hand.

I stole Kimarie Hunt from Cory and she helped look after the kids – and look after Melissa. Just like she took care of everything for me and Nasty when we were younger, she took care of everything for me again now. I really don't know what I'd have done without that lady. She was, like, my saviour when I needed saving. I didn't know which way to turn, but she guided me and stopped me going out of my mind.

Getting hurt like I did is crazy. It's like losing your job – one minute you're a paid BMX pro, the next minute you're on your ass with a family and kids to support. It's a fucked-up situation. How d'you pay your bills? What d'you do? I got no help from the health system in America, no help from the city of Los Angeles, no help from the state of California, or from the federal government. My limited insurance paid for a nurse to come see me for two hours a day, to do my bowel programme and help me wash. That was it. The only real help I got was from friends, family and fans. OK, you could say it was my own fault, I should've been more sensible with my money when I was earning it – and you'd be right, I'm the first to admit that. But when you're young and you haven't been used to money and suddenly you get it, you go a bit crazy. Any young guy would. And I wasn't like any young guy, I was just in it for the day, the minute, the second. I was full of life and lived it like there was no tomorrow. In the end, that proved to be ironic, didn't it?

I'd met Aaron Cooke on the gate at the Ontario ABA national during my first visit to California, before I moved out there to live in 1999. I knew his brother Allan better than I knew him, from the contest circuit. But I'd see him at Sheep Hills and the trails and places. Allan was at Baltimore the day I crashed and he called Aaron and told him I was gonna be paralysed. Aaron was working in the mortgage business at the time, but he was also an announcer for BMX and he knew all the riders and their families.

Aaron showed up at shock/trauma in Baltimore a couple of days after the accident. He immediately began helping my confused and vulnerable family. He set up a web page to get news out to my thousands of fans and gave them daily updates on my condition. He found my family a house to stay in, instead of the hotel, all fully paid for. He negotiated with sponsors for free flights to Denver and Altanta for my mum and Grotbags, to check out rehab hospitals. He co-ordinated with health insurance companies, which no one else had any experience of doing and was a fucking minefield. In other words, he was amazing and I'll never be able to repay the debt of his endless and relentless perseverance and resolve. I can't ever thank him enough!

Aaron knew I was gonna need money for medical bills and he wanted to get something going to help out, so he went into the Bank of America and convinced this cute girl behind the counter to let him open an account called The Stephen Murray Family Fund. There was supposed to be lots of legal form-filling and stuff, but the bank girl bought into the story and arranged it so donations could be paid in through a PayPal account.

Money started coming in from all over the world – the US and UK, and even places like Russia and the Philippines – one dollar donations, ten dollar donations, a hundred dollar donations, a thousand dollar donations, and so on. It was amazing! But, while people's hearts were in the right place, the money didn't always go to the right place and Aaron himself says that some rookie mistakes were made. Like, if people didn't want to use the PayPal account they could go into a Bank of America branch and pay directly. But it wasn't a good idea to put the account number online – some people took that info and fraudulently cashed big cheques. It blew Aaron away, he never thought anyone would do something bad like that. I guess it was a crazy time and it got kinda strange in the end – people just wanted to give the money straight to me and not go through the Stephen Murray Family Fund.

Despite the problems, Aaron raised hundreds of thousands of dollars and he started to pay my medical bills for me. Like, the insurance only covered $500 worth of home help and my wheelchair alone cost $40,000. But the money wasn't gonna last forever and Aaron went to ESPN and Dew Tour and ASA for support. People were saying the sponsors were using guys like me and not helping us when we needed it. The Dew Tour wanted to do something and ESPN suggested a scholarship programme. They all said it should be some kind of non-profit thing, because they weren't insurance companies and they needed a channel to go through. So Aaron created a fund called the ARF, Athlete Recovery Fund. Since then the ARF has raised millions of dollars and it's given great help to athletes who've been hurt, just like me. It's helped parents and families fly out to be with loved ones and stuff like hotels and financial support through the agony.

It all started with me, but it wouldn't have started at all without Aaron Cooke.

What a great guy!

Other people wanted to fundraise too. There was a social media site called MySpace and a BMX Talk website and they really got people involved in supporting me. Tens of thousands of messages of support came through on MySpace. Individuals all around the world did fundraisers and sent money. All my English mates rode BMX from London to Brighton – about fifty-five miles – and people organised BMX jams and sold Stay Strong Stephen Murray and Murray Strong wristbands. The UK cycling distributer, Fisher Outdoor Leisure, raised thousands of pounds through the bike trade by putting on auction events at their annual trade show, with sporting memorabilia from the world's best cyclists up for grabs and stuff like signed and framed David Beckham shirts and Arctic Monkeys Platinum discs.

My bother Martin did Land's End to John O'Groats in nine days on a bike – 924 miles! My cousin, Claudine Lee, ran the London Marathon and Ben Hall, my friend from high school, ran a half marathon. Geth Shooter, the old-school BMX racer and one of the best of all time, did a sponsored bike ride, and other BMXers rode from Crewe to Manchester and then on to Mansfield and then to Derby. Each rider had their own sponsorship and sent money to me. BMX racer Tristan Nunn and his daughter Megan rode the Trans Pennine Trail and covered 225 miles in two days. Dustin Grice sold bracelets and donated the money. Shanaze Reade, the three times UCI BMX World Champion, auctioned off her gear at national BMX race meets and signed stuff as well – she raised thousands of pounds for me and UK World Champion BMX racer Liam Philip's dad Pete bought loads of it.

At times there'd be thousands of dollars in the house and I guess nobody was keeping proper track of it all. Donations were coming in from all over the world, but as fast as the money was coming in, it was disappearing. My dad reckoned Melissa was suffering from some kinda PTSD and she wasted a lot of the cash. It was all going wrong. I still loved my wife and I needed her to be with me – but I also needed to live. Things were getting real fucked up. I wasn't fully compos mentis and, like, Melissa was my next of kin and she was in control of everything, even though she was disintegrating.

Neal Woods' wife Kelly had been trained as a lawyer at Chapman University in Orange and one of her mentors was Kathryn Turner. I don't know all the details but, in the end, Katherine Turner came to the house and she sorted out power of attorney for my mum. All cash money was paid into the Stephen Murray Family Fund and Melissa was given a monthly allowance.

It was just a real tough time and I guess everyone was struggling to cope with all the stuff that was happening. And I couldn't help them because of the way I was.

A few days before I left Craig Hospital, they got me a new chair, made by Invacare. After a while, there was a real problem due to my sitting position and the poor fit of the chair. I developed serious shoulder and neck pain and scoliosis – that's like abnormal twisting and curvature of the spine. I went to see a doctor called Suzy Kim and I was kinda shocked when I saw she was in a wheelchair too. But I reckoned who better to understand what was happening. She said my posture was causing the problems – my body position was constantly moving and going out of line and it was affecting my neck and shoulders. She persuaded the insurance company to pay for rehab at a specialist unit in Long Beach and I went there twice a week. The unit said my chair wasn't supporting me properly – I needed a proper chair. Oakley Sunglasses and the money fundraised paid for them to take a body mould of me, so a seat and back rest could be built around my shape. I could now sit in the chair with my weight distributed evenly and without flopping about all over the place.

One of the things Melissa had to do was regulate my medication. I mean, I was taking a lot of pills. Meds for blood pressure – to lower it at bedtime and to raise it in the morning – meds for spasticity, meds for bladder spasms, meds for acid reflux, antihists, painkillers, sleeping pills, antibiotics and other stuff. Being a quadriplegic wasn't just a matter of being stuck in a bed or a wheelchair, it was never-ending litany of health risks, ranging from minor to life-threatening. As far as I knew, Melissa was on top of what I should be taking and I trusted her to get it right.

After two weeks at home, I wanted to get back into rehab. The best place in the world for that was the Kennedy Krieger Institute, an international centre for spinal cord recovery where Dr John McDonald practised. Ironically, it was in Baltimore where I had the accident and it was my first time back there since shock/trauma. They planned for me to be there six weeks for rehab therapies five mornings and five afternoons a week. I was an outpatient and had to find a place to stay. It wasn't easy to find somewhere that could accommodate me and my wheelchair and, when we first arrived, my dad got us an apartment in a Starwood Hotel, in Arundel Mills, five miles southwest of Baltimore airport. Melissa and Clint came with us and Jeff hired a disabled van in Baltimore to get me around. The apartment was a long way from the Institute and we had to drive over cobbled stone streets to get there. This vibrated the fuck out of my neck the first time we went and caused massive pain and my jaw started clattering out of control. About a mile short of the hospital I had a seizure – I wasn't breathing and I was slumped in my seat. Melissa went hysterical and my dad had to boot it to A&E. When we got there, my neck was swollen up like a wrestler's and, after stabilising me, the doctors said the journey in traffic was too far.

One of the admin girls at Kennedy Krieger hooked us up with this millionaire from Argentina called Gonzo. Gonzo owned a lot of real estate and he gave us an apartment in the Inner Harbour area of Baltimore for the rest of my stay. It was close to the Institute and in a quiet neighbourhood that was perfect. It was out of the way of all the mess and shit of Baltimore – all the junkies and crazies. Dr McDonald would come and visit me there a couple of times a week. He wasn't treating me as his patient, but he'd come in and kick off his shoes and lay on the couch and we'd talk about football and BMX. He explained lots of things to me, like tapping into the spasms and movement in my wrist, and he was more of a guru than a doctor – always telling me I could recover.

I needed someone to tell me that sometimes.

Melissa was still taking drugs and she got kicked out of the rehab at Kennedy Krieger because of her abusive and disruptive behaviour in the gym while she was dosed up on some shit. I'm sure she meant well, but her viewpoint was distorted by the meds she was taking. She was popping pills all the time and she'd fall asleep in rehab or have massive rows with the trainers. So my dad came back over and stayed with us in the apartment. It was only a one-bedroom and he stayed on the settee, with Clint on a mattress on the floor. Pretty cramped, eh!

It soon became clear to Jeff that both Melissa and Clint were taking drugs and Melissa was over-medicating me because she wasn't able to cope – she wanted to take the pain away from me and keep me quiet and inactive. The doctors were concerned and said if the med situation wasn't sorted out, I wouldn't survive. My dad told Clint, if he saw him giving me anything that wasn't prescribed, he'd hurt him bad. That was Jeff alright! Clint was scared of him and told him Melissa was getting a package flown in from LA and delivered to the apartment block reception. My dad told reception to hang on to the package until he could see what was in it, but the people there had a fit when they found out they were being used as a drugs drop and they told us we had to get out. Jeff spoke to Gonzo and the guy just found us another apartment – no sweat.

Melissa stopped having her packages delivered. Instead, she was driving to a house in Laurel to collect them, that was about ten miles south of where we were staying – until my dad found out and wouldn't let her use the van. She had no means of transport after that and it aggravated her.

It was the start of a bad feud between my wife and my father.

The Institute suggested my dad have CCTV installed in the bedroom, where Melissa would lock us both in to medicate. Jeff decided against that, but when I wouldn't get out of bed to have a shower or do my bowel regime, he had a serious go at me – like, off the hook! It kicked off big time between me and him. OK, I trusted my dad, but Melissa was my wife and I believed she was helping me. Melissa banned Jeff from the apartment because of that, saying he wasn't easy to live with – like, he'd hang his wet Y-fronts on the lamp to air out and leave his socks over the kitchen taps and stuff like that. My father and my wife just never got on and I guess sometimes he did it just to wind Melissa up. Before he left, he warned Clint that he better not leave me alone with her. Jeff got a hotel room round the corner from the apartment so he could be close by.

Shortly after, when Melissa was back in California visiting the kids, I became seriously ill and wasn't breathing properly. Clint called my dad and he called an ambulance. I was completely out of it on meds and telling the ambulance crew I was OK and didn't want to go to hospital. Jeff insisted and the medics agreed with him. I was taken to the emergency room at John Hopkins Hospital. One of the doctors from Kennedy came over. He managed to get the triage nurse to see me immediately and, if he hadn't, I would've died. I was there for three days, recovering. They said I had so much medication in me that everything got suppressed and my heart and lungs were shutting down.

After that, my dad locked all the meds in a special box and he was the only person who'd give me what was prescribed. He could control the prescribed meds, but not the illegal ones. The atmosphere was completely crap because he had to come round the apartment four times a day to administer the meds and, when he did, Melissa was abusive to him, shouting and calling him names and being sarcastic to try and rile him. For the most part, Jeff just ignored her. He knew she was in a land of her own and wasn't really with it –

'Water off a duck's back, son!'

But I guess it wasn't easy for either of them.

Clint was still with me, but he'd been acting kinda strange for a while and been coming in to the apartment at all hours. He knew this player from the Baltimore Orioles baseball team and they hung out together. One night I found him smoking crack with the window open and I told him he couldn't do that – like, if he got caught by anyone else, we'd all be thrown out. After that he just disappeared and I never saw him again. I'm grateful for the help he gave me but I guess he was just out of his depth. The situation was intolerable and, in the end, I decided to go home. I never liked Baltimore and I missed my kids, I hated being away from them so, at the end of February, my dad flew back to England and I went back to California – with Melissa.

We needed someone to help lift me, so Jeff contacted Chris Mason. Chris was a jujitsu specialist and he came over from England to train at 10th Planet in Riverside and the Gracie Academy in Torrance during the summer months. We couldn't pay him, but we offered food and accommodation and this kinda worked out well for him. It was great for me too, because Chris was a funny guy and always up for a laugh and he was great for my morale. He told me who built the pyramids and where aliens live – he reckoned he'd been alive for four hundred years and he sure looked like it. He kept me laughing for days on end. Chris noticed immediately that Melissa had no handle on how to regulate my meds, especially painkillers. The painkillers were opium based and Melissa was taking them herself as well as dishing them out to me. OK, I had a lot of pain then and it was probably hard to know what the right doses were – my judgement was massively clouded and I guess both of us were just in a different place.

It turned out Melissa was taking more than I was and two weeks after we got home, she overdosed on a cocktail of muscle relaxants and painkillers and ended up in hospital. It was scary as fuck, man – she's on the bed with foam coming out of her mouth and there's pills and pill bottles all over the place. I'm shouting at her but she's not responding and I can't wake her up – luckily, the kids were staying at a friend's that night. My voice was very low at that time and didn't have the power to carry. After about half an hour of me shouting, Chris heard me and he came into the room. Chris turned her over to see if her airwaves were blocked and he did CPR as best he could, until Melissa started to respond. Then he phoned a neighbour called Cindy, who came round and cleaned Melissa up. Cindy sat with her for a while and got her talking, then everyone went back to bed.

About 7:30 in the morning it happened again and, this time, I thought she was gonna die. Chris wasn't asleep and he responded fast to me shouting and called 911. The police and ambulance showed up and they took her to the hospital and she was detoxed for twenty-four hours. She was supposed to go into rehab for two months after that. Chris asked for a list of my meds and he called my mum, who flew over immediately, and everyone thought there might be some better routine in the house with Melissa getting the help she obviously needed. But she turned up at about 5:30pm the next day and she's like –

'I can't afford rehab, so I'm gonna do it myself.'

She never did.

My mum found a bunch of empty soma bottles, the same stuff as Melissa overdosed on, and she got told they must be old bottles. But they were all dated for the same month and Melissa finally admitted she was getting them online from India and places like that and she said she was selling them for $3 a pill to make some money. Cynthia asked her how she could let people come to the house to buy drugs, with the two boys there – she said they didn't come to the house, she went to meet them. Mum offered to pay for Melissa to go into rehab, but she refused. Then there was a confrontation with Melissa's mother – she and her partner were supposed to move their trailer up to my yard to give Melissa some support, but they never did. Monika kept saying her daughter was just tired and dehydrated due to having no help, even though we had Kimarie and Chris at the time. Cynthia had to go back to England, but she was convinced something real bad would happen if nothing was done about the situation.

I'm not judging my wife. Melissa was in her own private hell back then and nobody except herself can say what was going through her mind. Our life together started out like a fairytale on that sunset beach in Maui, but now it'd turned into a nightmare. Some people can cope with disaster better than others, some people find the strength from somewhere and others just collapse inside. My wife wasn't responsible for what happened to me and she didn't ask for the consequences. It wasn't the life she expected when she married me and I can understand that.

After the overdose Melissa and me hit a rocky patch that lasted about six weeks. She was drinking fairly heavy and we were fighting and I couldn't make out what the fuck was happening. I guess I was still very overmedicated and kinda hallucinating and dreaming bad stuff. In the end we decided it'd be best if I went back to Baltimore for more rehab and Melissa stayed at home to be with the kids. The Institute offered to house and rehabilitate me free for a year and I was doing four hours rehab a day, five days a week, using electrical stimulation and it was fucking exhausting. Melissa gave me a medication box that I took to Baltimore with me. It had my allocation of meds – according to the way she was regulating them – that I was to take four times a day. After two days, I was completely monged, like a fucking zombie. There was a knock on my door and Colleen from shock/trauma came in – she was dropping off a shower chair and decided to see how I was. She takes one look at me and she's like –

'Are you on heroin, Stephen?'

I wasn't able to answer her, but I knew something was wrong. She shone her flashlight in my eyes. Then she called the staff and, when they checked the medication box that Melissa'd packed for me, they nearly had a fucking fit. Coleen told me if I'd kept taking the stuff in the box, I'd have been dead in a week.

Eve Wolf used to go out with Jerry Badders and her dad was a quadriplegic. She was from Denver and she flew out to help me get settled in for the first week in Baltimore. She was real cool because she used to make English food like shepherd's pies and stuff and bring it to me. Colleen explained the situation to her and she called my dad in England. He was in Baltimore two days later. Jeff spoke to the doctors and sorted out the right meds for me and he took complete control of what I should be swallowing from then on. You know what dad's like from what I already told you – he was fucking militant with the meds.

At the time I was so spaced out I couldn't even figure out why he was there, but he took ownership of the situation and bought lock-boxes with codes to get into and dispensed the pills to me as and when they were needed. A week later Melissa flew to Baltimore and she and dad went at it. The arguments were fucking intense! Thing is, in her mind, Melissa believed she was doing the right thing, even though she was still fucked up on the stuff she was taking, like somas and shit she was still getting from India over the internet.

On the first anniversary of my accident, on June 22, 2008, the Dew Tour in Baltimore arranged a repeat event and I invited Dr John McDonald and Dr Cristina Sadowsky, the two directors of Kennedy Krieger. It was at the M&T Bank Stadium, home of the Baltimore Ravens football team. All the riders wore black T-shirts with 'Stay Strong Stephen Murray'. TJ Lavin and Pippa Tabron, wife of BMXer Simon Tabron, had written and released a song called *Soldier*, which was a tribute to me. A video of *Soldier* was played on the big screen and it was my first public appearance since the crash. On the day of the event, Melissa was supposed to come with me, but she didn't turn up at the hospital to take me, so my dad got us a taxi there.

Nobody knew where she was.

After seven weeks in Baltimore, I went home again. It was a tough time for me because people were telling me this and that about my wife and how she was no good and a danger to my health. Thing is, in my little bubble, I could only see what I saw and hear what I heard and it was real difficult to decipher the truth of the situation with Melissa. She needed help, but wouldn't admit it and I was in denial.

OK, it's like this, when I got injured, I didn't know which way to turn, which questions to ask, which route to take – which direction. I was clueless and so was my family. The accident was an extremely traumatic experience for two young people like me and Melissa, in the prime of our lives, to deal with. There was no instruction manual to follow, no structured care system, no real advice that we could comprehend in the state we were in at the time, no guidance on how to deal with something so fucking extreme. The situation left both of us adrift in a crippled boat on a strange and turbulent sea of uncertainty – that's the only way I can put it.

It was chaotic. Adjusting to this new way of life was tough for me, but I reckon it was just as tough for Melissa. As well as the pills, she was drinking heavy. Her behaviour got real erratic and she'd be spending loads of money on computer games for the kids and designer clothes and pointless shit we didn't need. One day she crashed my Range Rover into a parked car while she was off her head, then drove away from the scene before the cops came, so there'd be no consequences. I guess being a mother, a wife and a nurse was breaking her and she just felt trapped.

See waking up after the accident on stysrg.com

16
MELISSA

As the song goes, things got bad and things got worse – Melissa was still drinking heavy and she started acting real hostile. She was still taking a lot of meds and sometimes she'd scream at me out of frustration. Once, she took off her wedding ring and told me it was over. I was angry and told her she'd talked the talk, now she could walk the walk. She didn't leave right then, but she went and slept in another room and left me in the bedroom on my own. I was bedbound and couldn't do much and, while I was lying there, the old feeling came creeping from the back of my mind.

Whispering. In my ear.

Maybe if I'd been someone else, I might've thought about ending it. Maybe if I'd had someone to help me – maybe if there was some dignity in it, or it wouldn't hurt my family. But I wasn't someone else, I was me, and it would've hurt my family. At times like that, the darkest times, the faces of my sons always appeared before me and gave me strength.

Nobody wants to hear that stuff, whether it has to be said or not. Nobody wants to talk about being scared, or about pain, or how it feels – not to be able to shit without help, not to be able to eat or dress or scratch your ass without someone to do it for you. Nobody wants to know about bladder infections, stomach ulcers, pressure sores, headaches, burning, pulsing, spasming. Everybody wants to look on the bright side – and they need me to look on the bright side too.

I said to Melissa after the accident, if she wasn't able to handle it, then we could split up amicably, with no animosity. To her credit, she didn't walk away – at least not until she got to breaking point, until it all got a bit ugly and seedy. I went through so much shit and I guess she did too. People said she was doing stuff behind my back and I didn't believe them. Maybe it was just that I didn't want to believe them, but then it was my family and close friends and I was being torn two ways – my family on one side and Melissa on the other. My dad said to me once –

'Son, one day the penny's goin' tuh drop.'

Then one day it did. Melissa had been fucking around when I was away at hospital and we had a massive argument and she left and took the kids to her sister's place. After a few days, she brought them back and said she couldn't manage. She left them with me. This went on for a while – like, to-ing and fro-ing – and it wasn't good for the kids. She was so out of it she didn't know where she was most of the time. The Child Protection Services were watching her because they'd been tipped off by a friend of mine, and they organised a meeting to decide what should happen with the boys. There was psychologists and counsellors and a whole bunch of people, and I showed up with Dale and Kimarie. Melissa came, but she was off her face. So they wrote a report saying she wasn't fit to look after the kids and they should stay with me.

And that was the end of that – or so I thought!

Kimarie was still coming round to help out and she'd drive me wherever I wanted to go and she was a real rock for me. Then, one day, she found this mobile phone down the side of the sofa with a video of Melissa filming me slumped in my shower chair, naked and medicated to the point where I didn't know what the fuck was going on. Melissa could be heard on the phone saying shit like –

'Look how fucking pathetic you are!'

Kimarie was shocked and she got in touch with my family in England. They started to get more involved in my life from that point, coming over more regularly and taking more control of things.

Melissa moved in with a guy called James Mulaney, who was a construction contractor. I knew James a couple of years before the accident and he seemed cool enough. He was always real friendly but I guess he had ulterior motives. When Melissa moved in with him, I wanted to kill that guy, but that's just the way I was feeling then – like, I still loved my wife and I felt she was deserting me and everything was falling apart. It hurt bad. I even asked Chris Mason to do for him and I'm like –

'Hey Chris, I'm gonna get Mulaney to come round the house.'

'What for?'

'I dunno ... I'll think of some excuse. When he gets here, you grab him and choke him.'

'What?'

'You can do that in America ... we can say he broke in.'

'No fucking way, Stephen!'

Chris chickened out on that one. I don't think he liked the idea of spending life in an American prison.

Another time I ran Mulaney over in my chair when he came round with Melissa to visit the kids. But time cools all the heat, don't it! I got myself more in control and eventually I didn't feel anything toward the dude. Thinking back, maybe it wasn't just about Melissa. This fucker got an expensive Weekend Warrior motorhome on credit and couldn't repay the loan, so he took it into the orange groves and torched it. He told Melissa she could do the same with my Range Rover, the one she crashed, but the dumb-ass took it to the same place where he torched the motorhome. The insurance company smelled a fucking rat and sued Melissa for a fraudulent claim. She tried to frame me, saying I was the mastermind behind it all and I had to deal with the cops. Detective Jeff Joseph of Riverside Police Arson Task Force investigated the case and cleared me. Melissa and Mulaney were took to court on charges of fraud, but I can't remember how it all played out. I think there was no hard evidence against Mulaney, and Melissa got out of it some way or other. Who cares?

But here's the twist – I got a phone call from the mother of James Mulaney's child, a woman called Kristi Dietzel and – OK, this is probably a bit Jerry Springer – but we started talking about stuff and she came to visit first and then ended up moving from Vegas to my house in Riverside with her daughter, who was the same age as my son Mason. We got along great and she paid special attention to my boys, which they really needed at the time, after their mother left. She was down to earth and didn't drink or take drugs or nothing and, after a few weeks, we became intimate.

After you suffer with a spinal cord injury, it's real difficult to maintain an erection. I tried all sorts of impotence stuff, but nothing really worked. I could get an erection OK, but I couldn't keep it. This was beating me up because, don't forget, I'd fucked more women than Mick Jagger and now I was only twenty-eight and in a shagless desert. It didn't do much for my confidence. Because of the infections I was getting, I was seeing this urologist at the time and he suggested I try some medication that's injected into the base of the penis. Man, this freaked me out for a while and I didn't know whether to try it or not, but I was desperate and went for it. A vial of the stuff cost about $100 – I kept it in the fridge and got ten or fifteen hits from it. Kristi injected me and, sure enough, this shit did the trick and the results were fucking outstanding.

Over the next few months, Kristi injected this stuff into my penis hundreds of times and we were having such a fucking ball – until my dick started to swell up and turn black. All the blood went to the wrong area, it got redirected sideways and there was a lump like a tennis ball on the side. It just got bigger and bigger and I thought the fucking thing was gonna explode. In the end, I had to call 911 and the paramedics came out.

'What's the problem?'

'I got an exploding dick.'

I let them see it.

'Holy cow! How did that happen?'

I told them what I was doing and they took me to hospital. I stayed there overnight and they gave me meds to bring the swelling down. My dick took twelve hours to deflate. OK, that was a scare, but it wasn't enough to stop me. Me and Kristi did it loads of times after that and my dick never swelled up again – don't ask me why, maybe the meds they gave me in the hospital made me immune?

I had two agency nurses, Betty and Arlene, paid for by the Athlete's Recovery Fund. Arlene was real wacky and she came from the deep south – maybe Louisiana or someplace like that. She was a big woman and she'd talk all the time and tell random stories about segregation. She was fascinated by English aristocracy and she called my dad 'Duke of Wellington' because he told her he met the duke once and done business with him.

Betty was small and slim and she came from Loma Linda. She was a lovely woman and went beyond the call of duty in taking care of me. They were both great characters and they'd show up on alternate mornings to clean me up and do my bowel programme by sticking their fingers up my ass to stimulate it to crap. I guess there's weird people who'd pay good money for that kinda thing but, all joking aside, I hated it and still do. It's not a great way to start every day. Then they'd do stretches until Chris arrived and got me out of bed with the electric hoist.

Like I said, since the accident, Kimarie really stepped in to help me and she lifted my spirits up to the moon, man. She was there for me when I was at an all-time low and she gave up a lot of her own personal life to be with me. She helped me steal Erika Diaz from Cory – Erika was looking after Nasty's kids, but she became a full-time nanny to my boys, thanks to Kimarie. She had an outrageous laugh and you could hear her coming a mile off because she dragged her feet along the ground. Erika became my partner-in-crime and we played tricks on Chris Mason – I'd tell her to do stuff and she'd do it, like putting fish in his pillow and dogshit in his shoes. He'd go fucking mad for a few minutes, but he always took it well in the end.

After Melissa left, I had all these people to help do the things I couldn't do for myself – drive me around and give me my meds and help me with rehab – and life got more stable. I tried to lead as normal a life as possible – I'd go watch jujitsu, take the kids boxing and watch them trampolining, go to the cinema and the BMX track. I started getting trails built around the house because I wanted BMXers to come and ride. Visitors cheered me up – made me feel good – like, that way I'd know people hadn't forgot about me. Mat Hoffman came over, and Pip from Guana Batz psychobilly band – who Chris Mason idolised like a girl groupie – Big Daddy, a BMXer who used to lie on the floor and put bricks on his stomach and let the kids smash them with a sledgehammer, Adam Aloise would show up and make BMX films – and the doubts and negative thoughts receded again.

Melissa opened up a women's boutique called Eye Candy – she had a shop and she also sold stuff online. I don't think it worked out, because she got a job selling golf equipment in Orange County – but I was told she regularly missed work and was always late and got put on a warning. Then she fell asleep in a sales meeting and got fired. She was in trouble with the police on a few occasions for driving under the influence. Her mother got cancer and she went into a downward spiral – as if she could spiral any worse than she was already. She came to the house looking like she was spaced out, with her eyes half shut, saying she wanted to see the kids. I'd had enough of this shit and I needed to do something to protect the boys.

Kathryn Turner, who sorted out power of attorney for my mum, was an expert in family law, like divorce and custody and stuff. My dad came over and we hired Kathryn – I was earning royalties from Oakley Sunglasses at the time and could just about afford her. I showed her the CPS report about Melissa and she suggested I file for sole legal custody of the kids because their welfare was at risk. Seth was living with me, but I wasn't his biological father. Like I said already, his real dad was a drug dealer and addict – he was in and out of prison and never had anything to do with Seth. Even so, I believed I'd have big problems getting custody of the boy, but I had to try. Even though Seth wasn't my biological son, he was still my son, if you know what I mean. I loved him just as much as Mason and was equally responsible for both of them. Kathryn made an application to the court for an emergency meeting so I could ask for sole custody of both boys.

To make the hearing legal, we needed to serve Melissa with notice, so my dad called her and told her the boys wanted to see her and could she meet with them at McDonalds in Van Buren. Jeff and Kathryn took the kids with them when they went to serve the papers. Melissa kicked off and the police had to be called. The cops wouldn't let her take the boys with her from McDonalds, like she wanted to do – they said she should go to the court and make her case there. We went to court and Melissa was OK – I mean, she wasn't out of it like she was at the CPS meeting. I was able to show that I had the resources in place to support the boys, like a house and enough money and support and I was clean. She was all sober and upright on the day, but she had so many things going against her she had no chance and the judge only took a few minutes to rule it'd be unsafe for her to have custody. I got temporary sole custody of the boys while an investigation took place and a full report came from the CPS.

After the CPS investigation, in December 2008, the judge ruled that the boys should live with me, but Melissa could have visitation rights, two hours a week to begin with. She was also ordered to undergo drugs tests at her own expense. During the next thirteen months, there was nine more court hearings. Like, it's normal in California for a judge to try to split custody 50:50 whenever they can. We kept the same judge throughout and he kept asking for reports and the results of drug tests. I guess he was trying to give her a chance, as he didn't want the kids to be deprived of a mother. Melissa kept stringing things out – I guess she had her pride and didn't want to be seen by all our friends as an unfit mother, but she didn't want to get clean either. Or couldn't. Every time we went to court, the judge extended her visitation rights, until she got two days a week. The kids were handed over at the local police station in case there was any trouble. It ended up with her entitled to have the boys from Friday at 5:00pm to Sunday 5:00pm – forty-eight hours. The judge also made a ruling that the custody would be 50:50 during school holidays, provided she wasn't in any more trouble with the cops.

But Melissa couldn't show she had a real home or income or job, and she never took any of the drug tests like she was ordered to. The boys didn't know whether they were coming or going and it really wasn't a good situation for them. Like, when they were with her they were either late for school or missing school altogether and I didn't know what was going on. OK, I wasn't a great role model when I was partying, but they were very young back then and now they were growing into impressionable boys. I was worried. Kathryn did the first few hearings and she proved to the judge that Seth was my son, because he'd never known anyone else as his father. It was classified under California law that I was legally Seth's dad.

Then, tragically, Kathryn died of heart failure. I needed another lawyer, as the court hearings were still dragging on because Melissa was still using delaying tactics. Kelly got us a meeting with Marisa Cianciarulo, the professor of law from the university, and she recommended another lawyer called Robyn, who wanted to get the custody sorted first and then she said I should divorce Melissa.

One day a letter of notification of the divorce hearing turned up. It was for the week before and I'd missed the hearing. We couldn't get in touch with Robyn and then we found out she died too, on the table while having an operation. I'm like –

'For fuck's sake, man, what else is gonna happen?'

Robyn had all my custody and divorce files. She operated from home, but had a convenience address for clients. Her phone wasn't being answered, so we went to the address and some guy there gave us a PO box number and told us where it was. We went along and asked the dude behind the counter if he could help us out. There was a young girl sat next to him and she's like –

'That's my mother.'

'We're real sorry for your loss, miss, but we need some case files.'

'What case?'

'Stephen Murray.'

'You're the BMX guy, ain't you?'

'That's me.'

'Sure, I know all about your case.'

She knew where all the papers were too, at an office in a place called Brea, near Anaheim. We met the girl there and she gave us everything we needed.

We went back to Marisa at the university and she gave us her star student, a Vietnamese lawyer called Van Ho – a beautiful young lady in her early twenties. She had to get the court to agree that she could represent me and that I could continue the divorce proceedings without having to start from scratch. I went for a clean break – I wanted nothing from Melissa, just to get clear of all the crap. She never even showed up and the divorce was granted without any more hassle

The other thing was, after my accident, it was clear that my sports visa wouldn't be valid no more, meaning I'd be kicked out of the US. I needed permanent residency. I tried to apply for it immediately after the accident, but Melissa didn't post the forms off. There was, like, five hundred envelopes stuffed into the top of a cupboard. I guess she just didn't want to deal with anything, everything was just too much for her to handle on her own. But it felt like, as well as everything else, she dropped me in all that immigration shit – as if I didn't have enough problems. Like, how much crap did I have to take? It was like everything was just constantly trying to beat me down, and I had to keep getting back up. Now I had to apply for residency all over again as a single adult, which was a helluva lot more difficult.

It's like, while I was living in America on the sports visa I was entitled to stay and work as a pro athlete. After the accident I wasn't a pro athlete no more, but I still needed to be able to stay in the country. My dad sorted out the paperwork while I was in Craig hospital but, as my wife, Melissa was the only person entitled to apply on my behalf. I finally realised this was never gonna happen and the lawyer made applications to the court, giving reasons why I should be able to apply for my own permanent residency – like, my wife was too traumatised by the accident to be able to make the application and I had to be in America to look after the kids. Van Ho went to work, but it still took nearly two years to get it sorted. In the end, I got my permanent residency through and it was a first in California history – although it was a massive struggle at the time.

Then I went through the courts to change Seth's name from Kelly-Sweeney to Murray. I applied for a birth certificate showing the name Seth Murray and me as his father. I could then get him a British passport. Me and my boys now have dual nationality through citizenship.

I never really held any resentment toward Melissa, even though, like I said, I wanted to kill James Mulaney, the fucker she moved in with. It was a crazy situation, with me seeing his daughter's mother and him with my ex-wife. I was getting abusive messages on my phone for a year and a half and things were real fucking messy for a while. A couple of times they showed up at my house and pulled up outside the gate, absolutely fucking wasted. He'd shout out abuse at me and say shit stuff about my dad – what a cowardly thing to do. If I could've jumped out of my chair, I'd have kicked him down the fucking street.

But, I guess you gotta take the rough with the smooth – the good with the bad.

The good was, I got invited to lots of BMX events and one of them was an Extreme Thing show in Las Vegas, organised by Ricardo Laguna, a pro BMX rider and television personality who was TJ Lavin's Mexican shadow and I knew him from Lake Perris. We went in my shitty old van that I bought from a BMX rider called Justin Wheatley, who got hurt and was quadriplegic like me. It was a Ford E150 Camper that had a lift at the side and could take my wheelchair and you had to start the fucking thing with a screwdriver. I mean, the screwdriver was jammed right into the ignition, up to the hilt, and you turned the handle to start the van. You couldn't see out the back window past the folding lift and Chris Mason reversed it into a telegraph pole outside Luke Parslow's house once.

Another time we got stuck in freeway traffic and I asked Chris to come back and give me a Soother sweet – I sucked hundreds of the things just to keep my throat moist. Chris didn't know how to drive the van; like, you had to put the brake on, not leave it in drive, which he did. So, while he's back with me, the van rolled forward and hit this Mexican guy's pickup. Chris and the Mexican get out and I'm in the back of the van shouting –

'Jujitsu! Do your jujitsu on him, Chris!'

Chris will try to say the van was difficult to drive, but that's just him making excuses. The truth is, he was a flapper – a granny – a shit driver – ha! We had some crazy rides in that old van – it looked like it'd topple over when I was going up on the lift in my chair. Bits would fall off it and the wing mirrors were smashed from Chris' crap driving and he called it the Scooby-Doo van.

Anyway, we're driving up to Ricardo's event in Vegas and there's me, Adam Aloise, Big Daddy and Chris Mason in the back. We're drinking Big Gulps and, as it's a five-hour trip to Las Vegas and whoever's driving doesn't want to stop the van in case he can't get it started again, they all piss in the empty Big Gulp cups. We pull up at Planet Hollywood behind Rolls Royces and BMWs and all kinds of super cars and, as they're getting me out, I knock over some of the Big Gulps and there's piss running down the side of the van and on to the red carpet. The valets are fucking horrified and I know they're thinking the van's stolen or something and maybe they should call the cops. Then they think, maybe we're some really eccentric rock group and we have comp tickets and they better just play it cool. So they get in and twist the screwdriver handle and take it away. We stay at Planet Hollywood that night and all the guys sleep in my room on the floor. We don't see the van again until it's time to go home.

Kristi Dietzel got real obsessive about me, even though I was paralysed. I liked Kristi and she was a great mother, but the obsessiveness got too intense. She didn't like anyone else feeding me or giving me drinks and she got increasingly jealous when I was talking to other women. Look, I consider myself to be a fairly easygoing dude – and I think people who know me will agree – but I wasn't in love with Kristi like I was with Melissa and I couldn't let this relationship go on – for her sake as much as my own. I had to break free. In the end, we separated amicably enough and Kristi became a carer for another quadriplegic. I guess she was just a real good samaritan and it was a kinda vocation for her to be looking after someone who needed her.

Eventually she moved back to Vegas with her daughter.

17
STAY STRONG

I just need to say a few words about Stay Strong here.

To do that, I gotta go back a bit.

Back to when I busted myself up in 2007.

As I said already, after my accident in Baltimore, riders wore black T-shirts with the words 'Stay Strong' on the front and my name on the back, like in that well-known photograph with everyone's back to the camera on the dirt jump at the Dew Tour in Cleveland, a couple of weeks after I got hurt. In the beginning they were printed by Steve Mateus from Rockstar, Rockstar gave them to every rider in Cleveland that weekend, so everyone rode in those colours. At that time, nobody had any intention of selling the stuff, it was just for athletes to show support. It started out as an empowering message and kinda evolved into a brand name. All the messages of support I was getting said 'Stay Strong Stephen!' and it originally came from the aftermath of that horrific crash.

Kimarie Hunt was distributing the shirts and wristbands – she was there again just like she helped out every time I needed her. She gave her time and set up stalls at events and paid for her own flights and for stock and, when people started contacting her on MySpace and asking how they could get their hands on the black and yellow shirts, she made reprints and distributed them.

Although I was going through such a crazy time in my life, I started travelling to different events where I'd meet with Kimarie and we'd go promoting Stay Strong and its ethos. It was a challenge getting on aeroplanes and taxiing about, but I needed to keep my mind occupied to overshadow all the chaos going on around me. I'd deliver motivational speeches about my life and the message behind Stay Strong at high schools and universities and business venues. It was great, because I got to work with different foundations, like the autism charity Taca, where I made some speeches and learnt about the difficulties these people experience in life. I had total stage fright in the beginning – the thought of talking in front of a room full of strangers terrified me. But, gradually, I was able to step into the role of a guy who'd been to hell and was coming back. I didn't realise it at the time but, by helping others, I was helping myself mentally.

Eventually the shirts started making a small profit and Kimarie plodded on like that for a couple of years. My dad got involved and, as you know by now, he's got a pretty militant way of dealing with things. By then, most of the Stay Strong support was in England, so he reckoned it needed someone in the UK to take it over and run things. Stay Strong was Kimarie's life and Jeff told her he was taking it away from her at the bike show in Vegas. I was told it hurt her bad and she took it real personally.

It's tough for me to write about what happened with Kimarie and I don't know the full extent of it, all I know is I lost a good friend who I loved and trusted and who helped me when I was down and in a dark place.

I guess Jeff was trying to save the brand and what he did was right in his eyes – but what's right to one person might be wrong to another. And there's different ways of handling things and everybody's got their own take on the best way to go. If I hadn't been in a wheelchair maybe things would've turned out different – I don't know. My dad will always do what he thinks is best for me – that's human nature, isn't it. A father will always protect his son, no matter what, and Jeff has his own way of doing things – everybody knows that. But, for what it's worth, I never meant for Kimarie to get hurt. I loved her then and I still love her now. I hope she can put whatever happened behind her and I hope she can be my friend again – I miss her a lot.

I think my dad wanted to set up a trust fund or something – I'm not sure, as I wasn't involved in that side of things. Anyway, it was decided to end the US set-up and concentrate on the UK. My BMX buddy Marco Dell'isola took over from Kimarie. I'd raced all over the world with Marco as a kid and he was a two-time world champion. He's a good salesman and he knows everyone in BMX – like, he knows the brands and he's a good hustler. He was brand manager for Zoo York for a couple of years and he has a great knowledge of the industry.

Stay Strong started out as a slogan of support, a message that people were rooting for me. Now, ten years later, it's a brand that's recognised throughout the world.

I already told you that various friends and fans were putting on BMX jams and fundraisers, raising awareness of quadriplegia and athletic disability and money for my hospital bills and ongoing care. Then Ogio, the bag manufacturer, released a signature backpack for me and Vans released a signature shoe that sold out in four hours. When I was a little better, we did signature Oakley sunglasses. I'd had a long relationship with Oakley, especially a guy called Mark Scurto who was their marketing manager. He gave me the opportunity to design these glasses and Chris Mason helped me out with a style that's based on the pattern I have tattooed on my chest – the three lions of England. In fact, I did two models of signature sunglasses for Oakley, over a three-year period and, for a long time, it was my only source of income.

My friend Mike Aitken nearly lost his life after crashing in Pennsylvania in 2008, and another good friend, TJ Lavin, had a bad accident at the Dew Tour in LA in 2010 – he crashed and was rushed to hospital and put into a medically induced coma. Both those riders had crashes that resulted in traumatic brain injuries and I couldn't believe two of the most bad-ass dudes on a bike came so close to death, just like me. So I started to work closely with Aaron Cooke at the Athlete Recovery Fund to support a campaign on bicycle approved helmets. So many people were wearing flimsy skateboard headgear and I'd seen the damage that could be inflicted in a serious crash.

Everybody thinks, 'it won't be me, it'll always be the other guy', but like the song says 'it only takes once'. Even the best riders in the world make mistakes and they end up paying for it. Any rider out there who thinks it's cool to ride without a helmet, think again! Even at the Mikey Aitken benefit jam at Fox there was friends of his riding without helmets. I was sat there in support of Mikey in my wheelchair and I couldn't fucking believe it. One thing I know for sure, if I hadn't been wearing a helmet when I crashed, not only would I be paralysed like I am, but I'd be a fucking cabbage as well! Severe brain damage is a real risk to all action sporters – it's a risk that shouldn't be ignored! Wear your helmet!

OK, that's my speech on head protection over, but it's something I feel strongly about and I had to get it off my chest.

Apart from BMX, MMA was my big passion and I couldn't get enough of it. I don't know what it is, but I guess fighting's in my DNA – like, it's the rawest form of competition and I done my fair share of brawling, though I never got in the ring. Maybe I should have – it might've knocked some of the aggression out of me. When I was done with all the hospitals, I'd go watch UFC events with TJ Lavin in Vegas whenever they were in town and I had so much respect for the Diaz brothers – the biggest bad-asses ever to step in the octagon. Stay Strong supported MMA Tough Enough final winner Shaun Bollinger and paid him to represent the brand. They also formed and supported a world racing team called Stay Strong, managed by Dale Holmes. Stay Strong has some of the best dirt, street and park riders in the world representing it – guys like Larry Edgar and Ben Wallace and more.

Staying strong's the only way I know how to live my life now. I've been through so much pain, so many setbacks, but I always had the drive to push forward through the darkness and stay focused. I'm proud of the Stay Strong message and I'm gonna try to spread that mantra all over the world.

Stay Strong means just that. Maybe you got injured, or your wife or husband's left you, or you lost your job, or someone's died, or some other bad shit's happened – there's so many things in life that'll make you crumble. But you gotta reach deep down inside – when you think there's nothing left, you dig deeper!

Deeper!

As deep as it takes!

You STAY STRONG!

Stay Strong Tattoos

staystrongbmx

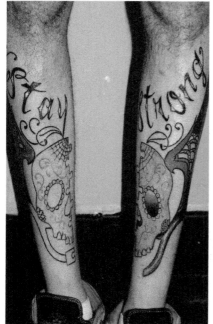

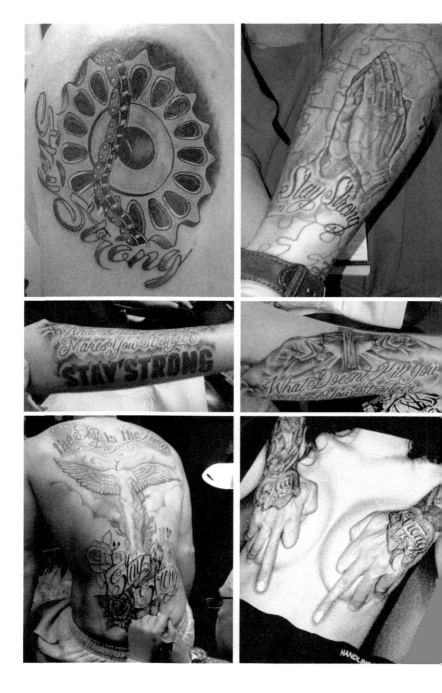

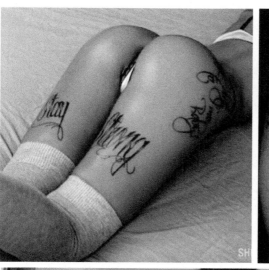

3.1 Stay Strong Signature Vans.

3.2 The Dew Tour after my crash. All the riders came together to show support. The beginning of Stay Strong.

3.3 360 flip sequence.

3.4 An American flag flown over Afghanistan in honour of Stephen Murray by the American Military.

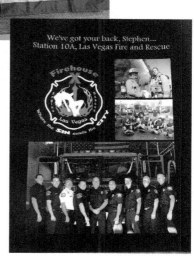

3.5 Las Vegas Fire and Rescue showing support for me.

18
LIFE GOES ON

The old van Chris Mason crashed so many times rattled like crazy and it was shaking me to fucking bits. My chair was chained to the floor and there was no suspension, so I'd get thrown about and vibrated like a dildo at an Ann Summers party. One day when Erika took the kids trampolining, me and Chris went out in it and we were driving around when there was a sound like a gunshot. We didn't know what was happening. Suddenly, there was another massive bang and my chair broke and I fell backwards and smacked my head and my legs went over my shoulders. The vertical stanchions that held my backrest snapped and I got flipped over like a rag doll. Chris slammed on the brakes and came back and lifted me up – he had to drive all the way home trying to balance me on his lap and steer at the same time.

This was a major setback because I didn't have a chair for two weeks and I had to stay in the bed. I was helpless, stuck in a fucking room all the time, and this was bad for me because it was at times when I couldn't get around that the doubts and negative shit came calling to me – promising an end to all my troubles.

One of my friends, Lonie Paxton, who played football for the New England Patriots and won the Superbowl three times, lived round the corner. Every St. Patrick's Day, he held a massive BMX jam in his backyard and hundreds of people turned up. Lonie had some rad trails in his yard that were built by my friends Heath Pinter and Corey Bohan.

The backyard was a tropical paradise, like something from MTV's 'Cribs' and, after the jam was over, everyone was partying. Then this bad-ass van comes out from behind the house – it's fully pimped out with fat rims and screens, a ridiculously loud sound system, a winch in case my chair breaks down and even a fucking fridge. Aaron Cooke's on the microphone and he announces that this is my new rig, on behalf of the Athlete Recovery Fund and my backers, Oakley, Rockstar and Vans. I couldn't fucking believe it. I was completely blown away! It meant I could now travel in style with my kids and their bikes – anywhere we wanted to go.

Aaron had seen the door of my old van opening by itself one day when I was being driven around by Chris and I nearly fell out. He pulled up alongside and used one of the tie-downs from his motorcycle to keep the door shut and it was then he decided I needed a proper vehicle. He got together with my dad and they bought a fleet van from a company in Arizona. It was just a bare bones vehicle when they got it and they took it to a fabricators and had the interior designed to fit me and my family. They tested it with my wheelchair when I was asleep, so I knew nothing about all this going on. The ramp was too short and too steep the first time they tried to get the chair up it – it was real sketchy, like I'd probably tip over. So they went away and got a longer ramp and, by the time they were finished, it was the baddest van on the roads. It was covered with two big tarps at the party and only a few people knew what was underneath – until Aaron presented me with it.

Man, that's what I call a surprise!

As well as thanking Aaron, while I'm at it I really need to thank all the people around the world who I don't even know – people who supported me and sent what they could to help. That really blew me away – it was amazing! I felt like I had the whole world behind me at times. I know I've mentioned fundraising before, but I want to say again that the world of BMX is a tight-knit family. Guys I haven't spoken to for years just pop up when they see on social media I'm going somewhere or doing something and they just reach out and help me. There's so many examples of this, the list's endless. Hall-of-Famer Tracer Finn, the 'Las Vegas Legend', got me an amazing viewing platform at La Reve show in Vegas when he saw I was in town. Mindy Brummett, who was in charge of the celebs who came into the Mandalay Bay, booked me a lush hotel gratis. All my old friends are forever fundraising.

BMX riders Craig Teague, Joe Baddeley and James Done performed bike shows at schools to raise money and awareness in England. Chico Hooke arranged the Brixton to Brighton sponsored bike ride. Jay Aliano and the DTR crew held a BMX jam at his trails every year after the accident and raised thousands of pounds. The Stay Strong Stephen Murray Jam became one of the UK's biggest BMX events for the next six years. In fact, it seemed like most of the trail spots in the world, especially California, were hosting benefit jams for me. If there's anyone I haven't mentioned here, then I apologise sincerely. But believe me when I say I appreciate everything you've done for me and do call me sometime so I can thank you in person. I was truly blown away by it all. It's like, when I needed help, the real people stood up and I'll be forever grateful to them!

My dad made fifty-seven trips across the Atlantic to support me in the nine years after the accident. He quit his job and his life to help me. Without Jeff I would've been lost. He took over things as much as he could, he got stuff handled, he got things done. My brother Martin was also amazing – all the effort he put into fundraisers and stuff. And my mum, it goes without saying she was a rock. She's the person I turned to when things were dark and I was confused – the one I talked to and got advice from – she calmed me down when I was going crazy and the world around me was closing in and choking me. Although she and my dad were divorced, they worked together for my benefit and always put me first. My granddad was a champ and my grandma Irene. Love them both forever.

One time I lived like there was no tomorrow. I pushed the envelope and partied and did all kinds of crazy shit. The journey I'm on now is harder than anything I've ever done. Harder than anything, man. You can't imagine how difficult it is just to try and twitch a finger – it's like, you gotta rewire your brain. You gotta figure your whole body out again – it's not the body you had before, it's a different thing altogether and you gotta come to terms with it. The worst times I got down was when I was confined to a bed and when I was alone – like, if people promised to come see me and didn't show up. But I guess I can't really blame them – a lot of people were struggling with the way I was now, finding it hard to accept – there but for the grace of God and stuff. Still, when people did turn up I always made the effort to lighten the situation – maybe crack a joke or something to put them at ease.

At this time, the rental period on the house in Grace Street was expiring and they gave me five days to get out – I needed another place to live. I'd been looking at houses and I stumbled on this place in Hoffa Lane that was perfect. There was a long driveway with a line of big trees on either side. It could get real hot in Riverside and it seemed like it was twenty degrees cooler in the shade of those trees. The house had an open plan design on one level and two acres of land around it on different elevations, ideal for building jumps. It was at the end of a cul-de-sac, where I didn't need to worry about the kids being near a main road. I had a mountain biker friend called Chad Hubbard who was in the real estate business – Chad offered to buy the house and rent it to me. What a guy, without Chad at that time, I'd have been up the fucking creek and no mistake!

I moved into 16510 Hoffa Lane on 6 December 2011.

I had to make some changes to make the place more accessible, and all my friends came to help out and get me settled in. Aaron Cooke's mum and dad, who were in their sixties, came and painted the house for two days – like, painting for ten hours a day. Jay Aliano came over from England and widened all the doorways and installed ramps and generally modified the building to make life easier. Thank you, guys!

Back when I was an able-bodied athlete, I spent countless hours constructing and shaping dirt jumps. It's kinda like a work of art, like a sculpture – you imagine it first, then you shape it out, and then refine it until it's created right there in front of your eyes. The more you look after jumps by maintaining them and giving them water, the more of a masterpiece you create. Some people just make jumps and then leave them, like they're gonna take care of themselves, but I always took pride in my work, making sure my trails looked immaculate and were smooth as glass. There's so many shapes and sizes to trails and you can make all kinds of sections – like, there's no limit to what you can create.

A couple of weeks after I got settled into the new house, it was time to feed my passion again, so I flew my friend Adam Aloise in from Philly to help make some bad-ass trails. Adam brought a guy called Randy Menenga with him, who had his own heavy equipment, and we started ripping up the yard. He was best friends with Jeremy McGrath, the great motocrosser, who'd built all types of jumps and trails and motocross tracks. They were the ultimate fucking team and responsible for building the best contest jumps of all time, like Red Bull's Dreamline – a BMX contest put on by Adam Aloise with the biggest jumps that were ever made.

Once they built the basics with the heavy gear, all my BMX buddies came to shape it up with their shovels. After it was ready, some of the best riders in the world came and sessioned in my yard on a regular basis. It wasn't possible to take my boys as many places as a regular dad and, as I was a single father raising them myself, it seemed the right thing to have trails on the doorstep for them – like, to compensate for all the stuff they might be missing out on. I'd hold massive jams at my house – you could feel the energy and the riding was off the chain. OK, after my accident, a lot of people stopped coming by to see me – I guess I reminded them of what could happen to them in action sports. Now riders were showing up again and I felt better than I had in a long time. It was so good for my morale, to be surrounded with the thing that defined me most – BMX.

Chris Mason had to go back and forth to England to take care of stuff over there, so a guy called John Jennings, who'd sent me a message in the form of a rap song, said he was willing to move from New Jersey to Riverside to be there for me as a carer. John came in December 2011 and he was someone I respected. He used to kill it on his bike, with his own unique style, and he kinda stood out from the crowd. Anyway, he came out to help me and he was completely different to anyone else around me. He believed in God, but he wasn't a typical churchgoer – like, he had dreadlocks and was covered in tattoos and everyone called him 'John The Baptist'. John was a real blessing and stood firm at a time when my whole world was falling apart and I really needed him. I also had a guy called Art Nava, who I knew from the Riverside party scene, Art came and helped out during the day to give John a break – then John took over at night.

Now I had my new ride it didn't make sense to have two vans sitting on my driveway. John Jennings got me going to the 777 Church in San Bernardino – the pastor there was called TJ O'Donnell and he dedicated his time to helping people in need. He told me about a local family whose son had a neurological condition and they were in some hardship – like, they had to take care of their boy and couldn't work. I had my old van tarted up and fixed and, one morning after church when we were all hanging out in the parking lot, John Jennings drove the van round and I presented it to them. Man, those people were overwhelmed and it was fucking emotional for me to see how grateful they were. To me, it was just a van I didn't need and now they could take their son where he had to be without a load of fuss and hassle.

I'd had my wheelchair for five years now and it was wearing out and starting to cause problems with scoliosis – just like the chair I came home from Craig Hospital in did. It was causing severe back pain because my body wasn't being supported properly. Aaron helped me raise enough to buy a wheelchair that'd support my back properly and allow me to drive it by using the head-functions. It had lights and all-terrain wheels and a really long battery life, along with suspension and even a phone charger. It was the Rolls fucking Royce of wheelchairs and it was a major breakthrough for me. Now I had more independence and freedom of movement than ever.

Then I got the opportunity to develop eye-tracking software through a company called Tobii, that was eventually taken over by Microsoft. There's this disease called Amyotrophic Lateral Sclerosis and it's an incurable type of motor neurone disease, like what's wrong with Professor Stephen Hawking. After a while, you can't move anything except your eyes, so this software helps people communicate as their body shuts down. Anyway, they tested the early models of Tobii PCEye on me and used me in their PR for company negotiations and the promotion of their software. I'd come to the point where I thought I'd never be able to use a computer again, but the Tobii PCEye made it possible. After that, I looked forward to waking up every day and working toward new goals in my life that would've been impossible previously, like writing this book.

The positive psychological effect was immense, man!

So, there's new stuff all the time, and rehab's ongoing too. I went to a bunch of rehabilitation centres in California before I found Next Step Fitness. Nothing came close to this place, it was on the cutting edge for people with spinal cord injuries and it was worth the one-and-a-half hour drive to Redondo Beach twice a week. I met a bunch of rad people there, who really wanted to help me. They got me standing in a harness over a treadmill, called 'locomotive training'. It was like walking again and I got up to a slow jog – that feeling was *sooo* good! I met some physios there who became good friends – one of them was a guy called John Gomez, he was always prepared to go the extra mile and try new stuff. I loved working with John because he always seemed to get the best out of me.

John Jennings was at my side for a year or so and he was just a great guy. Considering I was getting no state medical support whatsoever, he was a solid, non-judgemental rock in my life at that time. He gave me his honest opinion on everything and he helped me through such hard times – all the trials and tribulations we went through, and good times too, and I learnt so much from him and became a better man for it. I can never thank him enough! John met his girlfriend Vanessa and started seeing her on a regular basis. Things got real serious between them and, naturally, he wanted to spend more time with her. He let me know he wanted to move on.

I'd become complacent, thinking John would be there forever. I was so reliant on him and I started to worry about who'd replace him. I needed a carer urgently. This BMXer called Shaun Tarrant was coming round to jams on Saturdays. I got along great with Shaun – he was older, maybe about forty-five or so, and he was covered in tattoos from head to toe. Lots of them were cover-ups, because I think he'd been involved with gangs or Aryan white supremacists or some shit like that. I didn't want to judge him because he seemed like a real nice dude and I thought maybe he was over all his racist crap, because he said he'd just done a ten-year stretch for some kinda anti civil rights movement crime.

Anyway, Shaun had a girlfriend was called Cheianne Leonard, who worked at a hospital in Orange County, and she started travelling down from Long Beach to help me out. John Jennings moved out in January 2012 and Cheianne and Shaun moved straight in and lived in a big annexe at the back of my house. Shaun brought a set of drums with him and he was an amazing percussionist – he told me his dad played drums with Elvis Presley and some famous bands.

Shaun had a son called Nick who was about twenty. The boy was deaf, but he was a great kid and an aspiring BMX rider. His dad asked if he could move in and I had no problem with that because I wanted to help him out. Shaun and Cheianne loved a good time and I guess caring for me kinda got in the way of that sometimes and put a strain on their relationship. They were staying more and more in their rooms at the back of the house and drinking a lot. I could see it was kinda unravelling and it was time for us to part company. They moved back to Long Beach in October 2012, but Nick stayed with me. He was a cool guy who looked out for me a lot and my kids loved him. Eventually, Nick left too – he got his bike and a sleeping bag and literally rode all the way to Austin, Texas, where his mother lived. I hope he's doing OK down there.

After Shaun and Cheianne took off, I called Cory Nastazio and explained the situation. Cory had this kid he nicknamed '8-mile' – after the Eminem film – his real name was AJ Fox. He came from Tehachapi, or someplace like that, and drug dealers had come round his house and pistol-whipped him in the middle of the night. His mother threw him out after that and Cory found him living in a barn on the other side of the tracks and took him in and gave him a life. He helped Cory with his filming and editing and personal assistant stuff and he turned out to be a great kid, despite his background. Cory reckoned I needed AJ more than he did, so he sent the guy over to help me out and he was an intelligent, interesting kid and a good carer.

Pretty soon he took over from Erika the nanny, helping me pull strokes on people. My friend Ben Hall came over to visit with Lee Martin from England and, when they were going back, I got AJ to put a strong laxative in his juice. After they got to LAX, Ben disappeared and left Lee standing there with the cases. He came back about forty minutes later, wearing new trousers. He'd only gone and shit himself. He couldn't sleep on the plane because he had to keep going to the toilet and he didn't want to shit himself again. By the time they got to London he had bags under his eyes.

Melissa and James Mulaney split up in 2011 or 2012 – I'm not sure exactly when, but I guess it was always gonna happen. She moved in with an older guy named Gino who was mentally abusive to her – or so she said. I guess he had money and wanted a trophy girlfriend, but she still had some custody rights of the boys – we were a week on and a week off with the kids at the time. In January 2014 Melissa brought them back to me after her week and asked if they could stay at my house indefinitely, because she couldn't manage – again. She was having boyfriend, business and housing problems and wanted time to sort herself out.

That didn't happen and she never had the boys again.

I thought about going back to England, but I reckoned it'd be too cold for me there. My injury makes me suffer in chilly weather and my body temperature doesn't know where it is sometimes. I was living in a nice place, my boys liked it and I had trails all round my house. Like, if Muhammad can't go the mountain, the mountain must come to Muhammad – ha! If I couldn't go to the trails, they had to come to me. I taught my sons to ride and it wasn't long before they were ripping it and winning races.

Life was cool for a while, after all the mad mayhem.

One day the phone rang and, when I heard the voice on the other end, my eyes lit up. It was Erica from West Palm Beach and the sound of her voice took me back all those years to when we spent some great times together. I think she got my number from Kimarie, or maybe from Cory, but I was glad she did. She'd been married and divorced since our time together and she had a son called Chance, who was about eight, and a daughter called Brooklyn, who was twelve. She was coming out to California to visit a friend of hers and she wanted to know if she could swing by and see me. Man, I was over the fucking moon!

As soon as we met, all the old feelings came back and I was in love again. It's strange when I think back about the women who've had a real deep effect on my life, from among all the women I've known, like, up close and personal: Mindy, who I guess was too good for me; Fleur, who was probably more in tune with me than anyone else at the time, we were good together and that made us bad together, if you get my drift; Melissa, who I fell in love with and would've been happy to spend the rest of my life with; and Erica, who I loved in a different way to Melissa, a way I can't readily put into words. Me and Erica got close again and, eventually, I got the vial out of the fridge and explained the procedure to her. She injected the hard-on stuff into the base of my dick and we were away.

Erica came out to visit once a month for the next year and, one day in 2014, I'm thinking –

'Fuck it, I gotta go skydiving!'

I asked her if she was up for it and she was. Getting me out of the chair and into the jumpsuit was more than a bit difficult and it took forever. Like, everything I wanted to do took time and things could get pretty awkward. The jump site was at a military parachuting facility at Lake Perris and the organisers lifted me into the plane and got me sitting on the bench along the side of the aircraft, where I was supported by the instructors.

The plane was loud and knackered, but it managed to take off and ascended to 18,000 feet. I was sitting right by the door and the instructor got behind me and crossed my arms over my chest and put tape all around my legs. Shit got real when they opened the door – I could see the world below me and it was fucking gnarly. The instructor edged his way to the open door, with me attached to him by this harness. I was, like, hanging out of the fucking plane for a couple of minutes until he was ready and it was like I was weightless – like my body was no longer made of lead and there's no gravity, nothing pinning me down.

Then we jump! We start spinning and flipping to begin with and I've no idea what's up or down and it's like in Baltimore, just before the crash. I'm trying to turn like a cat in mid-air so I can land on my feet – until the instructor gets control and we're free falling. And for a minute or so I'm flying – free from the chair – I'm not a quadriplegic no more, I'm a bird. We seem to fall for a long time, even though it's not. Falling. Falling. Free! The air's rushing into my lungs and I'm finding it hard to breathe, but that don't matter. I want to fall forever. If my doctors could've seen me, they'd have had a fucking fit! They told me I shouldn't do it because I'd have problems with breathing and my blood pressure plummeting.

The parachute opens with a jerk and this is when the doctors are afraid I'll have problems, but I don't. We're gliding over the world and it's a great feeling and I forget I'm attached to the instructor by the harness – it's just me and the open sky – until he says from behind me –

'Welcome to my office.'

Everything's quiet and kinda serene and we can see for miles. Gliding. Soaring. The ground eventually comes up to meet us and he raises my legs so I land on top of him. Back to reality. But what an experience!

After that, I found out it was possible for me to go skiing. My brother Martin was over and he likes snowboarding, so we drove up to Big Bear, a mountain that was an hour's ride away from my house, with Erica and TJ Ellis. I was wondering how I'd get on the ski-lift – like, I'm at the bottom of this mountain and the lift's coming behind me. Then my brother and the instructor just picked me up and lifted me into it. I wasn't strapped in or anything, just the instructor holding me with his hand – it felt fucking sketchy.

We get to the top OK and it's time to shred the slopes. They had a sit-ski with one ski at the front and two either side. They lifted me on to the seat and crossed my arms and taped them on to my chest, so there'd be no flailing limbs. Then they taped my feet together. I couldn't believe how rigged the set-up was, but I trusted the instructors and I knew they'd done this many times before – at least, I hoped they had.

The instructor's skiing behind me, attached by a tether cord in case he crashes and I fall off the side of Big Bear. We take off and I tell the dude to go as fast as he can, so we're pinning it down the mountain. We go over rollers and catch some air and it feels fucking great! Then we ski over toward the super half pipe and the guy asks me if I want to hit it. I'm like –

'Fucking right!'

We drop in and start to carve the half pipe all the way down. It's a real rush and I'm fucking stoked, man.

I ended up going back to that place four or five times.

In 2015 I issued a summons to the family court for sole physical and legal custody of Seth and Mason. At the first hearing Melissa opposed me, but said she needed a lawyer to represent her, so the judge gave her time to get one. The next hearing was three weeks later and she turned up an hour late and said her lawyer was stuck in traffic. Our case was put to the back of the queue and we were the last in court that morning – but the lawyer was still stuck in Palm Springs, according to Melissa.

The judge asked her for the name of her lawyer and, when he checked the records, he found out the guy was no longer acting for Melissa. She wouldn't back off and insisted the guy was still her lawyer. So the judge called his office and got told he resigned from acting for Melissa two years ago. Needless to say, the judge nearly had a fucking baby in the court room, but he gave her one last chance and rescheduled the case for two weeks later. Melissa never showed up for the final hearing, so the judge issued sole legal and physical custody to me. Melissa was allowed limited visiting rights of seven hours a week, but her visits had to be supervised by a court official, who had to be paid for by her.

I was the first quadriplegic to be granted custody of children in California legal history. I was blazing a trail, man!

It was a tough time, all the court battles, trying to look out for the boys, trying not to have all this shit going on between me and Melissa. I never wanted to keep Seth and Mason from seeing their mother. I even told her if she took a drug test, she could come visit the kids anytime she wanted, but she wouldn't do it. The thing that was most important to me was, I needed my kids to have a stable, safe place to grow up. That's all. Like I said, I wasn't a very good role model, back when I was partying all over the place, but even before my accident, when I got clean and was getting back on top of my sport again, I was trying to be the kind of father they could look up to as they got older.

My kid's respect means more to me than anything else in the world!

At the end of 2015 I asked Erica to marry me. She said 'yes', so we got engaged. But she had problems with leaving Florida permanently, because she shared custody with her kids' father – that made it near enough impossible for her to come live with me full time if we got married. I had full custody of my boys by then and the other alternative was for me to move to Florida, and she was all for that. I mean, she didn't care about me being in the chair – she wanted to do it all, be my wife, a mum to my kids and my carer at the same time. But Melissa tried that before and I knew deep down it'd be too much for any one person to handle.

I was completely torn and didn't know what to do. It was a huge decision and I wavered this way and that for a while. Thing is, I really couldn't see myself living in Florida because of the heat and humidity and no support. Sure, Erica said she'd take care of me, but like I said, I'd seen Melissa try to do that and I didn't want to put Erica through the same pressure as Melissa – I knew it'd eventually be too much for her and she'd crack under the strain. I truly loved Erica and she was very special to me, a beautiful person who I wanted to be with. But my health was sketchy and I needed the support of my family. They wanted me to move back to England so they could be there for me all the time and Erica wanted me to move to Florida, so *she* could be there for me all the time. It was a crazy decision to have to make.

I'd had pneumonia a bunch of times in the eight years up to then and, although I didn't know it, pneumonia would make that decision for me in the end!

19
ENGLAND AGAIN

I wake up one morning in January 2016 feeling tired and disorientated. My nurse tells AJ I'm not making any sense. AJ gets me up into my chair and I want to phone my dad. I got a phone mounted on my chair and a stylus that I grip with my mouth, so I can call who I like. But I just can't figure out how to do it now, I'm all over the place. I don't know it at the time, but the carbon dioxide levels in my body have built up too high and become toxic due to shallow breathing at night.

I get pneumonia and black out.

I wake up in Riverside Community Hospital on a ventilator – my worst fucking nightmare. The thing I'd worked so hard to get off nine years earlier has literally gripped me by the fucking throat again. Because my right diaphragm's paralysed and 50% of my left diaphragm, I'm not able to breathe properly by myself and the CO_2 makes my body toxic. They gotta intubate me and I'm back not being able to talk, just croak like a fucking frog, and I'm gagging where they stuck the tube into me. Nurse Betty's there, along with AJ, and I'm trying to communicate with them, but it's impossible.

I'm fighting for my life – again!

I'm on the ventilator for sixteen hours, but it seems like fucking forever. I have no family, except my boys, and real friends I can count on one hand – and I could die here on my own in this room. I gotta fight.

I gotta hang in there.

AJ stayed for three days, until my mum could get over from England. Every four hours for two weeks, the respiratory doctors would come round and they'd stick a suction pipe down my throat and up my nose, to suck all the fluid from my lungs. They'd bring out a vibrating vest, like a kind of inflating lifejacket, that'd shake the crap out of me in an effort to loosen the secretions. I was in a bad way for a while, but the breathing treatments and respiratory exercise, along with heavy doses of antibiotics, eventually got me fit enough to go home. They were still worried about shallow breathing at night and the danger of building up high levels of CO_2 again, so they gave me a BiPAP mask that I had to sleep with. It's like being under water or out in fucking space – the thing measures the number of breaths I should be taking every minute and, if I go over the set time, the machine increases the air pressure and forces me to breathe.

When I came home, I found out that some of my so-called friends had been partying in my house and all hell broke loose. The fuckers were high on drugs and fighting and the house got smashed up, including my sons' rooms – it's fucking lucky they weren't there. It was a scene of carnage. I couldn't comprehend this – who the fuck goes and parties at a friend's house when he's fighting for life in hospital? I certainly didn't want my kids being brought up around this kind of stupid recklessness – that old lifestyle might've been OK with me once, but not anymore.

In April I got pneumonia again, with a temperature of 105, and ended up back in Riverside Community Hospital. This time, it wasn't as life-threatening as it was in January and, after five days, they let me fly to the Cleveland Clinic to have diaphragm pacers fitted. There was two electrodes on each diaphragm wire, coming out of my stomach, connected to stimulators – like, they electrically stimulated my diaphragms and allowed me to breath and talk better. But, with two bouts of pneumonia in four months and the dumb-ass fucks wrecking my house, my family were really worried about me.

That's when I made the decision to move me and my boys back to England.

Erica went back to Florida.

California always felt like home to me, like where I was meant to be. But to live there you gotta be fit and focused, like I was once upon a time. After the accident and all the things that happened between 2007 and 2016 – nine tough years – I finally agreed to come home. My family'd been asking me to do it for some time and I tried to resist them – I tried to tough it out on my own in California. I don't like the cold and the rain and wintertime in England, but I'm thinking – maybe it's better than being dead.

Once I decided to go back to England I had to go back to the courts as well. The conditions of the original court order stated the boys had to live in California. If I wanted to take them to England, I had to get their mother's agreement. I had to apply to the court and serve Melissa notice again – if she wasn't served, the case couldn't take place. At the time, Melissa was in the middle of being prosecuted for drug, alcohol and driving misdemeanours – driving with Class A drugs in her car, driving while banned, and driving while under the influence. We found out the date of her next court hearing and my dad went to the courthouse and served her there.

Melissa showed up this time and we talked to a mediator before going in to see the judge, who agreed that it would be in the kids' best interests to come with me. In the end she said she didn't object to the boys going to England – she said they couldn't live without their father and the judge amended the terms of the custody order so my sons could live permanently in England with me. She has no rights over the boys now, other than the right to come over to England to see them, under supervision.

Planning the move was difficult, but my family took control again. Jeff called Chad Hubbard and, as far as I know, the house in Riverside got sold on a handshake. Chad put the property online for sale on Thursday and it got sold on Saturday. My two retrievers and Rocky the St. Bernard all died of age-related problems within nine months of each other, starting in November 2015. Now I had an Alsatian called Axel and another dog and I wanted to take everything with me, including the mutts. Back in England, my mum was putting a superhuman effort into sorting out a house for me and making things right for when we got back there.

I already told you about a girl called Mindy Brummett who sorted out hotels for me in California. I met her through TJ Lavin and, like I said, she looked after hospitality at Mandalay Bay in Vegas. Her brother was manager of a logistics company called XPO and, when she found out I was moving, she called in a favour from him. Mindy, her brother, and two other guys drove down from Salt Lake City and got a forty-foot long, extra-high shipping container. The van needed the air-con unit on the roof taking off and the tyres letting down, so it fitted into the container along with all my other stuff. They took it to the docks at Long Beach where it was shipped out to Southampton via the Panama Canal.

The dogs were a different matter. Paperwork for their dog passports was fucking ridiculous and it took forever to sort out. My dad was running round everywhere, being pushed from pillar to post and, by the time he managed to get everything sorted, we had to leave without them.

Oakley threw a massive leaving party for me at their Foothill Ranch headquarters. There was a dirt jump event and everyone who was anyone was there – a helluva lot of people. Oakley even invited the old riders from forty years ago – guys who were there at the beginning, and it was just fucking awesome, man! After the dirt jumping, we went inside and there was food and drink and an auditorium with, like, ten rows of seats and a stage. They showed videos and made speeches and presented me with a gold shovel, in appreciation of all the digging I'd done on trails over the years – not, like, real gold, just gold-coloured. I still have that shovel. I love it!

Vans paid for three first-class tickets for me and nurse Betty and Adam Aloise, who flew over with me in case I needed lifting on and off the plane. Me and Betty and Adam were together during the flight, while my dad, Mason and Seth flew economy. We weren't in the air long when my oxygen levels started to drop – they fell so low nurse Betty thought I was gonna die on that plane. It's like, altitude causes oxygen levels to deplete and, even though I was using a portable breathing machine, my levels fell to 65/100. The average person's oxygen level is 99/100 – my oxygen level's 91/100 for most of the time, because I only work off half a diaphragm. I was delirious – completely out of it and in a bad state. Betty was panicking, but she kept me awake by talking to me through the flight.

Now, there's this guy called Tom Lynch who was awarded an MBE for setting up the London Ambulance Bike Response Unit – it put paramedics on bikes to cope with congestion in London and get quicker response times to emergency calls. My dad kinda anticipated that I might have problems on such a long flight and Tom was a friend if his for a bunch of years, and they arranged a reception for me in case the worst happened. Like, this took a lot of planning, with a lot of people, and Tom and his team treated it like an emergency training exercise. Anyway, when we touched down at Heathrow after nearly twelve hours in the air, three London ambulances were on the tarmac, waiting for us. I was real dehydrated and they immediately gave me oxygen and fluids to stabilise me. If Tom and his team hadn't been there, I'd have ended up in hospital again and who knows what would've happened.

After I was stabilised, Tom and his crews took us to a surprise welcome home party at Jay Aliano's house, between Tewkesbury and Upton. I went in one ambulance with my dad and Betty, and the boys went in another ambulance with Adam. The weather was pretty shitty, cold and rainy – which was a shame, as they planned for Mason and Seth to session Jay's trails. Instead, Jay fired up the wood burners in his massive garage and poly tunnels, to make sure I was warm enough, and we hung out there, with the boys playing table tennis, music and video games. There was Stay Strong welcome home banners, a load of buffet food and a proper buzz. I didn't feel that great at the party, after the nightmare on the plane, but I didn't want to ruin it because people had put a lot of effort into it – and it was important to me that Seth and Mason felt welcome. Anyway, everyone got merry and just had a great time. Like I said before, partying in England's so different to partying in California – the banter and craic in the UK are unbeatable, man! The ambulance crews hung out for a bit and cleared the buffet. They deserved it.

Thanks for your help, guys!

That welcome party made the transition positive from the beginning. It made me feel more at ease, because I was a bit worried about how the boys would deal with the change. Nurse Betty stayed for two weeks, it was her first time in England and she loved it – although she didn't get to meet the real Duke of Wellington and wouldn't be able to boast about it to Arlene when she got back. Maybe next time, Betty. That lovely nurse was with me for eight years, she was a very calming person and I had great respect for her. I missed her when she went back to America. Maybe I'll see her again some day.

BMXers TJ Ellis and Larry Edgar took my dogs to LAX on the Monday after we left and they eventually went with Virgin air cargo – in crates. We drove down to Heathrow to collect them when they arrived – Axel, the Alsatian, had chewed up his crate, but he was OK. The shipping container with my stuff arrived in Southampton a month later. It got taken to Jay Aliano's place until things at my new English house were properly sorted. I hadn't experienced an English winter for eighteen years, so I had to adjust quickly. I was used to being outdoors in the sunshine a lot and now, if it's cold, it hurts my bones and I gotta be wrapped up in many layers of clothes.

My mum and Tony Edgworth temporarily moved in with me and the boys while we got settled and carers could be arranged – it nearly killed Cynthia looking after everyone for the first few months, until I got the professional help I needed. I owe her more than I can ever repay!

Thanks for everything, mum!

I tried to get the boys involved in their new lifestyle as soon as possible: like Sunday roasts and UK skateparks;

showing them tourist places like London and the Cotswolds; watching Newcastle play football and going to music gigs at the O² Academy in Birmingham to see hot acts like the ska/punk band [SPUNGE]. I want to build trails round my house so my kids and all their friends can have a place to ride and a spot to chill. OK, at the moment I can't be a typical father to my boys and do typical things with them. But it don't stop me giving them all I can. I just want to make sure life's as regular as possible as far as the day-to-day stuff is concerned. They grew up seeing me in a wheelchair and it's kinda normal for them – I guess if I stood up and walked, that'd freak them out.

We live in a two-story house in a village near Stratford. Jay Aliano and his family came over and made the place accessible for my chair. It's a big house, but different to Riverside. The house in Riverside had way more land and was all open plan on one storey. The house in England's on two floors – open plan on the ground floor where I am – and it has a big decking area out back, overlooking the Worcestershire countryside.

For now my mum's taken over the vacant mother role for my sons. She's much more than a grandma to them and gives them the love and guidance that's often been missing from their lives. That don't mean she takes any shit – she doesn't, and I respect her for it. Seth goes to the same high school in Evesham as me when I was his age. It was a shock to my system back then and I'm sure it's the same for him now – but I reckon it'll do him good. I know he misses the trails and the Californian lifestyle, but he'll understand the world I came from and I hope it'll give him a stable grounding for his life to come. He's dedicated to BMX and skateboarding and I'll support him in whatever he does. I'm proud of Mason too, he's been through a lot, yet he's such a measured kid and I love him unconditionally. He's into gym and BMX and he did his first backflip on his scooter at Rush skatepark in Stroud. He reminds me so much of myself at that age – except maybe for setting fire to campsites and almost burning them to the ground. He won't do that – I hope.

I spent a lot of time trying to find the best rehab when I came back. I looked at a bunch of places, then I found

Neurokinex in Bristol, owned by Harvey Schota, a friend of my dad's. Neurokinex runs on the same principles as Next Step Fitness in Redondo Beach and now I've started working with those guys. Stoke Mandeville Hospital's in control of most of my holistic medication nowadays and – unlike the American system, where everything was disjointed and the different hospitals I went to didn't communicate with each other all that well – now everything's centralised and much more controlled and accessible.

Time's a strange thing, sometimes it moves so fast it can take your breath away, other times it feels like it's standing still. My life's slower here than it was in California, but that suits me right now. The people here are genuine and all my English friends have been real supportive and I feel strong. I love California, but I guess I love England too, and I feel at home in both places.

Being the way I am, like, in a wheelchair, I always need stuff to do to keep my mind healthy. I never thought I'd be able to write a book because my memory's so bad after all the concussions and medication. But I've surprised myself and, once I got started, the memories came flooding back like a home video. I guess, once you apply yourself, it's surprising what you can do. At times it's been difficult, talking about some of the darker episodes in my life, but I wanted to tell it all and not just the good bits. On the whole, however, it's been a real gas revisiting the craziness and it made me laugh as well as cry at times. I guess it's good if you can laugh at yourself and not be too pompous.

Melissa came to visit the boys toward the end of 2016. She seemed different – calmer and more stable. We spent a couple of weeks together and it was good to be like a family again – for a while. She said she bears no animosity to anyone and neither do I. She's happy I've found the level of independence I have in England and that the boys are settled in school over here. She's now with a Native American guy called Bobby, who's maybe 20 years older than her. He's had land, like forever, and the casinos lease the land from him. I met him once and he seemed like a nice guy and, despite all the craziness during our marriage, I genuinely wish her the best for the future.

No life is perfect – we're all human beings and human beings make mistakes. It's all about learning and trying not to keep making the same mistakes over again. Sometimes I feel like I've cheated death so often, I'm living on borrowed time – so I don't want to spend any of what I got left in the past – it's all about the future now. It's like I gotta make the most of every minute, good or bad, so I try to make every day a positive one and rise to every new challenge that's thrown at me.

Someone once said – '*life is what happens while we're waiting for life to happen*'.

Not me.

Not anymore!

20
THE FUTURE

OK, going forward to the future – there's this thing called a neural bypass that's half surgery and half engineering. It uses a brain implant to record electrical signals, which are decoded by a computer and routed to an electronic sleeve that stimulates the forearm muscles. It's like, if you *think* about doing something with your hands, you can *actually* do it. It sounds simple, but it's not. This research has been going on for years. Like, in 2006 a quadriplegic man used a brain implant to control a computer cursor; and in 2012 a quadriplegic woman used an implant to control a robot arm. It's kinda like they're combining engineering with physiotherapy so people can use their arms and hands again. They reckon, for now, it's just in a laboratory, but the long-term goal's to design a system that's safe and simple enough to use anywhere. I know this technology's only at the early stages, but regaining the use of even my arms would be a huge fucking achievement for me, no matter how it was achieved.

The Bionic BMXer – ha!

I guess the real hope for the future is with the Roman Reed Law in California. It was set up to fund research into spinal cord injury paralysis cures and it's had a couple of major breakthroughs. Barack Obama said this about it in his final speech as acting president, before he handed over to Donald Trump –

'I've seen our scientists help a paralysed man regain his sense of touch, and wounded warriors, once given up for dead, walk again.'

After that speech, Roman Reed texted my father –

'OMG!! President Obama just wrote about us and called me about his final speech!!'

Maybe I better explain this a bit more because it's kinda important – to me, at least. After his accident Christopher Reeve saw no money was being invested in research to cure paralysis. Like, everyone said you couldn't recover from a spinal cord injury because the spinal cord and the brain are two parts of the human body that don't regenerate. Once either is damaged, they don't repair, so you just have to change your life and get on with it. The Superman actor damaged his C2 falling off a horse and he was told he'd never get off the ventilator, just like I was told the same thing. Reeve started to fund research and raised millions of dollars to help the world's top scientists and doctors find the holy grail of making the spinal cord regenerate itself.

Joan Irvine, the well-known philanthropist, teamed up with Christopher Reeve and put ten million dollars into the Reeve-Irvine Research Centre in California. Top scientists were recruited to start finding solutions to spinal cord injury – guys like Dr Oswald Stewart from NASA and Dr Hans Keirstead, the neuro-biologist. They reckoned the way to get the spinal cord ends to grow back together was by using stem cells. Dr Keirstead had to prove to the FDA that growing embryonic stem cells and implanting them was safe and ethical. Like, some politicians and religious groups and activists are against stem-cell research, they reckon it's morally wrong. But this viewpoint, in my opinion, is a bit last-century and the benefits that could be achieved are nothing short of miraculous. Clinical trials in paralysed rats proved that implanting embryonic stem cells made them walk again.

Anyway, this guy called Roman Reed introduced Roman's Law into California and they're way ahead of the rest of the world at the moment. My biggest sponsor was Oakley and, like I said, they gave me the opportunity to design my own sunglasses that were sold around the world in 2008. Three years later a second pair were released and Oakley allowed me to donate some of the money raised to the Reeve-Irvine Research Centre. Me and my dad presented the cheque at Oakley's headquarters at Lake Forest and we met Roman Reed and Dr Keirstead for the first time there.

I met Roman again at the Unite2Fight Paralysis seminar in Orange County in 2012. They asked me to speak and I gave my personal message to encourage investment into stem-cell research and tried to be an inspiration to other paralysed people. From that point on, my dad has been in close contact with Roman Reed and they talk every week, just like when Roman sent him the text about what Obama said.

With my type of injury, they'll need to develop stem cells that can hang on to the spinal cord to regenerate, but they'll also need something to break down the hardened scar tissue. After any spinal cord trauma, the damaged cord goes into shock and scar tissue forms. After time, it gets difficult to break it down so that signals can pass through the cord again. But the plan is to wrap the wound in a placenta and allow the stem cells to grab on to the damaged area and then inject an enzyme to break down the scar tissue at the same time. When the scar tissue softens and the cord repairs, the signals should be able to get through again. I have 100% belief and confidence in this – I know it'll happen.

It's only a matter of time – and money.

In the meantime, life goes on and it's all a matter of quality. I know able-bodied people have a hard time understanding that a quadriplegic like me can have good quality of life. But I do – most of the time. People look at me and they get stuck for something to say – and I totally understand that they might be afraid of offending me. But I'm not that thin-skinned, I'm really not. What does makes me cringe is when someone talks down to me, like I'm a kid or retarded or something, just because I'm in a wheelchair. My head's still right. I think the same way as someone with a normal body thinks – that hasn't changed. My situation and my body might be different, but my mind's the same as it was.

People sometimes have trouble looking straight at me, like they're too polite or something. They do this weird thing, like trying to make it obvious they don't notice I'm disabled, but I catch them sneaking a look out of the corner of their eye. Guys I once rode with – you can tell some of them feel a mixture of pity and discomfort around me, and relief it didn't happen to them. I guess they mean well and just want to be kinda diplomatic, but there's only so much of that shit I can take. I'd rather people were straight-up than pussyfooting around.

Another thing people don't like talking about is state of mind. I guess most people assume that quadriplegics struggle mentally and are in a dark place for most of the time. I can't answer for everyone in my situation but, for me, the first part of that assumption might still be true sometimes, and even the second part at times in the past. I know a lot of people couldn't hack being where I am now – I mean, I saw dudes in Baltimore shock/trauma who broke down and lost it when the realisation of their predicament dawned on them. They lost the drive for survival. Their spirit was broken. New patients turned up all the time when I was there and new patients are constantly turning up in shock/trauma units all over the world – and that's not gonna stop any time soon. Losing functionality of your body's a shit thing – it's inconvenient, to say the least!

But life is far from over and life's a gift that I cherish.

When I was first pinned to a bed in that hospital and my wife at the time was losing it, I was in a bad place. I went into the darkness, but I came back out again. And, from time to time over the years, suicide's sat on my shoulder and whispered in my ear and I wished it would end – no more pneumonia, no more wheelchair, no more fingers up the ass in the morning, no more pain and no more bacteria in the lungs, no more fever from out of the blue. But I've always managed to resist. Why? Because of my kids – they're the reason I'm still alive. If you got the love, you can go on. Without it, you'll sink.

I'm not saying depression doesn't still affect me – man, sometimes I get so pissed off with stuff! But so does everybody. What I'm saying is, depression doesn't affect me any more or less than the average person. Why? Because I don't let it! People say I'm 'strong', but I'm not trying to be, like, fucking superhuman or anything. I guess I've just always been positive and I still love human interaction and fun – nothing's changed there.

The way I look at it is, I'm still alive, I'm still breathing, I'm still in the game and real lucky to be here. Maybe I'd get depressed if I wasn't surrounded by friends and family who really support me. Like, if I had nobody, then things might be different. But I have two amazing boys and I love watching them grow and mature into decent adults. OK, if I could hug them every now and then it'd be even better, but the fact is, I'm here and I'm witnessing them grow up. I'm involved and I'm trying to teach my sons how to live good lives through the journey I've taken and the lessons I've learnt. Looking back on my crazy life, I personally don't regret anything. I did what I did and it's easy to see now that, although I worked my ass off to achieve success, I wasn't mature enough to handle the money and fame and the 'party' scene. I've talked this over with my boys so they understand the pitfalls in my life and hopefully they'll take the good points into their future and leave the crap behind

I guess you could say I'm wiser now than I've ever been in my life. I talk. I reach out to others who need help. I make time for people. I connect with people I feel comfortable with – like, I have a sixth sense and I know within seconds if someone has that look in their eye. One time I never stopped moving – I was here, there and everywhere, never stopping to think or take a long look around me. Now I got time to do that, I see things from a different angle, I think about things more deeply. Don't get me wrong, I'm still always up for doing something outrageous, that hasn't changed. I still want to be as active as I can and get out and about – but it's not at the same breakneck pace. I'm constantly learning stuff I had no time to learn when I was younger and crazier. I have time to think about relationships, the way I engage with people, how I can help others and how I can help myself. I think about goals and strategies and challenges I want to set myself and how I can achieve them. I study behaviour in people and I'm still a big practical joker – always on the lookout for ways of having fun.

I love going places when I can and it's great when people stop to talk to me – I really love that! Just like when I went skydiving and skiing, if I listened to the doctors and did everything they told me, life would be pretty dull. Like, once I'd settled into my house after coming back to England, my mate Jeff Dovey, who I've known since I was a kid at BMX races, came over from Worcester to see me and brought his Lamborghini. Jeff, Martin and Marco lifted me into the car and, once I was supported properly, it was time to take that baby for a spin. I'm, like, pinned to the seat when he puts it in launch mode and accelerates to 180mph – man, I hadn't felt that good for a while. When I got home, it was like I'd been on a boat for two days – from going 180mph to being static in the chair was an adrenaline dump and it took a couple of hours to feel right again.

There's all kinds of things quadriplegics can do now, like bungee jumping or swimming with dolphins or canoeing or horse riding with a special frame. There's scuba diving and floating chairs for fishing and adapted quad bikes and stuff I've already done, like skiing and skydiving. There's a whole online community of people with spinal injuries out there. Thousands of men and women leading hidden lives, some with friends and family, some alone. People looking for info about the latest equipment, or for advice on rehab, or just for someone to talk to who understands. People struggling to cope with disabled husbands or wives, just like Melissa was, people feeling guilty, exhausted, in despair. People joking about exploding catheter bags, or getting drunk and falling down kerbs or out of their chairs, or spasming in the cinema and sending popcorn flying everywhere.

There's threads about suicide – like those who want to and those who try to persuade them not to – persuade them to give themselves more time and learn to look at life in a different way. When you read the threads, you get an insight into the secret workings of a quadriplegic's mind – the inner things you don't see on the outside. Most people probably think that being a quad's the worst thing that could happen

– for me it's not, I could be back on the vent or not able to talk again, just croak like a frog.

Or I could be dead.

I look forward to new experiences and I'm constantly reminding myself that you only live once – and facing your fears and overcoming them's just the greatest feeling in the fucking world! It's all about trying to live as 'normal' a life as possible for me, and carrying on doing the things I like doing. But then, I guess my life's never been 'normal' – I always tried to push the envelope on my bike, and now I'm doing the same thing in my chair.

I'm really proud of what I achieved on my bike. BMXing took me all over the world and made me see the bigger picture in life – something I might not have done otherwise. Travelling to other countries and experiencing so many different cultures was an education in itself and made up for the schooling I neglected when I was younger. I made so many great friends and met role models who influenced and motivated me to be the best I could be, both on and off the bike. I understood what it took to be at the top of what you do.

All the stuff I mentioned before is still with me. Like, I can't blow my nose or scratch an itch or brush my teeth or hug my kids. Waking up every morning, I need someone to help me go to the bathroom and get washed. My bowel and bladder still have to be manually emptied by a nurse before the day can start. I still get contractions and pins-and-needles and my skin still feels like it's burning – the closest description would be like falling into stinging nettles, you can feel the burn and discomfort for hours. I still gotta try to avoid pressure sores and I still get bouts of pneumonia and this makes me real sick, to the point where I could die. I get nerve pain on a daily basis and sometimes it comes in waves and is real difficult to deal with. Sometimes I suffer from autonomic dysreflexia, which is a sudden rush of excessively high blood pressure – this happens when I'm in pain – and it's the worst nightmare after pneumonia, like it's the damaged nervous system trying to be in control. It can come out of nowhere and send the body into meltdown with severe headache, sweating, blocked up nose, high blood pressure, slow heart rate and anxiety. Sometimes I get severely spastic – so spastic I'll literally rip myself out of the chair after contracting so hard. I still need the help of friends and family – someone needs to be my left hand and my right hand.

The way my body feels is kinda like if you immersed yourself in an ice bath for a couple of hours – when you get out you're numb, but you can still feel a slight touch.

That's what I'm like – right from my neck down to my feet.

OK, I really miss being free, like in the days when I was able to walk and run and ride. I miss it – the freedom. All the stuff I took for granted and never gave a second thought to. But I've learnt through the years to accept it and deal with it. I guess there's things you don't notice much until you're in a wheelchair, like how crap most pavements are – uneven with lots of holes and every jolt causes you pain. Things you gotta steer round, like cars parked on footpaths, and kerbs with no ramps, and unsafe road crossings where it's difficult to see. Shopping in crowded stores, having to be fed in restaurants, getting on and off trains, not being able to go anywhere too hot or too cold. Things that people with freedom of movement take in their stride. But, if I don't have complete freedom, I have a sense of freedom. I have some independence, even though I gotta rely on and trust other people to help me through the day and night. Best of all, I'm alive and I got my sons and I'm thankful for that. My dad told me once that the world's constantly evolving and you gotta learn to adjust – as long as you can adjust, you'll be OK.

Life's pretty busy, despite my injuries. Like I said, I go to BMX events and music festivals and down the pub with my friends. I'm currently organising the Murray Invitational Dirt Contest at Lakefest Music Festival at Eastnor Castle in Herefordshire. I take the boys snowboarding at Tamworth Snowdrome and I regularly visit skateparks and trails all over the UK. I'm helping to organise the UK BMX Dirt Series, which is a series of events that gives amateurs a platform to qualify for the Murray Invitational and I spread the word as much as I can about the world of BMX. I even had a rider from Australia representing Stay Strong in the 2016 Rio Olympics. Anthony Dean made the final of the BMX Supercross and was favourite to win. He won every lap to qualify for the final, but crashed in the main event and didn't make the podium.

Maybe next time in Tokyo?

But I guess my full-time job is being there for my kids and meeting people with injuries like mine and trying to encourage them to stay positive. I have a completely different perspective on life now. Every day I wake up with a genuine longing inside my soul to try to make life better for someone who's suffering – and this isn't some kinda selfless philanthropic bullshit, I have an ulterior motive. Helping people helps me, it gives me a purpose in life and keeps the darkness away. I started doing motivational speeches at Corona High School in California, back in 2008 – I must've done it about fifteen times. It was amazing. Thousands of kids sat there listening to my story. I'd really like to do as much of that as I can. It means a lot to me when people come up and say how I inspired them. I kinda make it my mission to bring courage to anyone who needs it. I'd like to think people who've seen my struggle and determination to push through will be able to take the message of Stay Strong to their own life situations, so they're able to reach inside and dig deeper.

Recently I've been meeting with the people from Wings for Life, a spinal injury research foundation. They want to find a cure for spinal cord injuries and they fund world-class research and clinical trials around the world. I'm looking forward to spreading the word about the important work they do and maybe being a kinda ambassador for them. It's like, Wings for Life depend entirely on donations to do their work and 100% of the money raised is used for research, that's because all their admin costs are covered by Red Bull. How cool is that! So, if anyone wants to help out, we'd be real grateful.

The lack of Californian sun and heat affects my body, like I said, but I feel good inside. My hopes are to regain as much movement as possible. That's my number one goal now, as well as taking care of my boys. People have asked me if I made a full recovery would I get back on my bike? For sure! I'd ride, but it'd just be for fun. Just for recreation – just to pedal round and feel the free breeze on my face.

While I'm waiting for the scientists to sort things out with stem cells and bionic stuff, I don't have to be the thing that defines me – the chair doesn't define me. I loved my life, really loved it. I loved my sport and the person I was – a physical person, a champion, partying, having fun – but most of all riding my bike. I wasn't designed to exist in a chair, but I don't let it define me. I'm not the chair and the chair's not me. Inside, I'm the same person I always was. Would I change things if I could go back? For sure, I'd change a lot of stuff. I wouldn't let my life hit rock bottom through the false promises of drugs – and I'd prefer if my left foot hadn't slipped off that pedal in 2007.

But it's a hypothetical question and I can't change any of what happened. I am where I am now and it's no use regretting stuff I can't do anything about.

Don't you think?

Who really knows what the future holds? I didn't know what it held for me when I got on the roll-in for that final jump in Baltimore in 2007. But, whatever comes, I guess I'm just gonna keep fighting like I always have – fighting to get better – and see what happens. I got many battles still ahead of me, I know that – some I'll win and some I'll lose. But never count me out. I might be down sometimes, but I always get back up. One day, I truly believe I'll be walking again.

If anyone can beat the odds, it's me.

There's this saying, '*it'll be alright in the end – if it's not alright, it's not the end*'.

Stay Strong!

See the Stay Strong van surprise on stysrg.com

I'm staring at the poster on my wall the one you signed
With wanker as the words yea that you left behind
To me as a friend yo when I was at your crib
You showed me such love yea we just wanna live
Just wanna keep doing what we do we wanna pursue
What God brought us to what he brought us through
What we begin to know how it shows with dough
How we get the fix with the sticks shift the drift I'm higher than the cliff
Yes the piff but I wish that we could do the twist because I miss
this father this is so important please adopt another orphan
that can swim through the mud covered by the blood
of the lamb the plan to make him stand
with the power of your glory see the story
is all yours but the choice is all his in this period of time
give him strength to live fill him up with your love
your presence is a free gift just know that God has definitely got your back
and I try to show his love I laid all on this track I want you back
to your feet staring at the defeat the heat
is getting hot just know what you supposed to be and what you supposed
to do
to keep your eyes to the sky never fall down to the lies of the guy
you know you're fine and in time
We will remember this song so cherish everything because it will all be
gone
But right now you still living and your heart still beating and you always
in season
for a miracle from God he's the reason
you still alive and I pray when I cry and I know deep inside
that the day will arrive
It's written in the book here take a look
When I speak about jesus please to believe me there is a way to see this
and a way to achieve this
I'm praying to the same god that raised Jesus from the dead
so that's enough proof that you're getting up again so get all those
thoughts out of your head and fill it up with life
You have the word of God and you really understand what's that drive
inside
Just know that God's got your back
And I lay it all down in this rap
I don't know how you'll react
Whether you think it's whacked
Either way I still love you back
And that's a matter of fact.

Stephen Murray Rap – a Tribute to Stephen Murray by John Jennings

ACKNOWLEDGEMENTS

in alphabetical order

Jay Aliano
Adam Aloise
Jerry Badders (Vans)
Rick Bahr
David Beckham
Jamie Bestwick
Steve Blick (Oakley)
Corey Bohan
Sir Richard Branson
Mindy Brummett
Marisa Cianciarulo
Michael 'Hucker' Clarke
Aaron Cooke
Marco Dell'isola
Daniel Dhers
Kristi Dietzel
Jeff Dovey
Larry Edgar
Cynthia Edgworth (my mother)
Scott Edgworth
Tony Edgworth
TJ Ellis
Andre Ellison
Colleen Flanaghan
Kye Forte
AJ Fox
Melissa Giles
John Gomez
Dustin Grice
Ryan Guettler
Ian Gunner

Kelly Gunner
Shane Guillen
Tobias Gutteridge
Matt Helders
Mat Hoffman
Dale Holmes
Chico Hooke
Chad Hubbard
Kimarie Hunt
John Jennings
Jade Keylock
Janne Kouri
TJ Lavin
Cheianne Leonard
Tom Lynch
Pat Mac (Oakley)
Lee Martin (Lakefest)
Chris Mason
Steve Mateus (Rockstar)
Chris Moeller (S&M)
Keith Mulligan
Jeff Murray (my father)
Martin Murray (my brother)
Mason Murray (my son)
Seth Murray (my son)
Cory Nastazio (Nasty)
Nate
Art Nava
Tristan Nunn
Ryan Nyquist
Mindy Pantus
Travis Pastrana

Jim Patrick
Lonie Paxton
Heath Pinter
Paul Roberts (Grotbags)
Mark Scurto (Oakley)
Alan Smith
Greg Steele
Kelly Suckling
Simon Tabron
Nick Tarrant
Shaun Tarrant
Craig Teague
Tyler Truman
Steve Van Doren–(Vans)
Van Ho
Ryan Van Kesteren
Erica Vizzo
Kendra Webber
Alistair Whitton
Kelly Wood
Neal Wood

Also

Dr Bizan Aarabi
Dr Hans Keirstead
Dr Suzy Kim
Dr John McDonald
Dr Cristina Sadowsky
Dr Oswald Stewart

Also

The Aliano Family
The BMX Family
The Ream Family
  (Woodward Camp)
The Wells Family
The Staff at Craig Hospital
The DTR Crew
The Stay Strong Team
  (past, present and future)
Next Step Fitness
SHL
Virgin Atlantic

Also

Anyone who picks up a shovel to keep their local trail
  scene alive.

Anyone who's sent a message of support, bought a product
  or helped raise money over the past ten years. There's too
  many of you to thank individually, but your support has
  always overwhelmed me. THANK YOU!

Anyone I've forgotten – my memory isn't what it used to
  be – if I've left you out, let me know and I'll include your
  name in the next edition.

A big THANK YOU to these special companies that have
supported me and played a massive part in my recovery

HIPPIE

a metaphysical pseudo-biography

ANYWHERE BUT HERE

LEE MARTIN

"A roller-coaster hallucinogenic ride through the hippie years and beyond" Tim Abbot, Creation Records (Oasis)

www.thehippiebook.com